History of
GEOGRAPHIC THOUGHT

History of GEOGRAPHIC THOUGHT

Dr. C.D. Kathuria

CENTRUM PRESS
NEW DELHI-110002 (INDIA)

CENTRUM PRESS

H.O.: 4360/4, Ansari Road, Daryaganj,
New Delhi-110002 (India)
Tel: 23278000, 23261597, 23255577, 23286875

B.O.: No. 1015, Ist Main Road, BSK IIIrd Stage,
IIIrd Phase, IIIrd Block, Bengaluru-560085 (INDIA)
Tel: 080-41723429

Email: centrumpress@gmail.com
Visit us at: www.centrumpress.com

History of Geographic Thought

First Edition, 2011

ISBN 978-93-81293-47-8

PRINTED IN INDIA

Printed at Suman Printers, Jagatpuri Extn., Delhi

Contents

Preface

History of geographical thought is the domain, which joins in itself two different disciplines, that is to say, history of geography and philosophy of science. This is in accordance with an age-old tradition of putting them together. This subject is concerned with the history and philosophy of geography and is designed to introduce students to key debates, both past and present, on the nature and scope of geography as an academic discipline.

It therefore sets out an essential context for understanding contemporary research in human and physical geography. The early origins of the subject are traced back to the revolutionary intellectual climate of enlightenment and empire, a time when geographical knowledge.

Since the natural part of the reality worked with no essential changes, and simultaneously the contemporary people acted more and more divergently in relation to natural laws (due to science and technology), both natural and human elements of the reality (the Nature in Humboldtian terms) must have created, paradoxically, the more and more coherent whole. And the source of this coherence was nothing but the diversity in the functioning of those two different parts of the system. This example shows that history of geographical thought is in fact the reservoir of socially important ideas, which still expect their rediscovery.

The future right now points to more technology like remote sensing and especially GIS. But the geography has been known to switch directions quickly before. Maybe the globalized world at war will led to the rise of regional geography with elements of cultural studies. Maybe the potential of climate change will cause physical/environmental geography to become more popular. What is known; however, is that multidisciplinary studies are becoming more frequent in academia. The big struggle hear is for geography to remain unique and not be absorbed into things like "environmental studies" or "international studies."

The book will be central to courses in geographical thought and the history of geographical thought, and as part of virtually all courses in human geography which entail philosophy and theory.

—*Editor*

1

Introduction

It is a universally accepted fact that the necessary condition of harmonious development of every field of knowledge, whether natural or humanistic, is that it should care for its humanistic element, which embraces the history of the field and its philosophy. In spite of that, historical and philosophical problems are in the field of interest of a rather few Polish geographers. Polish geography is deprived of journals, commissions, symposia and seminars devoted to historical and philosophical research, and at our universities there exists neither a chair nor a department dealing with such problems.

Historical topics appear in our journals exclusively on occasions of celebrated anniversaries. Such celebrations and accompanying publications are however not a good place for controversies and philosophical discussions. It could be said then, that in the frame of history of Polish geography, there exists only the documentary (or antiquarian) aspect, while the history of geographical ideas and philosophy of geography have deteriorated. And it is highly symptomatic that some aspects of history of geography are more interesting for historians of science than for the very geographers. It is mainly due to the fact that important elements of geographical knowledge, which before the Second World War were the most fundamental and necessary for educational aims, have been later abandoned and have fallen into oblivion. This is the direct response to the changes in the system of geographical education in Poland during the 1950s. History, which was the area necessary to understand the cultural landscape, has been replaced with mathematics – the discipline useful for the explanation of spatial relations.

WHAT IS TO BE THE HISTORY OF GEOGRAPHICAL THOUGHT

History of geographical thought is the domain, which joins in itself two different disciplines, that is to say, history of geography and philosophy of science. This is in accordance with an age-old tradition of putting them together. In this spirit during the International Geographical Congress in Warszawa in 1934, Professor Boleshaw Olszewicz proposed that a Société Lelewel should be formed with the French geographer, Lucien Gallois, as the chairman. The name of the society has been chosen to commemorate the 19th century Polish historian and geographer, Joachim Lelewel, author of the "Géographie du Moyen-Âge", "The Ancient History with Regard to Geography", and "Geographical description of the Polish Lands" (in Polish, ed.1858). The name "Lelewel" is a short Polish form of the German original Löhlhöffel von Löwensprung. Joachim's father was just Karl Moritz Löhlhöffel von Löwensprung, who came from Prussia to become the citizen of the Kingdom of Poland. In 1768 he gained the indigenate (recognition as a Polish nobleman) along with the name correction. In accordance with Joachim Lelewel's interests and style of research, Olszewicz's intention was that such a society should be concerned with history of geographical thought including philosophical and ideological issues. However, there is no sign that such topics were actually discussed during the Warszawa Congress or at the next Congress in Amsterdam in 1938. In spite of that, the idea was not completely forgotten and finally led to the formation of the IG U Commission on the History of Geographical Thought at the New Delhi Congress in 1968. From the very beginning the Commission worked mostly on the border between two established fields: history of ideas and philosophy of science. For example, the Commission's Objectives 1996–2000 formulated during the IG U Congress in Den Haag state that "the current and often violent conflicts linked to the political and cultural fragmentation of the world invite us to a renewed study of the ways of conceiving the human occupance and use of the Earth, as well as of the means of making these views compatible". In particular, the activity of the Commission included the following questions:

- how ideological concepts have influenced the social and institutional construction of geographical knowledge;
- how ideologies and religions have shaped geographer's conception of the human use of the Earth; and
- which geographical concepts promoted or prevented mutual understanding in the situation of growing political conflicts and cultural fragmentation.

Such were also the main topics of the special symposium held in Sandomierz, Poland, in 1997. These problems are still valid and even more and more important, but today the reasons for a revival of the history of geographical thought are manifold and are to be found in the societal, scientific and educational contexts in which we practice geography. These three contexts are considered further separately but it must be borne in mind that they are often intermingled and their complete isolation is rather an artificial measure. In spite of the fact that Polish geography has a long and very rich tradition, the history of geographical thought does not seem to be an attractive area of study for Polish geographers. Contrary to our British, French, German and American colleagues, we have published no academic handbooks in this area of knowledge for the last fifty years, we have no historical-geographical journals, no conferences, no commissions within our national geographical society, and there are no departments and chairs dealing with the history of geographical thought at our universities and geographical institutions. Consequently, it could be ascertained that history of geographical thought in Poland is dead.

Societal Context

The aim of this chapter is to prove that history of geographical thought embraces ideas and concepts that could be useful from the point of view of contemporary social and political problems. Recent history in many parts of the world has in fact challenged geographers to contribute to explanations as well as to reconciliations between different visions of reality in the circumstances of the more and more conflicting situations. History of geographical thought contains numerous ideas which could turn out to be useful in such situations, since geography from its very beginning is the study of diversity, understood as a source of unity, complementarity, coherence, harmony and beauty. For example, one of the banner slogans of contemporary Europe is "Unity in diversity", but none of the users of this idea seems to realize that this is just one of the fundamental principles of geography, formulated originally by one of our classics, that is to say Alexander von Humboldt. To recognize and understand the unity which exists in the diversity of terrestrial phenomena was, according to Humboldt, the key purpose of geography.

This statement was a logical consequence of the so-called Humboldt's paradox. According to this principle, every unit is the more coherent, the more divergent are the functions of its constituent parts. That is to say, if any unit is to form a coherent whole, its particular parts have to work divergently, or according to different principles. Humboldt applied this paradoxical principle to the idea of Nature, understood as the whole embracing both the natural and human elements of reality. It must be emphasized that the contemporary understanding of nature is strongly reduced in comparison to the classical, Humboldtian idea of Nature.

For Humboldt it denoted exactly all beings and things, whether man-made or existing independently of man. At that time the main distinction was not between the natural and the cultural (human), but between the natural and the supernatural. Then the supernatural things were effectively excluded from research, and in the frame of the former natural, the natural (in narrow sense) and the cultural parts were distinguished.

Since the natural part of the reality worked with no essential changes, and simultaneously the contemporary people acted more and more divergently in relation to natural laws (due to science and technology), both natural and human elements of the reality (the Nature in Humboldtian terms) must have created, paradoxically, the more and more coherent whole. And the source of this coherence was nothing but the diversity in the functioning of those two different parts of the system. This example shows that history of geographical thought is in fact the reservoir of socially important ideas, which still expect their rediscovery.

The question of diversity constitutes only one example of the broad array of contemporary social problems which could be investigated by historians of geographical thought. A lot of important problems are connected with the inequality in the social, economic, technological and mental developments of societies. During the fourth and fifth Kondratieff waves we witness unprecedented developments in science and technology. People have gained access to numerous mechanical and electronic devices, which have significantly changed everyday life and landscape, particularly in the economically advanced countries. Most of the necessary everyday activities have become easier and more pleasant. Unfortunately, the developments in the mental (spiritual) sphere are not fast enough to keep pace with the changes in technology and economy. Again and again, people show that their mental maturity does not correspond to their economic wealth and technological power. This situation is a source of numerous social problems, pathologies and sicknesses, which affect mostly the economically wealthy societies. Also in Poland, where the so-called Western way of life suddenly has become available for most of people, we can notice the appearance of social problems that were not known during the previous epoch. Classical geographers were conscious of these problems and their consequences and we can expect that their ideas could prove to be useful again. Since the inequalities between particular developments of human societies are connected with some aspects of development in science, they will be considered.

Scientific Context

Contemporary disproportions between technology and consciousness are the reflection and consequence of the gap which exists between arts and sciences, or the dichotomy between fact and value. This distinction came to be the basis on which the sciences and the humanities were differentiated and separated. To avoid values scientists adopted a doctrine of moral neutrality. The result was such estrangement of the sciences from humanities that scientists generally lost the desire and ability to communicate with non-scientific scholars. After these attitudes had been defended by positivism in the middle of the 19th century, the gap grew to the point, that many scientists were no longer willing to accept that the work of humanists had any meaning at all. By the middle of the 20th century the sciences and the humanities were generally considered to be so different from each other, that they could appropriately be characterized as two different cultures. Few scholars understood the need of interdisciplinary cooperation and tried to formulate special humanistic-scientific projects. Among them one can find mainly the representatives of theoretical physics, medicine, and geography. Huge expansion of science and its growing specialization make it difficult to develop a coherent view of the world, and to gain understanding of the very essence of human life. This has led to the mental crisis oppressing contemporary human civilization and to the serious social and environmental problems. It was expressed by the great Polish writer, Nobel Prize winner, Czessaw Miosz, who said that

"*The pollution of the natural environment with the by-product of technology* should be considered a direct response of the pollution of human mentality with *the by-products of science*" (Miosz, 1990).

The pull-push tensions of humanism and science are an age-old theme that lately has attained particular pertinence in the world of exploding technology and economic growth. For geography this problem should be one of the key issues. It is due to the fact that geography was a discipline which covered both the natural and cultural phenomena. According to the concept of the first Polish geographer, Wincenty Pol, geography was essentially to be an original idea of integration of particular areas of studies. Pol realised the abstractiveness of strictly scientific considerations and the fact that they disturb the natural unity and order. He saw geography as a necessary supplement to the particular sciences, getting a coherent picture of *cosmic unity*, which raises human intuition and cognitive abilities, which are far beyond the reach of perceptual experience (Pol, 1877).

The Polish geographer seems to be close to the view of Varenius, who wrote, that geography possesses special value *(excellency)*, which allows geographers to see synthetically *Kingdoms and Properties of the Earth*, with the eyes of the soul. This kind of recognition is available to geographers only and no specialist can reach that: *neither Divines, Physitians, Lawyers, Historians nor other Professors* (Kish, 1978: 377).

Geography was seen as a counterweight to an unavoidable specialization process in science also in the writings by another Polish 19th century geographer, Wacsaw Naskowski: "*The specialist prevents the geographer from shallowness and from too quick* generalizations, and the geographer in turn prevents him against the one-sided views of limited horizons of thought; he prevents the specialist from straying amid the oppressive weight of details in one exclusive area of study, he teaches to understand these details as an integral part of a coherent and harmonious *whole – the Gaia*".

So geography has a long tradition as a "great synthesis", but the far reaching consequences of the quantitative revolution and the fragmentation of study areas have led to the situation in which geography loses its identity and autonomy as an unified area of knowledge. Today geographers seldom refer to the classical synthetic concepts, and they even deny the role of geography as the great synthesis. Even one of the most eminent contemporary geographers, Roland J. Johnston, turned out to be the representative of the reductionist view of geography. In the contemporary discussion he showed no inclination to accept that geography... "*is* the discipline with the mind-set to take all of the pieces, position them, integrate *them and explain the big picture*". In his critical review of A. J. Pitman's paper (Pitman, 2005, pp. 137–148) he argued:

"*It is unclear when and where geographers first made the claim to be the* grand synthesizers, the only members of the academic profession with a mind-set so skilled across the wide range of disciplines that we can put them all together and see the big picture that others are to myopic to discern. But have we ever really been able to do that? Certainly as a student 45 years ago I had no training *in 'synthesis*'" (Johnston, 2006, pp. 7–11).

It is hard to say, like Johnston, seems to be completely unaware of some key achievements of modern philosophy of science. He also did not understand the 20th century psychological experiments, which showed that the subjective and synthetic character of perception and knowing is one of the characteristics of human personality. The position of Johnston seems to be particularly difficult to understand in the face of the fact that the synthetic (or interdisciplinary) concept of geography seems to be attractive for the younger generation of geographers (comp. e.g. Lau and Pasquini, 2008). The attitude of Johnston is quite popular among Polish geographers and this is the main reason why we are not in the position to decide what the essence of geography is. Is it the "great synthesis" or is it not? We are even not in the position to state what exactly geography is. Is it a natural science or a humanistic area of study? We do not know if there is a possibility to define exactly its subject-matter or not? And if not, how one can describe its essence? To answer all these questions we have to arrange epistemological studies and to examine and reinterpret numerous old ideas. And the necessary condition of that is the research in the area of the history of geographical thought, understood in the way designed by Joachim Lelewel.

EDUCATIONAL CONTEXT

It was the common conviction among the geographers in pre-war Poland that geography, thanks to its unlimited scope and its closeness to the everyday life, is a field which could be a basis for creation of a coherent vision of the world, joining all ways of knowing. Geography was believed to be a field, which suited best the needs of general education. It was expressed by one of the leaders of Polish pre-war geography – Ludomir Sawicki of the Jagiellonian University, who wrote some 80 years ago:

"*The hitherto existing education of societies has been performed at schools,* which have cultivated separately the arts or the sciences. And there have emerged two camps. The first consists of people, who are mainly influenced by aesthetics, belles-lettres, history, and philosophy, who look at the world with the eyes of idealists, fixed on the past. The other camp in turn is coming from the empirical and looks at the world with the eyes of realists. Failing to embrace with their senses, and to grasp the whole of terrestrial phenomena, both camps have judged *reality falsely, making mistakes in the arena of public life* (...). *Geography forces* us to put both points of view together, and join the scientific and humanistic perspectives to create an organic whole, it makes us see simultaneously with the *eyes of scientists and humanists* (...). *Modern geography is a field, which wants* to unify the whole of terrestrial phenomena, to comprehend them in a coherent view. If we make the cosmos, the eternal order of things intelligible for us, we will master our land and our people with care, and will lead them to where common *needs and our conscience tell*".

As you can see, Sawicki wanted geography to provide pupils with the broad, general knowledge useful in everyday life. He expected geography to become the core of general education. He wanted it to be a source of practical wisdom instead of the mere knowledge limited to the specialist areas. He saw geography as the only discipline which could fulfill the requirements of the pedagogical axiom, by which I mean the basic principle of pedagogy, formulated in 1920 by German humanist, Georg Kerschensteiner; and popularized in Poland mainly by Bogdan Nawroczyński (1987).This principle says that not all kinds of knowledge can be effectively utilized in the teaching practice. In the process of education only that knowledge can be applied the structure of which is closely related to the structure of human psyche, that is to say, which can simultaneously engage and influence all human psychic powers. This is also in accordance with the Kantian category of synopsis.

Due to the specialization and fragmentation of knowledge people have lost the primary feeling of unity of the world. The whole world seems to be fragmented and the knowledge of it divided into separate categories and domains. And in each of them different laws and values happen to be in force. In the sphere of material bodies, force and energy are the most important elements. In the world of biological life the ability to survive in the face of changing conditions is most essential. In economy money is the most important thing, meanwhile in the domain of humanities the spiritual values are in force. Which values should we follow in our own lives then, and how should we teach our children? What is more important: physical force and violence, biological wealth, economic power, or humanistic ideals?

How to reconcile the contrary values arising from different teaching subject areas? We have to admit that the values preferred by the particular fields of knowledge have not too much in common. Where should we then look for wisdom, which could help us to choose the right directions and ways of life, to reconcile the divergent tendencies, which influence us depending on where we are and what we do? Where should we look for the values, which could allow us "*to master our land and our people, and to lead them to where common needs and our conscience tell*".

Looking for the answers to these questions we should keep in mind, that it was also one of the main problems for geographers and that they resolved it decades ago. We have to remember, that it was geography that was the only field, which transcended all boundaries, in which all sharp distinctions between different disciplines and particular paths of knowledge, even between the natural and the human, disappeared. Looking at the Polish classical geography one can say that it was an effort taken in order to reconcile particular fields of knowledge and to create a necessary tool for the selection of the knowledge which could be essential from the point of view of education. What are then the values which arise from geography? Contrary to particular sciences, for a geographer there is no universal set of values. They are changing from culture to culture, from place to place. For a geographer, the most important value is always the value, which is the most important from the point of view of society, on the local, regional, and global scale. To make a selection of knowledge for educational purposes, a geographer has to know what is important from the point of view of ordinary people. This is the reason why geography has always been fascinating and interesting. It simply concerns the problems and phenomena, which are connected with the everyday life of societies. And this is the fact that makes true the old Kantian sentence: "*nothing is more able to enlighten the sound human intellect than exactly geography*".

The history of geographical thought is probably the only discipline, which is in the position to restore geography's rationale and to create new lines of thought, which could make geography a socially relevant field of knowledge. If we need to create new geographical concepts, we can do it only on the condition that we utilize the past ideas. We will discover nothing new if we fail to lean on the shoulders of our predecessors. This is because no discipline, neither scientific nor humanistic, can develop without special attention paid to its humanistic component, which embraces its history and philosophy.

MODERN GEOGRAPHIC THOUGHT

Environmental Determinism: In the latter half of the nineteenth century Darwinism was all the rage. An increase in the interest of biology combined with old geographic ideas of the Greeks. German-trained geographers like Ellen Churchill Semple and others began to study groups of people and cultures through the framework of the environmental conditions. This became known as environmental determinism.

In short, these geographers believed people, cultures, civilizations, et al. could only develop as far as the environment would let them. Examples would be island people are isolationist because they live on an island or no advance culture could develop near the equator because it is too hot and when it is hot people do not work as much.

Environmental Determinism quickly got involved with Social Darwinism and racist ideals. It became a tool for those who supported imperialism; the justification was that the natives were environmentally-capped and needed those from a better climate to care for them as best as possible.

CULTURAL AND REGIONAL GEOGRAPHY

Around the 1920s there was a fundamental shift against environmental determinism. Two theories of thought more or less joined together and became the leading forces in geography. The Berkeley School of Cultural Geography was based on the works of German geographers who believed that Culture (with a capital "C") was the highest unifying force of a group of people. Culture was everything from the arts, to beliefs, to customs, and more. Cultural geographers believed a person and people were capable of doing anything from making a desert bloom to adopting a new style of government; the only thing that imposed limitations on what was possible was the person or group's Culture.

Regional Geography was the lead in education at the time. Regional Geography what people think most often when they hear the word "geography." The study of countries and regions of the world is regional geography's domain. However, over time regional geography was narrowed down in schools to become memorization of capitals and the three major export products. It was this that led to what Catholicgauze refers to as "The Really Bad Times."

Quantitative Geography

The end of World War II was a good time for geography. Regional Geography with a cultural emphasis helped win the war. Geographers were highly sought after by the government, universities, the private sector, and the opposite sex. It was an era of money, fast cars, and cute bunnies who sang to geographers as they left for work. In reality it was a time of crisis. Was geography a science or an art or something else? Quantitative geographers promised to make geography a respected science. They proposed geography be done with numbers as well as maps. Means, correlation, t-values, and much more became known to geographers as they took statistics classes to understand what was going on in a spatial and numeric world. The number crunchers had geography by the neck. To be considered a geographer one had to prove their data with numbers or be exiled. It looked like the establishment was victorious. Black suits with ties for everyone. Cold, square numbers held the throne of geography.

MARXIST GEOGRAPHY

David Harvey was one of the leaders of the quantitative junta which controlled geography. But in the late 1960s he discovered Karl Marx. Harvey rejected the quantitative revolution and embraced Marxist Geography. He saw geography as a tool to make the world "better" by imposing a Marxist viewpoint and goal on his studies. Everything became seen as a struggle between the has and has nots. The counter culture of the 1960s and 1970s help fuel the rise of Marxist Geography in departments in America and England. The journal Antipode became a sort of Bible to Marxist and other "critical geographies."

Sedevacantism Geography

At the same time Marxist Geography and its critical relatives were taking on the machine there were many other geographic ideas. Behavioural Geography sought to study human behaviour by combining elements of psychology and statistics. Humanistic Geography sought to understand "the emotions" of geography and rejected statistics completely. Meanwhile regional geography laid abandon in academia. The Berkeley School of Cultural Geography dwindled in numbers and the term "cultural geography" became the domain of the critical geographers. Sedevacantism can sum up geography today. There is no one leading idea which is guiding everything else. While the big tent is nice for those who were on the outs with the establishment, geography is certainly suffering. Recently the geography department split at the University of Nebraska-Lincoln over the long debate of human geography versus physical geography. In other universities geography is frequently grouped with geology, anthropology, or even political science. This gives geography the label of "whatever is left science."

THE FUTURE FOR GEOGRAPHY

What will become of geography? The future right now points to more technology like remote sensing and especially GIS. But the geography has been known to switch directions quickly before. Maybe the globalized world at war will led to the rise of regional geography with elements of cultural studies. Maybe the potential of climate change will cause physical/ environmental geography to become more popular. What is known; however, is that multidisciplinary studies are becoming more frequent in academia. The big struggle hear is for geography to remain unique and not be absorbed into things like "environmental studies" or "international studies."

THE HISTORIES OF GEOGRAPHY

From the Renaissance onwards, the geographical works of antiquity have served both as a scientific model and also as a corpus of data which could be used for modern purposes. Estrabón or Pomponio Mela furnished chorographic models that were followed and esteemed time and again from the 16th to the 18th centuries; moreover, the information which these authors-as well as other authors of antiquity and of the Middle Ages-provided, and also itineraires and accounts of journeys, were also useful, after due criticism and authentification, in constructing the map and developing the description of the earth's surface, more particularly to the benefit of historical geography. All of this generated great interest in the old texts, in the careful editing of them-which involved the collaboration of geographers, historians and philologists-and in the study of them, as in the case of other sciences. In spite of the advances made since the Renaissance, a grasp of historical knowledge continued, until the 18th century, to be an extremely important prop in the development of modern geography. We have dealt elsewhere with the usefulness of the ancient sources and of the works of the 16th and 17th centuries in the solution of geographical problems of the 18th, and there is no need to reiterate this. We need only remind ourselves here of the interest of a D'Anville, a Homann or a Tomás Lopez in the information of ancient geographers for the construction of their maps, or how closely Buache, Torrubia and others studied the voyages of discovery in the 16th and 17th centuries in order to attempt a solution of the geographical enigmas related to continents that were still little known.

If all this is granted, it is, however, also true that from the 16th century onwards, with the great discoveries, there arose an increasing awareness of the insufficiencies and the limits of the works of the classical geographers. These works began to be supplemented and superseded by new observations from all parts of the planet. There is thus a parallel growing process of obsolescence of the ancient texts, and their role changed so that they were invoked as classical models to be imitated, both because of the diversity of the integrated data and the systematization as precedents that lend value and prestige to science. In the introductions to geographical works, in discussing the value and dignity of the science, the forerunners and ancient authors were carefully given a distinguished position, which meant that one often finds, in the histories of geography, celebrities like Moses or Homer, thus lending to the science the most illustrious ancestors.

It could be argued, therefore, that in a way the history of geography appeared with the purposes of providing dignity and legitimacy. It is an attitude which, if we look further back, we find in those same classical geographers. This may be seen, for example, in Estrabón's Geography, where in Book 1, after claiming that it is a "proper (study), no less than any other, for a philosopher", he accepts Hipparchus' thesis that its founder was Homer, and he delves into the history of geography in order to show "those who followed him were also illustrious", all of them philosophers (i.e. scientists), viz.: Anaximander, Hecataeus, Democritus, Eratosthenes, Hipparchus, Polibius and Posidinius, among many other names.

In general, up to the 19th century, the history of geography stood both as a history of the advances in our knowledge of the earth, that is to say as a history of geographical studies and explorations, and also as a history of maps. While it was, just like other histories at that time, above all a history of progresses-a "historical picture of the progress of geography", in the words of Malte-Brun-from the second half of the 18th century, due to the impact of Buffon's description of the earth, it could become an epocus of geography. The history of geography was also related to historical geography, that is to the reconstruction of the geographies of the past, particularly-from a European viewpoint-the Greek, Roman and Jewish past. As a history of journeys, there was also in connection with the discovery of possible prior claims which would assure the juridical legitimacy of political possession of those territories.

At the same time, in a geography that was essentially a descript..on of countries and regions, the history of the journeys and discoveries could continue to play its part, as is shown in the use to which it was put by two great figures at the beginning of the 19th century, Humboldt and Ritter. Thus, with reference to the so-called "comparative method", which he took over from anatomy and applied widely in writing his Erdkunde, Hanno Beck, a great specialist in his field, could write: "what Ritter understands by the comparative method is, in the first place, no more than the compilation of historical sources, ordered chronologically, above all the accounts of journeys". It is thus not surprising that these accounts, which reflected the widening geographical horizon, continued to form the essential part of the histories of geography down to the beginnings of the 20th century; histories which some authors now considered part of the history of science, and particularly useful in the study of the discipline because, as Vivien de Saint Martin wrote: "simply by following science as it passes through its successive stages one can see the place it occupies in the general development of humanity".

In the second half of the 19th century, coinciding with the spectacular growth of the scientific community of geographers, the history of geography turned its attention to new topics. The resonance of the Historical Essay conceming the Progressive Development of the Idea of the Universe, which was published in Alexander de Humboldt's Cosmos (1845-1862), and the development of physical geography, brought to these histories the evolution of ideas about the physical structure of the world and about the interrelationship between different natural phenomena. At the same time as developing a growing interest in human concerns-which was to lead to the creation of a systematic human geography-attention was also directed towards the history of the techniques and procedures used to establish the wealth and population of countries (censuses, tax-lists, etc).

At the same time, the development of a new regional geography in the second half of the 19th century implied the search for antecedents in order to delimit the chorographic units. In this respect, certain 18th century geographical contributions, such as those of Buache or the geographers of the Reine Geographie, could now be highlighted. Meanwhile, the issues of the theoretical foundations of the discipline in relation to other scientific fields led to a study of figures in the past, such as Varenius, who had reflected on the contents and methods of this science.

During the last decades of the 19th century, the academic institutionalization of geography was made by affirming the notion of a break with the past. The "new geography" that appeared in the 1880's reduced everything prior to Humboldt and Ritter to being considered as a pre-scientific stage that was now superseded, and converted it into simply an object of attention in the search for antecedents of current ideas. At the same time, the history of cartography and the history of discoveries-which, as we have seen, were traditional ingredients of the history of geography-acquired an independent development and, although they continued to be the subject of attention for certain geographers, began to be increasingly studied by specialists: the former mostly by cartographers and historians of science; the latter by the historians of society and of techniques.

From the end of the 19th century, every important theoretical change in the science of geography, and every debate concerning its foundations and methods, has been accompanied by incursions into the history of the discipline with a view to using arguments from the past to support one or other of the contesting conceptions. Important theorical works, like those of Alfred Hettner or Richard Hartshorne, also contain a historical dimension which seeks to illuminate current thinking "in the light of the past".

Our discipline had a difficult struggle towards the end of the 19th century in order to achieve recognition in the universities; moreover, because of its situation at the crossroads between the natural sciences and the social sciences, it has not only had serious problems with its foundations, it has also had numerous critics and competitors. This underlies its felt need for a justification of the discipline and the affirmation of its dignity and independence from the other natural and social sciences. Introductions to university handbooks as well as longer and shorter compendia have approached this task, and frequently there has also been a debate concerning its relations with the sciences that are "adjacent" or "auxiliary" to geography. In general, as in other disciplines, one has attempted to show the route that has led to modern, truly scientific geography.

However, as one might expect in a subject with both ancient roots, a powerful institutional development, and also a long tradition of historical studies, the histories of geography that have been written throughout the present century are richer and more varied. While it is true that a large number are written out of concern for current issues, there has also been, in past epochs, an important school of histories of geography that were directly linked to the history of science and the history of culture: specific research as well as general works on the geography of the ancient world, of the Middle Ages, of modern times, and of 19th and 20th centuries. Interest in the biographies and the individual contributions of the most illustrious geographers has more recently given way to the ambitious attempt to produce a complete biographical inventory of every geographer who has contributed to the science, and to a concern to collect the testimony of those still alive concerning their training and their ways of working.

Emphasis on the origins and evolution of geographical ideas, as well as on their intellectual and social context, appear again-and with increasing intensity-in certain works that have responded to the call that J K Wright made in 1926, and they continue, more or less explicitly, the line laid down in the works of Lovejoy.

Anthologies of geographical texts have put at the disposal of students selected fragments from the most important geographers, in some cases alongside evidence of the geographical knowledge of other historical authors (poets, philosophers, theologians, travellers, etc.).

The changes that have taken place since 1950 have caused a fissure in the unity, which the discipline had maintained since the beginning of the century, based on the acceptance by the whole scientific community of the regional paradigm and the historicist approach. These changes led to new generations of historical works, some of which have sought to recount the vicissitudes and the protagonists of the transformations that have taken place. All of this meant, first, greater attention on the present; second, a search for appropriate antecedents for each revolutionary change; and finally, a greater attention to geography's relations with the general evolution of the natural and social sciences, as well as with the general evolution of ideas and of philosophical frames of reference. It has also reinforced the tendency towards a shortened chronology of the history of the subject, one that restricts itself to contemporary geography, that is to say developments subsequent to the contributions of Humboldt and Ritter, who are solemnly considered by all sides as the fathers of present-day geography.

The attempts that have recently been made to present in a global form the discipline's historical development since antiquity faithfully reflect, as always happens, the authors' standpoint vis-a-vis the changes that have been taking place. By way of an example, we only need to cite the case of Preston James's work published in 1972. The different chronology of the changes in different countries becomes evident if we compare this work with that of the German Hanno Beck published the following year. While in the latter the quantitative revolution is totally absent, in the work of James-some 20 years older than the German-we see reflected both his acceptance of the regional paradigm and also his sensitivity to the changes that had been taking place in the discipline in its Anglo-American context. James insists that geography deals with the differences in the earth's surface (geodiversity) and investigates "what things are combined in different places to produce the complex characteristics of the world's landscape"; this shows that James is set in the same line as Hartshorne, that is to say in the conception of a geography of regions and landscapes. However, at the same time, the allusions to the mental images, to the importance of relative location, and the statement that "scientists have formulated many different kinds of explanations to make the mental images plausible and acceptable, and their explanations, in turn, often determined what features they choose to observe", all of which demonstrates that the work was written after the debates of the 1950's and 1960's.

One sentence in particular reflects his awareness of, and his reservations about, quantitative geography: according to him, scientists "sought and found mathematical regularities separate from the processes of change, that nevertheless satisfied the urge to explain the images of geodiversity". In this "nevertheless" we see unconsciously reflected his disqualification of those mathematical discoveries which, faced with the urgency to find provisional solutions, provide only momentary satisfaction. In other words, we see in him all the dissatisfaction of a traditional-though sensitive and open geographer with one of the fundamental aspects of the quantitative revolution. Thence arises an excellent history, conceived in a particular place and time (USA, 1970), with a wide perspective, and with great attention to the most recent developments (in the 1960's), though at the same time without renouncing his own viewpoints.

With all this evolution, the history of geography is today an extraordinarily rich and diverse field, with a long tradition of research carried out within the discipline. Ever since the first International Geographical Congress in Amberes in 1871, practically all meetings have devoted attention to these topics, usually in specific sections dedicated to "The History of Geography and Historical Geography". More recently (since 1968), within the International Geographical Union a commission devoted to "The History of Geographical Thought" has been formed; this has stimulated new research, and there have been discussions on reports of the most varied types: journeys, the history of ideas, philosophical frames of reference, biographies of scientists, history of the language and methods of geography, institutions, etc. As one might expect, in all these works there is a mixture: of those who approach history from concerns that arise in current scientific or professional practice, and those whose interest is in history itself; those who use traditional historical techniques, and those in search of new ways, using philological, bibliometric or iconographic techniques; those who aim to set their research in the most general area of the history of science, alongside those who still see their research as serving to legitimize and dignify the discipline.

HISTORY OF GEOGRAPHY IN SPAIN

There has been a similar evolution in Spain. Studies in the history of geography in this country have a long tradition to which we can refer only briefly here. It has undoubtedly been a field of interest to geographers, but also to social historians, naval historians, and historians of science. These studies, together with those of historical geography, have also had great significance in the general development of the subject, since they were, for a long time, predominant among the different geographical studies. Owing to the intimate association which existed, as we have mentioned, between the history of geography and the history of discoveries, it has been sailors interested in naval history who have produced some of the most important contributions.

We find an example of this in the work of the erudite author of the Enlightement Martin Fernández de Navarrete, whose Disertación sobre la Historia de la Naútica y de las Ciencias Matemáticas que han contribuido a sus progresos entre los españoles, published by the Royal Historical Academy in 1846, is surely the most outstanding contribution of the whole of the 19th century. The founding during the Restoration-specifically in 1876-of the Geographical Society of Madrid (subsequently the Royal Geographical Society) allowed the gathering of a large number of geographers interested in all aspects of the discipline including, among the foremost, the history of geography. The historical topics that were developed by this nucleus of geographers, and by certain historians and naturalists connected to them, were mostly very much in line with the traditional focus which associates the history of geography with the history of geographical discoveries. Although there were some works on antiquity and the Middle Ages (concerning journeys, or medieval geographical descriptions), the majority of the contributions were studies of the changes in our knowledge of the earth from the 16th century onwards. Special attention was paid to navigation and to the Spanish cosmographs, as well as Spanish enterprises such as the Geographical Reports, ordered by King Philip ll, or of Spanish enterprises in America. Obituaries and commemorative tributes formed another important line of work, to which should be added the historical accounts of certain geographical institutions, from the Casa de Contratación in Seville, to the Geographical and Statistical Institute, and the Geographical Society itself. Finally, the zeal to keep abreast of the geographical advances of the times and to report one's participation at international congresses gave rise to a last line which are today valuable contributions to the history of geography, although at the time, of course, they did not have this purpose. At all events, this is the reason why in current bibliographies on this topic we notice a heavy concentration on the 1 9th and the beginning of the 20th centuries.

The general historical works that were published during the Restoration continued to set forth the progress in geographical knowledge of the earth in general and of its continents and countries, and they therefore continued to be histories of discoveries and explorations-which at this time reached as far as the polar regions-but devoted ever more attention to geographical descriptions and to geographers and their individual works. Among all the published works, that of Jerónimo Becker deserves a special mention. The introduction of the new French (and, to a lesser extent, the new German) geography also led to certain theoretical debates published in particular after 1910.

In referring to the content and focus of the studies that were made before the civil war, one expert, Professor Joaquín Bosque Maurel, has seen fit to write that the studies in the history of geography were produced "with a greater concern for description than for explanation, of the facts and of the protagonists". In the years immediately after the Spanish civil war (1936-1939), geographers went on writing this type of history, which continued to concentrate on the usual topics: discoveries, chorographic studies, biographies, and the contributions of individual geographers.

Certain authors who had started to publish before the war continued to do so,. The celebration of certain jubilees meant that certain figures received repeated attention, both from geographers and from historians: the cases of Humboldt and Jorge Juan particularly stand out because of the number of studies that were devoted to them. The history of cartography, of geodesic triangulation, and of the scientific institutions aroused renewed interest, centered in particular on the figures of Ibañez de Ibero and Francisco de Coello. There appeared also more general works on specific topics, such as Spanish military cartography in the 19th century; at the same time certain new topics were tackled, such as the history of administrative divisions or the history of certain geographical concepts. In certain cases, the concern for the history of the discipline in a broad, general perspective was united with an interest in the most recent changes and in the theoretical foundations of geography; there was also an appreciation of less well-known traditions such as the Catalan tradition. Meanwhile, the most recently published anthologies adopted a short chronology, only including texts from the 19th and 20th centuries. Handbooks and more general works have on occasions continued to incorporate historical contributions that, by through legitimacy and self-justification, serve a socializing function.

The contribution of social and naval historians continues to stand out and, thanks to these, we have new and valuable studies: of the geographical institutions, like the Casa de Contratación by J. Pulido, or the Geographical Society of Madrid an excellent study by E. Hernández Sandoica; of cosmographs such as Alonso de Chaves, by P. Castañeda; of the role of geography in the economic development of the Enlightenment, by J. Muñoz Pérez; of the development of American geography, by F. Morales, J. Muñoz Pérez, R. Serrera, et al. Historians of science show a growing interest in navigation and journeys; in expeditions (Lucena); or in the process of geometrication of the earth (A. Lafuente). At the same time, institutions like the

Naval Museum, the Museum of Natural Sciences, The National Library, the Geographical Service of the Army, and others tackled the publication of systematic catalogues of their richly documented archives or the publication of manuscripts and other works of great geographical interest which had become out of print.

Without doubt, the range of Spanish studies in the history of geography is today richer and more varied than was the case in years gone by, both with regard to available sources, and also to individual papers and interest in new topics. In general, though, there is still a predominance of descriptive and monographic studies, while those of an interpretative nature remain a minority. At all events, one frequently notes a failure to set these studies within a more general frame of reference linked to the great theoretical concerns, or within the history of science at the time in question. In one sense, however, this should be the main concern in setting up research programs, since these urgently need to go beyond a scope restricted to the discipline itself, and shed-if it is still there-the concern with apologetics for, and self-justification of, the discipline, and instead, in close collaboration with philosophers, epistemologists, historians and sociologists, adopt a more general frame of reference.

GENERAL FRAME OF REFERENCE

The beginning of the research program in the history of geography undertaken by our Department team at the University of Barcelona was closely linked to the changes that began to take place in the science of geography in the 1950's, and which were felt in Spain towards the end of the 1960's. In those years, the delayed impact in our country of the quantitative revolution and, immediately following it, the first echoes of the antipositivist revolution forced us to question the theoretical presuppositions that had prevailed in the geographical community up to that point. This gave rise to theoretical reflections which soon led to an epistemological, historical and sociological enquiry into the foundations and development of the discipline.

In the first phase we had to come to grips with the theoretical and methodological presuppositions of the "new geographies", and spread the word. Some of the first works whose aim was to systematize and proselytize were published in the Revista de Geografía of the then recently founded Department of Geography at the University of Barcelona, and also in the collection "Geographical Thought and Method", where we published a translation-some 20 years after its original publication-of the particularly important theoretical paper by Fred K. Shaeffer, Exceptionalism in Geography. The promotion of a systematic understanding both of the basic theoretical texts of thenew movements and also the standpoints that criticized the prevailing ideas was what lay behind the founding of Geo Crítica, subtitled "Critical Papers in Human Geography" the first issue appeared in January 1976, and its aims of criticism and renewal were manifest right from the start.

The changes that took place revealed, time and again, the need to answer questions concerning the definition and goal of geography, concerning the strands of continuity that existed between the new developments and the old geographical tradition, concerning the validity of geographical synthesis and the integration of physical and human aspects into the discipline, concerning the position of geography in the system of the sciences and its relation to other scientific disciplines, particularly to those that had hitherto been considered as "adjacent" or "auxiliary" sciences. There was a constant recurrence of the subject of continuity and change, while the changes that had recently taken place were so momentous that they appeared to question the notion of the linear development and progressive accumulation of the science. All of this led to a consideration of the subject of "normal science", of scientific revolutions, as well as of the paradigms, concepts that had earlier been applied in Geography in an attempt to explain the changes that were taking place.

Without doubt, Kuhn's work on scientific revolutions had crystallized many ideas-still diffuse in the early 60's-about the farreaching nature of the revolutionary changes which various branches of science had undergone during the 1950's. Geography was one of the subjects most profoundly affected, and the notion of "revolution" had come to be widely accepted in the geographical community. It is no accident that in 1963 lan Burton published an article on "The quantitative revolution and theoretical geography", where he emphasized the importance of the change and defended the view that the revolution had triumphed in geography. Shortly afterwards, Kuhn's ideas were applied directly to geography in order to justify the change of paradigm, and they became standard in the discipline.

In early 1970, when all of these issues were making themselves felt in geography in Spain, the debate over Kuhn's proposals was very lively, and serious criticisms had already been leveled at his scheme, which nevertheless proved to be enormously stimulating. This is why we need to look at alternative views, especially starting from Gaston Bachelard's and Michel Foucault's ideas of "epistemological breaks" and epistemic changes, and ending with the positivism-historicism contrast proposed by Ernest Cassirer, Von Wright and other epistemologists, which in one form is found implicitly in geography in the work of Shaeffer, whose theory is closely linked to German neopositivist circles.

This last cited theoretical frame of reference provides us with a basis for presenting the history of contemporary geographical thought in terms of the recurrent contrast between positivism and historicism. This interpretative scheme was also applied to the evolution of contemporary physical geography, as well as to the development of Spanish geography and to the thought of certain contemporary geographers.

Just as Kuhn predicted, every revolutionary change in a science leads to the rewriting of its history. Right from the outset, this is precisely what quantitative geographers did: they quoted new accounts and authorities in their struggle to gain acceptance for the new ideas. But this at the same time threw doubt on the whole of accepted history, since it put in question the value and significance of the historical precedents that had been commonly accepted for much longer than the strictly contemporary period.

From 1974 on, in the collection "Pensamiento y Método Geográficos" (Geographical thought and Method), we aimed to re-examine the authorities and the significant works in the history of modern geography, including both figures who had little direct impact on the Spanish tradition and texts that had been forgotten or were little known. This is the reason behind the partial translation of Varenius' Geografía Generalis (1650) and of the study concerning the significance of this work, as well as certain later publications.

It was becoming increasingly clear that the revolutionary scientific changes affected both theory and methods, while at the same time producing decisive changes in questions of prestige and power relationships within the scientific community. In the 1950's and 1960's the debate surrounding the introduction of quantitative geography had turned into a real civil war within the community; what was at stake was not merely scientific conceptions, but also social factors relating to control over the community. At the same time, the early research that we carried out into the institucional development of contemporary geography showed the importance of the opposition and social conflicts which it had produced within the scientific community in the 1 9th century. It also highlighted the decisive role played by the defence of the geographers' interests, and the strategies that were adopted for this, in the configuration of academic geography from the turn of the century on.

What began to emerge from all of this was an autonomous program in the history of geography which sought to encompass the whole development of modern geography, from the Renaissance and the Scientific Revolution up to the present. Right from the start, due to the nature of its origins and goals, this program necessarily implied profound historical, theoretical and sociological dimensions. As it has unfolded, we have been led to forge ever increasing links with other specialists studying the same topics but from different angles.

This research program, in which we have been fully engaged for the last fifteen years, makes certain presuppositions which need to be made clear. Above all, an acceptance of the usefulness of historical research in the work of today's scientists. Faced with different and succeeding "new geographies" and faced with the diversity of theoretical and methodological options in our subject today, historical research, guided by well-defined theoretical goals and permanently and dynamically in touch with current scientific practice, offers a perspective that allows us to discriminate, evaluate and select among different approaches and methods, and allows us to compare the different theories that are put forward.

From the educational point of view, the history of a subject, and in general the history of science, plays an important part because it helps us to respond undogmatically to questions concerning the boundaries of each branch of knowledge and their relations with other sciences. Moreover, and perhaps more importantly, it allows us to show that scientific problems have in variably been formulated historically, and this underlines that what is important in science is never the answers but the formulation of the questions.

The history of geography, like that of any subject, also has a value for its own sake; not in its search for legitimacy, but as a contribution to the history of science, and in general to the history of society. Our interest is in the history of geography in relation to other aspects of scientific activity in the past, that is to say as history of science, of culture and of society.

Although our program touches on general issues, the prime focus of our research is on the history of geography and the history of science in Spain and in the Iberoamerican countries. This tradition is richer and more important than is normally appreciated by historians brought up in the Anglosaxon, French or German schools; indeed it is essential in our discipline in order to understand the origin of modern geography. Finally, our project also has a political dimension in that we are convinced that the history of hispanic science can contribute to eliminate the feelings of inferiority often found in our countries. This has grave consequences for our university students since they accept uncritically the stereotypes of superiority of other traditions, without a due appreciation of their own history; they are thus easy prey to cultural colonization and become incapable of conceiving and carrying out ambitious scientific projects.

CONTINUITY AND CHANGE

The problem of continuity and change within the scientific disciplines is felt acutely in a science like geography, which has been studied without a break for-at least-virtually three thousand years: The comparison of present-day geographical works with those of the past reveals immediately profound differences of goals and method. While the term that is used for this branch of science, "geography", i.e. description of the earth, has remained constant, and while members of the community tend to affirm the notion of continuity, an examination of the evolution of the discipline allows us to see the great differences in the work of the geographer, not only from the ages of Herodotus and Estrabón, but even between what was done in the 18th century and what is today undertaken by these scholars.

This led us to set up a line of research that would attempt to reconstruct an unprejudiced history of geography from the Renaissance and the Scientific Revolution up to the present. We hold that the modern era is essential to the modifications to the content of the discipline, but that changes from classical times up to the Renaissance may, for our purposes, be disregarded. As well as the analysis of the changes within the subject, we are interested in its relations with other branches of knowledge, and the interchanges and reciprocal influences that there may have been. The study of these relationships is very important, both at times when there was no marked scientific specialization, with scientists often simply changing the boundaries between the various sciences, and also from the 19th century on, when as a rule we find institutions and scientific communities clearly structured and differentiated.

From the very beginning, geography has had a dual nature, partly mathematical and partly historical, making this study of great interest, but at the same time creating a danger because of the breadth and diversity of the directions that could be followed.

The traditional division of general geography into mathematical (or astronomical), physical (or natural) and political (or civil) reflects the different facets of this branch of knowledge. This division was clearly made as early as the 17th century. As a mixed mathematical science it studied the geographical characteristics that derive from the shape and movements of the earth, made measurements and produced maps. As a physical or natural science, it was concerned with the composition of the planet, with the shape of its surface, with the distribution of land and sea-this latter being the specific subject matter of hydrography-and of the distribution of vegetable and animal life. Finally, as a political science, its concerns were the characteristics of the peoples of the earth and the nature of their societies.

At the same time, the special, particular or chorographic side of geography described continents, countries and regions in all the complexity of their physical and human traits, and this became an enormously ambitious encyclopedic undertaking. As a descriptive science geography was a "historical" subject, and it figures as such in many of the classifications of the sciences from the Renaissance on; however, at the same time it was included, closely related to astronomy, as a mixed mathematical or physicomathematical science.

As a mixed mathematical science, geography was studied as part of Mathematics at the universities, and it has been present in practically all the great scientific institutions of modern times. In the 17th century it was in the vanguard of scientific knowledge, and it was associated with the solutions to some of the great problems of the Scientific Revolution. This relationship and the growing separation which took place between geography and mathematics in the 18th century have been the subject of some of our papers. The publication of the work of Manuel de Aguirre (1782) made accessible a basic text of 18th century Spanish geography; it was representative of the "new geography" which was possible thanks to the definitive resolution of the problem of the size and shape of the earth.

The study of the mathematical dimensions of geography naturally leads to the history of cartography in the modern and contemporary eras; some of our work has already dealt with this topic, and it is one of the fields we would like to tackle in greater depth in the future. The republication and study of the first great scientific bibliography of the Hispanic world-Andrés González de Barcia's edition of A. León Pinelo's Epitome (1737)-puts at our disposal a copious source of references to works on geography, cosmography and navigation, as well as ancient maps, which could prove extremely useful for later studies.

We must also look at the relationship between physical geography and the physical sciences, and our project began by turning to the study of the specific contributions of geographers to the development of theories concerning the earth, and also to the influences that have made themselves felt from other branches of science. The systematization of data from diverse sources on relief, rivers, seas and lakes, and the speculations concerning the laws of their distribution over the surface of the earth, are contributions of the first order that geographers made to the study which we today call geology. Issues that particularly interest us are: how physical geography became today's geology and similarly, what were the changing relations between the former and both the geology of plants and zoogeography.

Through political and regional geography, relations were established with a wide range of social sciences, which only started to become scientific disciplines in the 18th century. In that century, political economics, statistics and ethnography-in particular-overlapped with geography, both in aims and methods. As in the cases already quoted, their development as independent disciplines could not help affecting the integrative ambitions of the latter.

The evolution of the names of the branches of knowledge reflects the trials and changes in the evolution of science. The first thing that strikes us is the large number of branches which appeared in the luxuriant trees of earlier classifications of the sciences, but which today are not recognized as such. Another noteworthy fact is the semantic changes that affect the meaning of names of the sciences. Geography itself is an interesting example of this.

As the 17th century progressed, the description of the earth (geography) gave way to the scientific study of the earth (geology), but the new science-which finally acquired this name among other possibilities that were also current-developed only one of the facets that made up classical and modern geography. With the development of astronomy, geophysics, botany (especially botanical geography), statistics, political economy, etc., geography was becoming reduced essentially to chorography (the description of countries and regions) and topography (the description of places and counties). The former, however, which could have turned into chorology, was used for one part of geography (regional geography), and the latter turned into a new branch of science with different aims. In fact, in the 19th century "topography" was used in two different senses. One was the traditional sense, and was widely used in medicine at the time, which had not yet undergone the bacteriological revolution and which still laid great emphasis on the old Hippocratic line of environmental causes. We are referring to the "medical topographies", occasionally on the grand scale-and therefore truly topographic-but sometimes medium or small scale-and thus chorographic; in all of these we see reflected the old geographical line of regional studies. The second sense was new: it referred to the appearance of a new science in the hands of new practitioners for the geodesical and cartographical operations in the territory.

The persistence and the changes in the names of branches of science are certainly of great interest; they give us a shifting panorama of the system of sciences in relation to the transformations in the bases of scientific activity.

After the process of specialization-starting in the 18th century and increasing in the 19th-geography might have disappeared, with its functions being taken over by other sciences: geology; cosmography, an old name now in desuetude but which was used institutionally even up to the 1 9th century; statistics, or the study of a state's data; physiography, or the descriptive study of the earth's surface in all its complexity, which was on the point of replacing geography in education; ecology, or the science of relationship between living creatures and their habitat; political economy; chorography; topography... But it did not disappear for various reasons, among which we should emphasize the educational: the presence of Geography in the educational system as well as its educational and cultural role.

In the whole of this diachronic process, one event in the 19th century was to take on an ever-increasing significance. This was the formation of well structured scientific communities with strong institutional backing.

These were the cause of the crystallization of science into clearly demarcated disciplines that competed among themselves for the well defined fields of learning. It began as a problem in the rational classification of libraries-which presupposed a classification of the subjects; it thence turned into a philosophical question concerning the classification of the fields of knowledge; it continued in the 18th century as a more or less successful exercise and effort to propose new names; and it reached its conclusion in the 1 9th century with the crystallization into rigidly demarcated disciplines that were studied by mutually competing scientific communities.

MODELS OF PROFESSIONALIZATION AND INSTITUTIONALIZATION

Institutionalization and professionalization, with the concomitant training in the scientific communities, has in reality played an essential part in the formation and development of the scientific disciplines. It is these communities, backed by teaching and research institutions, that have made possible the process of specialization, which was fundamental to scientific progress in the 18th an 19th centuries. The sociology of science has shown quite clearly how important a community focus and institutional factors are in the process of academic socialization and in the selection and acceptance of scientific concepts. It is through the creation and consolidation of scientific communities that social action normally makes itself felt in the development of scientific thought. This is why, we might say, the old controversy between internalists and externalists can be given a new perspective, focusing on those institutional and community aspects.

The scientific community, which is a subsystem of society, is in its turn broken down differentiated, disciplinary communities, with varying prestige and social power. In these communities, when the practical, applied or technical side is more important than the purely scientific, we may speak of professional bodies. Although the communities have intellectual interests in common, they also have to defend corporate interests, vis-a-vis both their individual members and also competing communities. In pursuing these interests, they display-both within the community and outside it-social and intellectual strategies that are sometimes essential for the evolution of scientific concepts.

Within this general view, the study of the community of geographers became a cornerstone of our research. We have distinguished two separate periods. During the first, reaches to the 18th or early 19th century, the profession of geographer existed, but there was little specialization and professionalization. By this we mean that geographers, just like other scientists, would often study different fields of learning. In the second, starting in the middle of the 19th century, national scientific communities were formed and these, through organizations and intersecting relations, became integrated into a supranational community of geographers with rigidly defined rules of access and modes of operation. Our project aims to establish: the specific and general characteristics of the community of geographers and their relationship with the rest of the scientific community; the different models of professionalization and of organization of the intellectual tasks; the rules of access and the internal operating norms; and in general the social strategies that are deployed and their influence on scientific activity and the concepts that are generated. We believe we have been able to demonstrate conclusively that, in the case of the community of geographers, certain aspects in the evolution of the subject are not fully comprehensible unless we take into account all these social aspects.

The process of socialization which takes place within a community is essential to the way in which practice is carried out; the vocabulary, the concepts and even the very theories put forward will be affected by entry requirements, syllabuses, reading and practical assignments, professional applications, etc. This is why, when different scientific communities tackle subjects that totally or partially coincide, the relation between the community structure and the intellectual output is of particular interest. This is a new, stimulating way of tackling the general issue of the connection between social factors and the development of scientific thought.

Geography is especially well situated for this type of comparative analysis. As a science that deals with the earth's spatial arrangement and relations, it well overlap more or less extensively with other subjects that deal with the same space. We feel that it is of great interest to observe how scientists or professionals from different communities approach the same goal.

Apart from geographers, some of the scientific communities that deal in their various ways with the earth's space are: geologists, geophysicists, soil scientists, botanists, oceanographers, economists, anthropologists, human ecologists, sociologists and historians. To these we need to add several technical-scientific communities whose work, which requires previous training of a scientific kind, impinges on that space: architects; highway, forestry, civil and mining engineers; agronomists; and the armed forces.

For all of these, just as for geographers, the earth's space is the ineluctable setting for the working out of their theories or for their professional operations that seek to change it. However, corresponding to the various aims, each one selects and highlights different aspects. It is an essential part of our research to show in what way this takes place and how the community structure affects the selection and development of spatial concepts and theories. This is why we have chosen some of these communities to start our project; we cannot deny that we would prefer to have the time and the means to embrace them all.

The methodology that we use includes the analysis of various dimensions. One is a study of the institutional structure: legislation concerning qualifications and functions; internal operational norms; recruitment, selection, quality control. Another looks at the process of academic socialization: syllabuses and courses of study; teaching institutions; degrees; ideological justification of the dignity and usefulness of the work to be done. A third is an inventory of the members of the scientific community; this should be as complete as possible, thus allowing subsequent prosopographic analysis. Finally, the study and appreciation of the scientific output, of the professional work and of the other intellectual activities of the members of the group, with special attention, in our case, to the publications and activities that refer to the earth's space.

The aim of all this is an understanding of the intellectual bases and the social interests that might have affected the development of concepts and scientific theories related to the earth's space; we must separate, on the one hand, any common aspects that are the result of ideas prevailing in the scientific community in general or in society at each moment in history, and, on the other, those specific, distinguishing features related to socialization in the discipline and to the intellectual and professional aims of the community.

With this methodology we have already undertaken a study of the corps of Spanish military engineers. Throughout the 18th and part of the 19th centuries-due to the late appearance of civil engineersthis group was essential to cartographic work, to the description and study of the land, and to spatial arrangement. For the 18th century we have produced a biographical index and inventory of the scientific and spatial work undertaken by the thousand or so members of the group, and also a study of their scientific training and institutional structure, as well as various analyses of their spatial operations. We are now carrying out an analysis of their scientific and cartographic output, relating it to the norms of the corps (orders that determined the type of maps and descriptions to be made), and to their training in the Spanish Military Academies of Mathematics in the 1 8th century. As to the 19th century, the study of this corps has been set in a more general analysis of the role of geography and the use of spatial concepts in military training.

At the same time we have tackled, either directly or in relation to other lines of research, the study of oceanographers, forestry engineers, agricultural engineers, highway engineers, soil scientists, anthropologists, and, as we have already said, geographers. If the whole project is allowed to continue for a few more years, we hope to be able to reach interesting conclusions, within our limited scope, concerning the general issue of the relation between social factors and the development of scientific knowledge.

In our view, this corporative and institutional analysis is also in close relation to the problem of the formation and evolution of the scientific disciplines. The differences in "these rational undertakings that are the scientific disciplines" have both an intellectual and a social dimension. From the intellectual point of view, the disciplines are distinguished by the key issues which they seek to resolve; from the social viewpoint, by the ecological, i.e. institutional, setting in which they have developed. Starting with the institutionalization and formation of the scientific community, there is a growing differentiation that leads to a vocabulary, concepts and traditions that become constantly more distinct. The disciplinary boundaries and the existence of conflicts between communities set limits, in certain cases, to contacts and intellectual interchanges; at other times they result in new relations that affect theoretical and methodological evolution.

Of the two dimensions that have to be taken into account in the definition and demarcation of the scientific disciplines, the social is probably the more fundamental. This is shown by the existence of communities who tackle a similar or practically identical key issue, but consider themselves, nevertheless, as separate communities and disciplines. Examples of this are: sociology and anthropology, geography and human ecology, or geography and regional studies as a branch of economics; we have devoted some attention to the last two of these. On many occasions, it is the profession that the scientist claims he belongs to-through his institutional connections-rather than the problems, methods and theories that distinguish certain disciplines from others.

All of this presupposes historical and sociological research that is of interest to current scientific practice. Issues that can be illuminated by this research are: the evaluation of the role of the scientific disciplines, and of the disciplining of the scientists, in scientific development; the academic and institutional strategies for the development of new fields of knowledge; or the question of the legality of using theories and methods from one discipline in another.

THE INTERNALIST PERSPECTIVE

Even if the sociological, "externalist" focus is essential in understanding scientific output, it nevertheless cannot be exclusive. Together with it we also need the "internalist" perspective, which considers scientific ideas in themselves, their genesis, their internal logic and their evolution, seeking to discover the intellectual influences that form them. In this respect our research up to now has favored, apart from the evolution of geographical thought (to which we have already referred), above all certain specific fields.

Theories of the physical structure of the earth, and the interaction between philosophy, theology an natural science. The concern for the continuity into the modern era of ideas from classical times led us to study the influence of the Platonic and Aristotelian traditions on the reformulation of the organicist conceptions that spread in Europe in the 17th and 18th centuries, particularly with reference to the theories about the central fire, volcanism and earthquakes. We studied with special attention the work of Father Kircher, which was profoundly organicist and had great influence on European thought towards the end of the 17th century. The problem of the late development of the Scientific Revolution in the field of what is today known as biology also became a basic issue. Here the fundamental factor was the biblical conception of the creation of the world and of the universal deluge.

The empirical facts of erosion and changes in the earth's surface shape are difficult to account for within a providentialist, anthropocentric or teleological frame of reference. Such a frame assumed that the world was created by God for men and that is was unchangeable since it was the divine plan which required no corrections. Many rationalizations of the biblical story were put forward in the 17th century by people with different backgrounds and concerns. These resulted in the formulation and diffusion of daring hypotheses that allowed the notion of change and evolution in the earth's surface gradually to gain acceptance. This led us to study the issue of the influence of religious beliefs and theological standpoints on the development of geology, and we have published a number of papers representative of that period.

Profoundly innovative ideas like those Descartes-who applied the spirit of the Scientific Revolution to the theory of the earth-or the cautious attitude and empiricist mentality of Varenius could only spread and have any real impact when there appeared hypotheses alternative or complementary to that of Genesis. Other topics of interest include the evolution of the notions of physical geography in Spains; the arrival here during the 19th century of modern geological theories; and also the appearance and spreading of geomorphological theories. Among these, one area that has received ample treatment is the problems relating to the action of glaciers and the foundation of glaciology; this is related to another line of research which we mention below.

The history of ideas about the environment constitutes the second major area tackled from an internalist standpoint. As in the previous case, the standpoint is never exclusively internalist, since at times it is very difficult to separate the internal from the social aspects. The view that prevailed in Europe until the 18th century was of a providentialist nature. There was no place for concern over natural resources since, in accordance with the divine plan of creation, man would find in nature everything necessary for life. The crisis of this providentialist, anthropocentric and teleological view, as well as the realization that certain resources-like woods and fish-might well be affected by human exploitation, gave rise to a conservationist attitude; this appears clearly formulated in learned Spanish thought towards the end of the 18th century. We find here the roots of a current of thought that increased in importance during the 19th century; it was related to the defence of the great forests, and to the struggle against the erosion and for the protection of natural spaces. In the mid-20th century it culminated in the movements of an ecologist nature and in concern over the issue of the earth's resources.

Linked in certain ways to the environmental tradition, we find the development of concern for health. In the field of medicine, the Hippocratic tradition gave way to a line of studies concerning the nature of the environment and its influence on human health and diseases. Here we find-as we have mentioned above-the origin of the "medical topographies", which were produced by these specialists and which had such great significance as paradigms of chorographic studies. Similarly, the concern over the environmental conditions in towns, and their effect on the evolution of epidemics, stimulated the development of a school of public hygiene which had great influence during the 19th century.

The third area deals with the theories of the social sciences. During the Renaissance and the 17th century, the formulation of these theories is to be found in very diverse places. Of these, history is doubtless the most fundamental; in this connection, it is worth looking at certain specialized fields which have largely gone unattended. The histories of towns, for example, form a well defined and significant corpus. From the early 16th century, works of this type reveal, on the one hand, the influence of classical historiography, especially Titus Livius, of the political works of Plato and Aristotle, and of St. Augustine's City of God, as well as the work of geographers and naturalists like Pliny.

On the other hand, they served as a starting point for the development of a new historiographic model, of an analysis of society at the service of certain social groups, and, subsequently, of ideals of social reform. We must therefore regard these works as representing a meeting point between historical learning and utopia.

Another important line of thought which gave rise to the development of social theories is to be found in statistical collections and in reflections on the growth in population. Up to the 1 8th century, this concern with number of people adopted an optimistic attitude linked to the providentialist view; it was only with the work of Malthus that it became a powerful pessimistic current, and this was soon felt in Spain. Throughout the 19th century, this concern with numbers was united to a concern for the quality of life; this, in the context of the positivist climate that arose in the middle of the century, became a concern for selection and eugenics. Thus was developed a powerful line of thought, in conflict with Christian tradition and with European Enlightenment; in the 20th century it would lead to political demographic proposals which tended towards a selection of people and which have generally been united to totalitarian political ideologies and racist attitude.

One conclusion which we can draw from all this research is the complexity of the intellectual influences that shape the development of scientific concepts and theories. Traditionally the historians of the physical and natural sciences have been insensitive to philosophy, religion and the arts; this has hampered a proper appreciation of the fact that scientific ideas are closely interwoven with the development of thought in general, and even with aesthetic and literary ideas. This was not only the case in the past-before the dissociation between what C. P. Snow has called "the two cultures"-but even today in that, in spite of this dissociation, the circulation of ideas is extremely rapid, and the interaction between science and the arts is greater than is normally believed. In this respect our research leads in the same direction as that of other researchers into the history of science-as we can see from recent congresses and publications.

What is also clear from our work is that empirical data on their own have a very limited value; with these alone it is very difficult to arrive at general theories. The same data can take on extremely varied values in different theories. Thus empirical observations concerning erosion only achieved true significance when the biblical conception was challenged and the idea of change on earth was accepted. Similarly, accounts of the depletion of fish populations could be seen very differently depending on whether one accepted the providentialist, teleological view or not. Again, information concerning the evolution of human populations acquires a different value from an optimist's and from a pessimist's viewpoint. How empirical date and theories interact is an issue which is still debated, and it deserves to be tackled from a historical standpoint.

TEACHING OF SCIENCE

The need for a new, integrated focus in the studies of the history of science is seen clearly when we recognize the dissociation that exists between the history of education and the history of scientific disciplines and ideas.

Our research program attempts to avoid this divorce. In this respect our options derive above all from an interest in the teaching of geography, which is not specifically historical. Our interest lies in the role and function of geography in primary and secondary education and in the renewal of teaching methods for geography. At first this led us to examine the supposedly innovative proposals that were put forward throughout the 1970's, as well as the alternative that were being developed both within the discipline and elsewhere. The analysis of these proposals requires a historical perspective to allow an evaluation of the new features that they claimed, rightly or wrongly, to include. Also we sought to reveal any valid critical elements that there may have been in similar debates in the past. At the same time, the continuous presence of geography in all the curricula of basic education ever since the Renaissance, as well as our hypothesis that this presence had been decisive in its institutionalization in the universities during the 19th century, forced us to view the topic from a historical standpoint.

Without doubt, geography has been a privileged subject, due to its long and important presence in basic education in both European and other countries for the last 500 years. However, the history of the teaching of an individual subject cannot be properly understood if we do not look at the overall structure of the curricula and at the relative weight that the different subjects have there; it is this which allows us to draw conclusions about the role assigned to them. We therefore need diachronic and structural studies of the curricula at the different levels of education. Thus our current research has undertaken a broad analysis of geography in Spanish education. Using things like the number of hours for each subject, we have reconstructed its relative position in the whole curriculum; we have also interpreted the changes in the educational system in the light of modifications both in the social structure and also in pedagogy.

The history of the teaching of geography has led us towards: first, the history of science teaching in secondary education; second, the history of primary education; third, the organization of colleges of education and the training of primary school teachers; and finally, the relation between workers' political movements and science teaching. This has forced us time and again to take up a position where we consider simultaneously the history of science, the history of pedagogy as well as social and political history.

SPREAD OF SCIENTIFIC IDEAS

Thanks to its continuous presence in the curricula and to its popularity, geography is á subject that has contributed greatly to the spread of scientific knowledge; like other subjects, it has also had important ideological functions. It is largely through geography that educated people have traditionally acquired knowledge about the position of the earth in the universe, about the physical structure of the planet, its surface features, its climate, the people that live there, and the characteristics of the different continents and countries.

The study of the content of geography textbooks is a fruitful line of research for an understanding of what has been taught and also to observe the persistence of old ideas or the arrival of new ones. To this end we started, some time ago, the analysis of elementary geography teaching in the 18th century by studying the syllabuses of the public examinations; we are now following this with a study of the geography textbooks used in Spanish schools in the first half of the 19th century, in the subsequent 50 years, as well as a bibliography of the geography textbooks used in Spain between 1800 and 1939 Our research has also included textbooks for history, and for agriculture and in the future we intend to take up other subjects and also stimulate similar undertakings in the Iberoamerican countries. There seems to be an enormous interest in this aspect of the research, though the task is certainly laborious. In its most ambitious form, it requires as comprehensive a list as possible of the textbooks for the different levels of education-primary, secondary, tertiary, and special education-with the number of editions and, if possible, the number printed. We must also identify the authors and learn about their training and whether they were specialists or not, as well as studying the overall structure of the books. Finally, we need to study the content itself, paying attention to the novelty or otherwise of what is taught, and relating it all the time to the development of the subject at the highest level. Starting from an inventory of the textbooks, it is possible to produce simple bibliometric analyses which, in a first approximation, will yield the names of the publishers, the most prolific and influential authors, the importance of translations, and the number of editions or how long they survived; our study has shown that on occasion they enjoyed a life of more than half a century.

Later on-and including the bibliographical references that they textbooks have-it will be possible to apply, though with due caution, more sophisticated bibliometric techniques in order to learn about the scientific activity. At the same time, although we feel that a qualitative analysis of the contents is still essential, the application of new techniques like lexicometry will perhaps yield quantitative data which reflect the conceptual evolution.

Our understanding of the true impact of scientific ideas, both on the general public and also on the scientific community, is an important topic which has recently been taken up. Bibliometric analysis of quotations is a commonly used technique and, although is has limitations, it is undoubtedly useful. This area can also be approached in a qualitative way through a careful analysis of the texts actually produced by scientists, particularly specific authors of note, and which are identified either through direct references or by implication. On a more general scale, the study of the spread of scientific ideas and of their audience can also draw on other sources: subscribers and purchasers of journals; publishers' and bookshop sales; library catalogues; post mortem inventories, etc. We have used these-with encouraging results-in the study of the spread of geography and its audience in the 18th century, and we intend to continue with this.

From the point of view of social history, it is important to encourage studies of the popular spread of science, of the acceptance or rejection of new scientific ideas, of how fast and through what channels new ideas have spread, now and in the past. One could claim that what today passes for popular culture is in large measure scientific culture that was vulgarized in the past through the pulpit, school, peasant calendars, religious works, or scientific periodicals and books. What popular sayings, proverbs and beliefs often contain simply fragments of classical culture, (for example, Aristotle, Pliny, Seneca, etc.), or Renaissance or humanist culture. These have been vulgarized and incorporated into folk lore in such a way that it is difficult to recognize them unless their origin is identified. We have data which demonstrate the truth of this in popular ideas concerning the structure of the earth, the climate and diseases. Geography is one of the sciences that has contributed most effectively to the formation of these popular beliefs; this is due to its long presence in education and to its traditional popularity. It is responsible for the spreading of ideas and stereotypes concerning the earth, its countries and its peoples.

We must not forget that, as well as the readers and textbooks in schools, geography has been available to the public ever since the Renaissance through widely distributed world geographies and through encyclopedic dictionaries. This long line of publishing, which continues with popular works up to our times, reached its greatest intellectual significance in the era of the encyclopedists during the Enlightenment and the first decades of the 19th century. These could still serve the useful function of systematization, as Madoz's dictionary shows.

Geography has also had a constant association with journeys: preparing them, undertaking them, and using the results. Geography has often been the point of departure and also the goals of these journeys: the former, since it provided the traveller with prior information indispensable for an appreciation of the countries to be visited; and the latter, in that the results, when they had been systematized, could be incorporated as news about a country or a region in a new encyclopedic collection of a geographical nature (chorographies, dictionaries and world geographies). At the same time, however, it was also an indispensable guide during the journey, since it was the chorographic method that provided the methodological framework to guide observations during the trip and, on occasions, in the subsequent systematization.

Within the framework of our research project, journeys are of interest first, with regard to the learning strategies-for geography and for science in general-both in the preparation and during the journey itself; this includes groundwork, previous knowledge, observations during the trip, selection of informants, use of bibliographies and maps, etc. Second, the results, when published, become a vehicle for the spread of ideas and stereotypes, whose impact depends on the success it enjoys. Travellers are undoubtedly influenced by the intellectual climate of their epoch, (ideas from philosophy or aesthetics, religious beliefs, political prejudices), and are supplied to a greater or lesser degree with scientific notions, (about population, resources, climate, terrain, etc.). Thus prepared-and probably also acquainted with essays and travel guides-the travellers produce work which sometimes contributes to scientific knowledge, and almost always to popular stereotypes (of the nature of peoples, the beauty of the landscape, "picturesque" or "romantic" spots, etc.) This was the case with the travellers of the Enlightenment, the ones who undertook the "grand tour" or the "petit tour", which did so much to establish models of conduct for these journeys.

The accounts of these journeys, with all the auxiliary material (guides to staging posts and inns, maps, tourist guides), make up materials that are very useful in understanding the formation of mental images and stereotypes concerning places and peoples. We feel that town guides are of particular importance at the moment since they allow the study of the evolution of opinions about towns and the sites that are deemed worthy of a visit by the traveller, and we can thus analyze images and ideas about towns. During the 19th century, concomitant with the rise in the standard of living and the educational level of the middle and lower middle classes, traveling became more common; the notion of excursions became more widespread, and these showed varied, but inextricable, facets: scientific, sporting, or simply out of an interest in nature. This social phenomenon, though it had earlier origins, expanded greatly during the 19th century. It served educational, cultural, moral and ideological purposes and, in certain cases, was closely linked with nationalist sentiments and extremism. At the same time, however, hiking, climbing and mountaineering clubs became a factor in the spread of science; in some cases they made outstanding contributions to the inventory and study of the environment, of our heritage, or of the ethnography and folklore in the countries of Europe and America.

In this connection, we are also interested in the spread of scientific ideas through other means. Literature in particular has on occasion played an important part, and the work of certain authors, such as Jules Verne, is especially significant.

IDEOLOGY AND SCIENCE

The study of textbooks, encyclopedias, accounts of journeys and trips and also literature is not only interesting from the viewpoint of social history and the spread of scientific ideas. It also holds interest from the viewpoint of ideology, both whether they are pervaded by an ideology and if they contribute to the spread of a "scientific ideology". The long confused debate about ideology has been keenly felt in the history of thought since the turn of this century and in the history of science since the Congress on the History of Science held in London in 1931.

This is a highly relevant topic which is attracting growing attention in international journals and congresses on the history of science. We are especially interested in two important aspects of this: on the one hand, the ideological presuppositions of scientific theories, and on the other, the ideological exploitation of these theories. Our progress in this area has been achieved through various lines of study. The first looks at the relations between ideology and science in the debates and the proposals concerning territorial organization. We are particularly interested in the use of scientific ideas to justify and support specific proposals for territorial organization, when these are put forward as objective and above discussion, when in fact they reflect the options of social groups or class strategies. In this respect, the study of the debates over the regional division of Spain in the late 19th and early 20th centuries has demonstrated the use of positivist ideas and organicist conceptions in certain proposals that were made. They also reflect the intense debate of that period between positivists and neoromanticists. If we apply this same focus to later debates, it is not difficult to recognize similar attempts at self-justification, using a methodology and scientific language (natural or functional region, systems theory, and so on) for predetermined social options.

In this same area of research we can set other studies: spatial ideas in Spanish military thought; the role of mental images, of myths and, in a way, of ideologies in the appropriation of less well organized areas; and the ideological aspects that may be present in the establishment of connections in a new state through the construction of a railroad network. A second area of study puts special emphasis on the subject of power and the control over space. This is research at the intersection of the history of penological ideas, the ideology of techniques and the evolution of the physical forms of territorial control, from prisons and barracks to the general organization of a city and industrial estates. The growing sophistication and reach of the mechanisms of social control, related to the social transformations since the Enlightenment, are precisely reflected in legislation, in ideological output, in scientific reflection, in technical proposals (for example, machines that flog scientifically), and even in the structure of the buildings (prisons, barracks, etc), which take on a symbolic function, or the whole of a town or a territory.

Finally, we are also interested in the ideological content of the scientific theories and debates concerning population. With respect to Spanish America in the 16th century we believe we have demonstrated that certain ideas were influenced not only by intellectual traditions and systems of belief that resulted in prejudices, but also by the strategies adopted by the social groups to which the authors belonged, since these-consciously or unconsciously-sought to defend economic interests, and political or very specific religious positions. These ideas include superiority or inferiority vis-a-vis the indigenous peoples, the origins of the Amerindians, and the demographic catastrophe that the Indians suffered after the conquista. In the following two centuries, Spanish America underwent social changes, especially the strengthening of the Creole groups and the appearance of important emancipation movements towards the end of the 18th century. These reflected a growing self-evaluation of these social groups in a process that would, after independence, find a symbolic culmination in the ideological acceptance of Ameghino's thesis of the American origin of man; one could thus understand the immigration movement as a return to roots.

Throughout the 19th century practically all scientific and general debates on population, as well as the demographic policies carried out in the South American cone, were strongly impregnated with ideology, ranging from the concept of "desert" used for areas occupied by indigenous populations to the justifications of the immigration policy or of the characteristics of the peoples.

Parallel to this, in Europe during the same period, the concern over selection of individuals and peoples resulted in the development of eugenics, a vigorous branch of science to which numerous important contributions were made. In these it is always fascinating to reveal and to separate what truly belongs to science and what has been introduced because of the authors' preiudices.

2

The Positivism

Positivism refers to a set of epistemological perspectives and philosophies of science which hold that the scientific method is the best approach to uncovering the processes by which both physical and human events occur. Though the positivist approach has been a 'recurrent theme in the history of western thought from the Ancient Greeks to the present day' the concept was developed in the early 19th century by the philosopher and founding sociologist, Auguste Comte.

OVERVIEW

Positivism asserts that the only authentic knowledge is that which is based on sense experience and positive verification. As an approach to the philosophy of science deriving from Enlightenment thinkers such as Henri de Saint-Simon and Pierre-Simon Laplace, Auguste Comte saw the scientific method as replacing metaphysics in the history of thought, observing the circular dependence of theory and observation in science. Sociological positivism was later reformulated by Émile Durkheim as a foundation to social research. At the turn of the 20th century the first wave of German sociologists, including Max Weber and Georg Simmel, rejected the doctrine, thus founding the antipositivist tradition in sociology. Later antipositivists and critical theorists have associated positivism with "scientism"; science *as ideology*.

In the early 20th century, logical positivism—a descendant of Comte's basic thesis but an independent movement— sprang up in Vienna and grew to become one of the dominant schools in Anglo-American philosophy and the analytic tradition. Logical positivists (or 'neopositivists') reject metaphysical speculation and attempt to reduce statements and propositions to pure logic. Critiques of this approach by philosophers such as Karl Popper and Thomas Kuhn have been highly influential, and led to the development of postpositivism. In psychology, the positivist movement was influential in the development of behavioralism and operationalism. In economics, practising researchers tend to emulate the methodological assumptions of classical positivism, but only in a de-facto fashion: the majority of economists do not explicitly concern themselves with matters of epistemology. In jurisprudence, "legal positivism" essentially refers to the rejection of natural law, thus its common meaning with philosophical positivism is somewhat attenuated and in recent generations generally emphasizes the authority of human political structures as opposed to a "scientific" view of law.

In contemporary social science, strong accounts of positivism have long since fallen out of favour. Practitioners of positivism today acknowledge in far greater detail observer bias and structural limitations. Modern positivists generally eschew metaphysical concerns in favour of methodological debates concerning clarity, replicability, reliability and validity. This positivism is generally equated with "quantitative research" and thus carries no explicit theoretical or philosophical commitments. The institutionalization of this kind of sociology is often credited to Paul Lazarsfeld, who pioneered large-scale survey studies and developed statistical techniques for analyzing them. This approach lends itself to what Robert K. Merton called middle-range theory: abstract statements that generalize from segregated hypotheses and empirical regularities rather than starting with an abstract idea of a social whole. Other new movements, such as critical realism, have emerged to reconcile the overarching aims of social science with various so-called 'postmodern' critiques.

PRINCIPLES

In its strongest original formulation, positivism could be thought of as a set of five principles:

1. The unity of the scientific method – i.e., the logic of inquiry is the same across all sciences (social and natural).

2. The goal of inquiry is to explain and predict. Most positivists would also say that the ultimate goal is to develop the law of general understanding, by discovering necessary and sufficient conditions for any phenomenon (creating a perfect model of it). If the law is known, we can manipulate the conditions to produce the predicted result.
3. Scientific knowledge is testable. Research can be proved only by empirical means, not argumentations. Research should be mostly deductive, i.e. deductive logic is used to develop statements that can be tested (theory leads to hypothesis which in turn leads to discovery and/or study of evidence). Research should be observable with the human senses (arguments are not enough, sheer belief is out of the question). Positivists should prove their research using the logic of confirmation.
4. Science does not equal common sense. Researchers must be careful not to let common sense bias their research.
5. The relation of theory to practice – science should be as value-neutral as possible, and the ultimate goal of science is to produce knowledge, regardless of any politics, morals, or values held by those involved in the research. Science should be judged by logic, and ideally produce universal conditionals:
    - For all conditions of X, if X has property P and P=Q, then X has property Q.
    - Statements must be true for all times and places.

There are now no fewer than twelve distinct epistemologies that are referred to as positivism. Many of these approaches dispose of a number of these claims. For example, most contemporary social researchers do not believe in the existence of general social laws.

SOCIOLOGICAL POSITIVISM

Comte's Positivism

Auguste Comte (1798–1857) first described the epistemological perspective of positivism in *The Course in Positive Philosophy*, a series of texts published between 1830 and 1842. These texts were followed by the 1844 work, *A*

General View of Positivism (published in English in 1865). The first three volumes of the *Course* dealt chiefly with the physical sciences already in existence (mathematics, astronomy, physics, chemistry, biology), whereas the latter two emphasized the inevitable coming of social science. Observing the circular dependence of theory and observation in science, and classifying the sciences in this way, Comte may be regarded as the first philosopher of science in the modern sense of the term. For him, the physical sciences had necessarily to arrive first, before humanity could adequately channel its efforts into the most challenging and complex "Queen science" of human society itself. His *View of Positivism* therefore set-out to define the empirical goals of sociological method.

Comte offered an account of social evolution, proposing that society undergoes three phases in its quest for the truth according to a general 'law of three stages'. The idea bears some similarity to Marx's view that human society would progress toward a communist peak. This is perhaps unsurprising as both were profoundly influenced by the early Utopian socialist, Henri de Saint-Simon, who was at one time Comte's mentor. Both Comte and Marx intended to develop, scientifically, a new secular ideology in the wake of European secularisation.

Comte's stages were (1) the *theological*, (2) the *metaphysical*, and (3) the *positive*. The theological phase of man was based on whole-hearted belief in all things with reference to God. God, Comte says, had reigned supreme over human existence pre-Enlightenment. Humanity's place in society was governed by its association with the divine presences and with the church. The theological phase deals with humankind's accepting the doctrines of the church (or place of worship) rather than relying on its rational powers to explore basic questions about existence. It dealt with the restrictions put in place by the religious organization at the time and the total acceptance of any "fact" adduced for society to believe. Comte describes the metaphysical phase of humanity as the time since the Enlightenment, a time steeped in logical rationalism, to the time right after the French Revolution. This second phase states that the universal rights of humanity are most important. The central idea is that humanity is invested with certain rights that must be respected. In this phase, democracies and dictators rose and fell in attempts to maintain the innate rights of humanity. The final stage of the trilogy of Comte's universal law is the scientific, or positive, stage. The central idea of this phase is that individual rights are more important than the rule of any one person. Comte stated that the idea of humanity's ability to govern itself makes this stage innately different from the rest. There is no higher power governing the masses and the intrigue of any one person can achieve anything based on that individual's free will and authority. The third principle is most important in the positive stage. Comte calls these three phases the universal rule in relation to society and its development. Neither the second nor the third phase can be reached without the completion and understanding of the preceding stage. All stages must be completed in progress.

Comte believed that the appreciation of the past and the ability to build on it towards the future was key in transitioning from the theological and metaphysical phases. The idea of progress was central to Comte's new science, sociology. Sociology would "lead to the historical consideration of every science" because "the history of one science, including pure political history, would make no sense unless it were attached to the study of the general progress of all of humanity". As Comte would say, "from science comes prediction; from prediction comes action". It is a philosophy of human intellectual development that culminated in science. The irony of this series of phases is that though Comte attempted to prove that human development has to go through these three stages, it seems that the positivist stage is far from becoming a realization. This is due to two truths. The positivist phase requires having complete understanding of the universe and world around us and requires that society should never know if it is in this positivist phase. Anthony Giddens argues that since humanity constantly uses science to discover and research new things, humanity never progresses beyond the second metaphysical phase. In this view, Comte's positivism appears circular.

Comte's fame today owes in part to Emile Littré, who founded *The Positivist Review* in 1867. As an approach to the philosophy of history, positivism was appropriated by historians such as Hippolyte Taine. Many of Comte's writings were translated into English by the Whig writer, Harriet Martineau, regarded by some as the first female sociologist. Debates continue to rage as to how much Comte appropriated from the work of his mentor, Saint-Simon. He was nevertheless influential: Brazilian thinkers turned to Comte's ideas about training a scientific elite in order to flourish in the industrialization process. Brazil's national motto, *Ordem e Progresso* ("Order and Progress") was taken from Comte's positivism, which was also influential in Poland.

In later life, Comte developed a 'religion of humanity' for positivist societies in order to fulfil the cohesive function once held by traditional worship. In 1849, he proposed a calendar reform called the 'positivist calendar'. For close associate John Stuart Mill, it was possible to distinguish between a "good Comte" (the author of the *Course in Positive Philosophy*) and a "bad Comte" (the author of the secular-religious *system*). The *system* was unsuccessful but met with the publication of Darwin's *On the Origin of Species* to influence the proliferation of various Secular Humanist organizations in the 19th century, especially through the work of secularists such as George Holyoake and Richard Congreve. Although Comte's English followers, including George Eliot and Harriet Martineau, for the most part rejected the full gloomy panoply of his system, they liked the idea of a religion of humanity and his injunction to "vivre pour autrui" ("live for others", from which comes the word "altruism").

The early sociology of Herbert Spencer came about broadly as a reaction to Comte; writing after various developments in evolutionary biology, Spencer attempted (in vain) to reformulate the discipline in what we might now describe as socially Darwinistic terms. (Spencer was in actual fact a proponent of Lamarckism rather than Darwinism).

Durkheim's Positivism

The modern academic discipline of sociology began with the work of Émile Durkheim (1858–1917). While Durkheim rejected much of the detail of Comte's philosophy, he retained and refined its method, maintaining that the social sciences are a logical continuation of the natural ones into the realm of human activity, and insisting that they may retain the same objectivity, rationalism, and approach to causality. Durkheim set up the first European department of sociology at the University of Bordeaux in 1895, publishing his *Rules of the Sociological Method* (1895). In this text he argued: "[o]ur main goal is to extend scientific rationalism to human conduct... What has been called our positivism is but a consequence of this rationalism."

Durkheim's seminal monograph, *Suicide* (1897), a case study of suicide rates amongst Catholic and Protestant populations, distinguished sociological analysis from psychology or philosophy. By carefully examining suicide statistics in different police districts, he attempted to demonstrate that Catholic communities have a lower suicide rate than that of Protestants, something he attributed to social (as opposed to individual or psychological) causes. He developed the notion of objective *suis generis* "social facts" to delineate a unique empirical object for the science of sociology to study. Through such studies he posited that sociology would be able to determine whether any given society is 'healthy' or 'pathological', and seek social reform to negate organic breakdown or "social anomie". For Durkheim, sociology could be described as the "science of institutions, their genesis and their functioning".

Accounts of Durkheim's positivism are vulnerable to exaggeration and oversimplification: Comte was the only major sociological thinker to postulate that the social realm may be subject to scientific analysis in exactly the same way as natural science, whereas Durkheim saw a far greater need for developing a distinctly sociological scientific methodology. His lifework was fundamental in the establishment of practical social research as we know it today-techniques which continue beyond sociology and form the basis for methodology in other social sciences, such as political science, as well in market research and further fields.

Antipositivism and Critical Theory

At the turn of the 20th century, the first wave of German sociologists formally introduced methodological antipositivism, proposing that research should concentrate on human cultural norms, values, symbols, and social processes viewed from a subjective perspective. Max Weber argued that sociology may be loosely described as a 'science' as it is able to identify causal relationships—especially among ideal types, or hypothetical simplifications of complex social phenomena. As a nonpositivist, however, one seeks relationships that are not as "ahistorical, invariant, or generalizable" as those pursued by natural scientists. Weber regarded sociology as the study of social action, using critical analysis and verstehen techniques. The sociologists Georg Simmel, Ferdinand Tönnies, George Herbert Mead, and Charles Cooley were also influential in the development of sociological antipositivism, whilst neo-Kantian philosophy, hermeneutics and phenomenology facilitated the movement in general.

Karl Marx drew upon historical materialism and critical analysis rather than positivism, a tradition which would continue in the development of critical theory. Following in the tradition of both Weber and Marx, the critical theorist Jürgen Habermas has critiqued pure instrumental rationality (in its relation to the cultural "rationalisation" of the modern West) as meaning that scientific thinking becomes something akin to ideology itself. Positivism may be espoused by 'technocrats' who believe in the inevitability of social progress through science and technology. New movements, such as critical realism, have emerged in order to reconcile postpositivist aims with various so-called 'postmodern' perspectives on the social acquisition of knowledge.

Modern Positivism

In the original Comtean usage, the term "positivism" roughly meant the use of scientific methods to uncover the laws according to which both physical and human events occur, while "sociology" was the overarching science that would synthesize all such knowledge for the betterment of society. "Antipositivism" formally dates back to the start of the twentieth century, and is based around the belief that natural and human sciences are ontologically and epistemologically distinct. Neither of these terms is any longer used in this meaning. There are no fewer than twelve distinct epistemologies that are referred to as positivism. Many of these approaches do not self-identify as "positivist", some because they themselves arose in opposition to older forms of positivism, and some because the label has over time become a term of abuse by being mistakenly linked with atheoretical empiricism. The extent of antipositivist criticism has also become broad, with many philosophies broadly rejecting the scientifically based social epistemology and other ones only seeking to amend it to reflect 20th century developments in the philosophy of science. However, positivism (understood as the use of scientific methods for studying society) remains the dominant approach to both research and theory construction in contemporary sociology, especially in the United States.

The majority of articles published in leading American sociology and political science journals today are positivist (at least to the extent of being quantitative rather than qualitative). This popularity may be due to the fact that research utilizing positivist quantitative methodologies holds a greater prestige in the social sciences than qualitative work. Such research is generally perceived as being more scientific and more trustworthy, and thus has a greater impact on policy and public opinion (though such judgments are frequently contested by scholars doing non-positivist work).

FURTHER THINKERS

Within years of the publication of Comte's book *A General View of Positivism* (1856), other scientific and philosophical thinkers began creating their own definitions for positivism. They included Émile Zola, Emile Hennequin, Wilhelm Scherer, and Dimitri Pisarev. Émile Zola was an influential French novelist, the most important example of the literary school of naturalism, and a major figure in the political liberalization of France.

Emile Hennequin was a Parisian publisher and writer who wrote theoretical and critical pieces. He "exemplified the tension between the positivist drive to systematize literary criticism and the unfettered imagination inherent in literature." He was one of the few thinkers who disagreed with the notion that subjectivity invalidates observation, judgment and prediction. Unlike many positivist thinkers before him, he believed that subjectivity does play a role in science and society. His contribution to positivism pertains not to science and its objectivity, but rather to the subjectivity of art and the way the artist, work, and audience interrelate. Hennequin tried to analyze positivism strictly on the predictions, and the mechanical processes, but was perplexed due to the contradictions of the reactions of patrons to artwork that showed no scientific inclinations.

Wilhelm Scherer was a German philologist, a university professor, and a popular literary historian. He was known as a positivist because he based much of his work on "hypotheses on detailed historical research, and rooted every literary phenomenon in 'objective' historical or philological facts". His positivism is different due to his involvement with his nationalist goals. His major contribution to the movement was his speculation that culture cycled in a six-hundred-year period.

Dimitri Pisarev was a Russian critic who showed the greatest contradictions with his belief in positivism. His ideas focused around an imagination and style though he did not believe in romantic ideas because they reminded him of the oppressive tsarist government under which he lived. His basic beliefs was "an extreme anti-aesthetic scientistic position." He focused his efforts on defining the relation between literature and the environment. Stephen Hawking is a recent high profile advocate of positivism, at least in the physical sciences. In *The Universe in a Nutshell* (p. 31) he writes:

Any sound scientific theory, whether of time or of any other concept, should in my opinion be based on the most workable philosophy of science: the positivist approach put forward by Karl Popper and others. According to this way of thinking, a scientific theory is a mathematical model that describes and codifies the observations we make. A good theory will describe a large range of phenomena on the basis of a few simple postulates and will make definite predictions that can be tested... If one takes the positivist position, as I do, one cannot say what time actually is. All one can do is describe what has been found to be a very good mathematical model for time and say what predictions it makes.

However, the claim that Popper was a positivist is a common misunderstanding that Popper himself termed the "Popper legend." In fact, he developed his views in stark opposition to and as a criticism of positivism and held that scientific theories talk about how the world really is, not, as positivists claim, about phenomena or observations experienced by scientists. On the other hand, continental philosophers like Theodore Adorno and Jürgen Habermas regarded Popper as a positivist because of his devotion to a unified science.

POSITIVISM IN SCIENCE TODAY

The key features of positivism as of the 1950s, as defined in the "received view", are:

1. A focus on science as a product, a linguistic or numerical set of statements;
2. A concern with axiomatization, that is, with demonstrating the logical structure and coherence of these statements;
3. An insistence on at least some of these statements being testable, that is amenable to being verified, confirmed, or falsified by the empirical observation of reality; statements that would, by their nature, be regarded as untestable included the teleological; thus positivism rejects much of classical metaphysics.
4. The belief that science is markedly cumulative;
5. The belief that science is predominantly transcultural;
6. The belief that science rests on specific results that are dissociated from the personality and social position of the investigator;
7. The belief that science contains theories or research traditions that are largely commensurable;
8. The belief that science sometimes incorporates new ideas that are discontinuous from old ones;
9. The belief that science involves the idea of the unity of science, that there is, underlying the various scientific disciplines, basically one science about one real world.

Positivism is elsewhere defined as "the view that all true knowledge is scientific," and that all things are ultimately measurable. Positivism is closely related to reductionism, in that both involve the view that "entities of one kind... are reducible to entities of another," such as societies to configurations of individuals, or mental events to neural phenomena. It also involves the contention that "processes are reducible to physiological, physical or chemical events," and even that "social processes are reducible to relationships between and actions of individuals," or that "biological organisms are reducible to physical systems."

While most social scientists today are not explicit about their epistemological commitments, articles in top American sociology and political science journals generally follow a positivist logic of argument. It can be thus argued that "natural science and social science [research articles] can therefore be regarded with a good deal of confidence as members of the same genre".

CRITICISM

Historically, positivism has been criticized for its universalism, i.e. for contending that all "processes are reducible to physiological, physical or chemical events," "social processes are reducible to relationships between and actions of individuals," and that "biological organisms are reducible to physical systems."

Max Horkheimer and other critical theorists criticized the classic formulation of positivism on two grounds. First, they claimed that it falsely represented human social action. The first criticism argued that positivism systematically failed to appreciate the extent to which the so-called social facts it yielded did not exist 'out there', in the objective world, but were themselves a product of socially and historically mediated human consciousness. Positivism ignored the role of the 'observer' in the constitution of social reality and thereby failed to consider the historical and social conditions affecting the representation of social ideas. Positivism falsely represented the object of study by reifying social reality as existing objectively and independently and labour actually produced those conditions. Secondly, he argued, representation of social reality produced by positivism was inherently and artificially conservative, helping to support the status quo, rather than challenging it. This character may also explain the popularity of positivism in certain political circles. Horkheimer argued, in contrast, that critical theory possessed a reflexive element lacking in the positivistic traditional theory.

Few scholars today hold the views critiqued in Horkheimer's work. Since the time of his writing, critiques of positivism, especially from philosophy of science, have led to the development of postpositivism. This philosophy greatly relaxes the epistemological commitments of logical positivism and no longer asserts the separation of the knower and the known. Rather than dismissing the scientific project outright, postpositivists seek to transform and amend it, though the exact extent of their affinity for science varies vastly. For example, some postpositivists accept the critique that observation is always value-laden, but argue that the best values to adopt for sociological observation are those of science : skepticism, rigor and modesty. Just as some critical theorists see their position as a moral commitment to egalitarian values, these postpositivists see their methods as driven by a moral commitment to these scientific values. Such scholars may see themselves as either positivists or antipositivists.

Positivism has also come under fire on religious and philosophical grounds, whose proponents assert that truth begins in sense experience, but does not end there. Positivism fails to prove that there are not abstract ideas, laws, and principles, beyond particular observable facts and relationships and necessary principles, or that we cannot know them. Nor does it prove that material and corporeal things constitute the whole order of existing beings, and that our knowledge is limited to them. According to positivism, our abstract concepts or general ideas are mere collective representations of the experimental order — for example, the idea of "man" is a kind of blended image of all the men observed in our experience. This runs contrary to a Platonic or Christian ideal, where an idea can be abstracted from any concrete determination, and may be applied identically to an indefinite number of objects of the same class. From the idea's perspective, the latter is more precise as collective images are more or less confused, become more so as the collection represented increases; an idea by definition remains always clear.

Echos of the "positivist" and "antipositivist" debate persist today, though this conflict is hard to define. Authors writing in different epistemological perspectives do not phrase their disagreements in the same terms and rarely actually speak directly to each other. To complicate the issues further, few practicing scholars explicitly state their epistemological commitments, and their epistemological position thus has to be guessed from other sources such as choice of methodology or theory. However, no perfect correspondence between these categories exists, and many scholars critiqued as "positivists" actually hold postpositivist views. One scholar has described this debate in terms of the social construction of the "other", with each side defining the other by what it is *not* rather than what it *is*, and then proceeding to attribute far greater homogeneity to their opponents than actually exists. Thus, it is better to understand this not as a debate but as two different arguments: the "antipositivist" articulation of a social meta-theory which includes a philosophical critique of scientism, and "positivist" development of a scientific research methodology for sociology with accompanying critiques of the reliability and validity of work that they see as violating such standards.

LOGICAL POSITIVISM

Logical positivism (also called logical empiricism and neo-positivism) is a school of philosophy that combines empiricism – the idea that observational evidence is indispensable for knowledge of the world – with a version of rationalism incorporating mathematical and logico-linguistic constructs and deductions in epistemology.

Logical positivism grew from the discussions of a group called the "First Vienna Circle" which gathered at the Café Central before World War I. After the war Hans Hahn, a member of that early group, helped bring Moritz Schlick to Vienna. Schlick's Vienna Circle, along with Hans Reichenbach's Berlin Circle, propagated the new doctrines more widely in the 1920s and early 1930s. It was Otto Neurath's advocacy that made the movement self-conscious and more widely known. A 1929 pamphlet written by Neurath, Hahn, and Rudolf Carnap summarized the doctrines of the Vienna Circle at that time. The doctrines included the opposition to all metaphysics, especially ontology and synthetic a priori propositions; the rejection of metaphysics not as wrong but as having no meaning; a criterion of meaning based on Ludwig Wittgenstein's early work; the idea that all knowledge should be codifiable in a single standard language of science; and above all the project of "rational reconstruction," in which ordinary-language concepts were gradually to be replaced by more precise equivalents in that standard language.

In the early 1930s, the Vienna Circle dispersed, mainly because of political upheaval and the untimely deaths of Hahn and Schlick. The most prominent proponents of logical positivism emigrated to United Kingdom and United States, where they considerably influenced American philosophy. Until the 1950s, logical positivism was the leading school in the philosophy of science. During this period of upheaval, Carnap proposed a replacement for the earlier doctrines in his "Logical Syntax of Language". This change of direction and the somewhat differing views of Reichenbach and others led to a consensus that the English name for the shared doctrinal platform, in its American exile from the late 1930s, should be "logical empiricism."

Origins

The chief influences on the early logical positivists were the positivist Ernst Mach and the young Ludwig Wittgenstein. Mach's influence is most apparent in the logical positivists' persistent concern with metaphysics, the unity of science, and the interpretation of the theoretical terms of science, as well as the doctrines of reductionism and phenomenalism, later abandoned by many positivists.

Wittgenstein's *Tractatus Logico-Philosophicus* was a text of great importance for the positivists. The *Tractatus* introduced many doctrines which later influenced logical positivism, including the conception of philosophy as a "critique of language," and the possibility of drawing a theoretically principled distinction between intelligible and nonsensical discourse. The *Tractatus* also adhered to a correspondence theory of truth which the positivists adopted, although some, like Otto Neurath, preferred a form of coherentism. Wittgenstein's influence is further evident in certain formulations of the verification principle.

Compare, for example, *Proposition 4.024* of the *Tractatus*, where Wittgenstein asserts that we understand a proposition when we know what happens if it is true, with Schlick's assertion that "To state the circumstances under which a proposition is true is the same as stating its meaning." The tractarian doctrine that the truths of logic are tautologies was widely held among the logical positivists. Wittgenstein also influenced the logical positivists' interpretation of probability. According to Neurath, some logical positivists disliked the *Tractatus*, since they thought it was full of metaphysics.

Contemporary developments in logic and the foundations of mathematics, especially Bertrand Russell and Alfred North Whitehead's monumental *Principia Mathematica*, impressed the more mathematically minded logical positivists such as Hans Hahn and Rudolf Carnap. "Language-planning" and syntactical techniques derived from these developments were used to defend logicism in the philosophy of mathematics and various reductionist theses. Russell's theory of types was employed to explosive effect in Carnap's early anti-metaphysical polemics.

Immanuel Kant also had an important influence on the positivists, both positive and negative. On the negative side, Kant was often treated by the positivists as something of a punching bag in their early debates, and Kant's doctrine of *synthetic a priori* truths was the doctrine they most wished to overthrow. On the positive side, Kant's views about the nature of physical objects pervaded the "protocol sentence" debate, and Kantian views about the relationship between philosophy and science were shared by the positivists to some degree.

Rise of Logical Positivism in Germany

Positivism in Germany is thought to have risen in response to Hegelian and neo-Hegelian metaphysics, which was the dominant philosophical view in Germany. Hegelian successors such as F.H. Bradley attempted to explain reality by postulating metaphysical entities that did not have any empirical basis. Logical positivists in response wanted to stop such metaphysical entities from being used as an explanation.

Another, less well-known factor that triggered logical positivism was the urgency of solving new philosophical issues raised by new scientific developments. The Vienna Circle under the influence of Moritz Schlick and the Berlin Circle under the influence of Reichenbach consisted of scientists, mathematicians, and scientists turned philosophers, who shared a common goal of solving newly raised problems in philosophy of science.

Basic Tenets

Although the logical positivists held a wide range of views on many matters, they were all interested in science and skeptical of theology and metaphysics. Early on, most logical positivists took the view that all knowledge is based on logical inference from simple "protocol sentences" grounded in observable facts. Many logical positivists supported forms of materialism, metaphysical naturalism, and empiricism.

Perhaps the view for which the logical positivists are best known is the verifiability criterion of meaning, or verificationism. In one of its earlier and stronger formulations, this is the doctrine that a proposition is "cognitively meaningful" only if there is a finite procedure for conclusively determining whether it is true or false. An intended consequence of this view, for most logical positivists, is that metaphysical, theological, and ethical statements fall short of this criterion, and so are not cognitively meaningful. They distinguished cognitive from other varieties of meaningfulness (e.g. emotive, expressive, figurative), and most authors concede that the non-cognitive statements of the history of philosophy possess some other kind of meaningfulness. The positive characterization of cognitive meaningfulness varies from author to author. It has been described as the property of having a truth value, corresponding to a possible state of affairs, naming a proposition, or being intelligible or understandable in the sense in which scientific statements are intelligible or understandable.

Another characteristic feature of logical positivism is the commitment to "Unified Science"; that is, the development of a common language or, in Neurath's phrase, a "universal slang" in which all scientific propositions can be expressed. The adequacy of proposals or fragments of proposals for such a language was often asserted on the basis of various "reductions" or "explications" of the terms of one special science to the terms of another, putatively more fundamental one. Sometimes these reductions took the form of set-theoretic manipulations of a handful of logically primitive concepts; sometimes these reductions took the form of allegedly analytic or *a priori* deductive relationships. A number of publications over a period of thirty years would attempt to elucidate this concept.

CRITICISM AND INFLUENCES

Early critics of logical positivism said that its fundamental tenets could not themselves be formulated in a way that was clearly consistent. The verifiability criterion of meaning did not seem verifiable; but neither was it simply a logical tautology, since it had implications for the practice of science and the empirical truth of other statements. This presented severe problems for the logical consistency of the theory. Another problem was that, while positive existential claims ("there is at least one human being") and negative universal claims ("not all ravens are black") allow for clear methods of verification (find a human or a non-black raven), negative existential claims and positive universal claims do not allow for verification.

Universal claims could apparently never be verified: How can you tell that *all ravens are black*, unless you've hunted down every raven, including those in the past and future? This led to a great deal of work on induction, probability, and "confirmation," which combined verification and falsification.

Logical positivists' response to the first criticism was that logical positivism is a philosophy of science, not an axiomatic system that can prove its own consistency. Secondly, a theory of language and mathematical logic were created to answer what it really means to make statements like "all ravens are black."

Many commentators (including the preceding section) on logical positivism have attributed to its proponents a greater unity of purpose and creed than they actually shared, overlooking the complex disagreements among the logical positivists themselves.

Karl Popper's Objection

Karl Popper was a well-known critic of logical positivism, who published the book *Logik der Forschung* in 1934 (translated by himself as *The Logic of Scientific Discovery*, published 1959). In it he argued that the positivists' criterion of *verifiability* was too strong a criterion for science, and should be replaced by a criterion of falsifiability. Popper thought that falsifiability was a better criterion because it did not invite the philosophical problems inherent in verifying an *induction*, and it allowed statements from the physical sciences which seemed scientific but which did not meet the verification criterion. Popper's concern was not with distinguishing meaningful from meaningless statements, but distinguishing scientific from metaphysical statements. Unlike the positivists, he did not hold that metaphysical statements must be meaningless; he also held that a statement which was "metaphysical" and unfalsifiable in one century (like the ancient Greek philosophy about atoms) could, in another century, be developed into falsifiable theories that have the metaphysical views as a consequence, and thus become scientific.

Popper denied that science need rely on inductive reasoning, or that inductive reasoning actually exists, although most philosophers think it obvious that science does rely on it.

A.J. Ayer's Objection

A response to the second criticism was provided by A. J. Ayer in *Language, Truth and Logic*, in which he sets out the distinction between "strong" and "weak" verification. "A proposition is said to be verifiable, in the strong sense of the term, if, and only if, its truth could be conclusively established by experience." (Ayer 1946:50) It is this sense of verifiable that causes the problem of verification with negative existential claims and positive universal claims. However, the weak sense of verification states that a proposition is "verifiable... if it is possible for experience to render it probable". After establishing this distinction, Ayer goes on to claim that "no proposition, other than a tautology, can possibly be anything more than a probable hypothesis" (Ayer 1946:51), and therefore can only be subject to weak verification. This defense was controversial among logical positivists, some of whom stuck to strong verification, and claimed that general propositions were indeed nonsense.

Hilary Putnam's Objection

According to Hilary Putnam, a former student of Hans Reichenbach and Rudolf Carnap, making an observational/ theoretical distinction is meaningless. The "received view" operates on the *correspondence rule* that states "The observational terms are taken as referring to specified phenomena or phenomenal properties, and the only interpretation given to the theoretical terms is their explicit definition provided by the correspondence rules." Putnam argues that introducing this dichotomy of observational terms and theoretical terms is the problem to start from. Putnam demonstrates this with four objections:

1. Something is referred to as "observational" if it is observable directly with our senses. Then an observation term cannot be applied to something unobservable. If this is the case, there are no observation terms.
2. With Carnap's classification, some unobservable terms are not even theoretical and belong to neither observation terms nor theoretical terms. Some theoretical terms refer primarily to observation terms.
3. Reports of observation terms frequently contain theoretical terms.
4. A scientific theory may not contain any theoretical terms (an example of this is the original Darwin's theory of evolution).

Subsequent Objections from Quine and Kuhn

Subsequent philosophy of science tends to make use of certain aspects of both of these approaches. W. V. O. Quine criticized the distinction between analytic and synthetic statements and the reduction of meaningful statements to immediate experience. Work by Thomas Kuhn has claimed that it is not possible to provide truth conditions for science independent of its historical paradigm. But even this criticism was not unknown to the logical positivists: Otto Neurath compared science to a boat which we must rebuild on the open sea.

Influence of Logical Positivism

Logical positivism spread throughout almost the entire western world. It was disseminated throughout the European continent. It was spread to Britain by the influence of A. J. Ayer. And later, it was brought to American universities by members of the Vienna Circle after they fled Europe and settled in the United States during and after WWII. Logical positivism was essential to the development of early analytic philosophy. The term subsequently came to be almost interchangeable with "analytic philosophy" in the first half of the twentieth century.

Logical positivism was immensely influential in the philosophy of language and represented the dominant philosophy of science between World War I and the Cold War.

Contemporary Status within Philosophy

Most philosophers consider logical positivism to be, as John Passmore expressed it, "dead, or as dead as a philosophical movement ever becomes." By the late 1970s, its ideas were so generally recognized to be seriously defective that one of its own chief proponents, A. J. Ayer, could say in a interview: "I suppose the most important [defect]...was that nearly all of it was false." It retains an important place in the history of Analytic philosophy as the antecedent of movements which continue today, such as Constructive empiricism, Positivism and Postpositivism.

POSITIVISM & POST-POSITIVISM

Let's start our very brief discussion of philosophy of science with a simple distinction between *epistemology* and *methodology*. The term epistemology comes from the Greek word epistêmê, their term for knowledge. In simple terms, epistemology is the philosophy of knowledge or of how we come to know. Methodology is also concerned with how we come to know, but is much more practical in nature. Methodology is focused on the specific ways — the methods — that we can use to try to understand our world better. Epistemology and methodology are intimately related: the former involves the *philosophy* of how we come to know the world and the latter involves the *practice*.

When most people in our society think about science, they think about some guy in a white lab coat working at a lab bench mixing up chemicals. They think of science as boring, cut-and-dry, and they think of the scientist as narrow-minded and esoteric (the ultimate nerd — think of the humorous but nonetheless mad scientist in the *Back to the Future* movies, for instance). A lot of our stereotypes about science come from a period where science was dominated by a particular philosophy — *positivism* — that tended to support some of these views. Here, I want to suggest (no matter what the movie industry may think) that science has moved on in its thinking into an era of *post-positivism* where many of those stereotypes of the scientist no longer hold up.

Let's begin by considering what positivism is. In its broadest sense, positivism is a rejection of metaphysics. It is a position that holds that the goal of knowledge is simply to describe the phenomena that we experience. The purpose of science is simply to stick to what we can observe and measure. Knowledge of anything beyond that, a positivist would hold, is impossible. When I think of positivism (and the related philosophy of logical positivism) I think of the behaviorists in mid-20th Century psychology. These were the mythical 'rat runners' who believed that psychology could only study what could be directly observed and measured. Since we can't directly observe emotions, thoughts, etc. (although we may be able to measure some of the physical and physiological accompaniments), these were not legitimate topics for a scientific psychology. B.F. Skinner argued that psychology needed to concentrate only on the positive and negative reinforcers of behaviour in order to predict how people will behave — everything else in between (like what the person is thinking) is irrelevant because it can't be measured.

In a positivist view of the world, science was seen as the way to get at truth, to understand the world well enough so that we might predict and control it. The world and the universe were deterministic — they operated by laws of cause and effect that we could discern if we applied the unique approach of the scientific method. Science was largely a mechanistic or mechanical affair. We use deductive reasoning to postulate theories that we can test. Based on the results of our studies, we may learn that our theory doesn't fit the facts well and so we need to revise our theory to better predict reality. The positivist believed in *empiricism* — the idea that observation and measurement was the core of the scientific endeavor. The key approach of the scientific method is the experiment, the attempt to discern natural laws through direct manipulation and observation.

OK, I am exaggerating the positivist position (although you may be amazed at how close to this some of them actually came) in order to make a point. Things have changed in our views of science since the middle part of the 20th century.

Probably the most important has been our shift away from positivism into what we term *post-positivism*. By post-positivism, I don't mean a slight adjustment to or revision of the positivist position — post-positivism is a wholesale rejection of the central tenets of positivism. A post-positivist might begin by recognizing that the way scientists think and work and the way we think in our everyday life are not distinctly different. Scientific reasoning and common sense reasoning are essentially the same process. There is no difference in kind between the two, only a difference in degree. Scientists, for example, follow specific procedures to assure that observations are verifiable, accurate and consistent. In everyday reasoning, we don't always proceed so carefully (although, if you think about it, when the stakes are high, even in everyday life we become much more cautious about measurement. Think of the way most responsible parents keep continuous watch over their infants, noticing details that non-parents would never detect).

One of the most common forms of post-positivism is a philosophy called *critical realism*. A critical realist believes that there is a reality independent of our thinking about it that science can study. (This is in contrast with a *subjectivist* who would hold that there is no external reality — we're each making this all up!). Positivists were also realists. The difference is that the post-positivist critical realist recognizes that all observation is fallible and has error and that all theory is revisable. In other words, the critical realist is *critical* of our ability to know reality with certainty. Where the positivist believed that the goal of science was to uncover the truth, the post-positivist critical realist believes that *the goal of science is to hold steadfastly to the goal of getting it right about reality, even though we can never achieve that goal*! Because all measurement is fallible, the post-positivist emphasizes the importance of multiple measures and observations, each of which may possess different types of error, and the need to use *triangulation* across these multiple errorful sources to try to get a better bead on what's happening in reality. The post-positivist also believes that all observations are theory-laden and that scientists (and everyone else, for that matter) are inherently biased by their cultural experiences, world views, and so on. This is not cause to give up in despair, however. Just because I have my world view based on my experiences and you have yours doesn't mean that we can't hope to translate from each other's experiences or understand each other. That is, post-positivism rejects the *relativist* idea of the *incommensurability* of different perspectives, the idea that we can never understand each other because we come from different experiences and cultures. Most post-positivists are *constructivists* who believe that we each construct our view of the world based on our perceptions of it. Because perception and observation is fallible, our constructions must be imperfect. So what is meant by *objectivity* in a post-positivist world? Positivists believed that objectivity was a characteristic that resided in the individual scientist. Scientists are responsible for putting aside their biases and beliefs and seeing the world as it 'really' is. Post-positivists reject the idea that any individual can see the world perfectly as it really is. We are all biased and all of our observations are affected (theory-laden). Our best hope for achieving objectivity is to triangulate across multiple fallible perspectives! Thus, objectivity is not the characteristic of an individual, it is inherently a social phenomenon. It is what multiple individuals are trying to achieve when they criticize each other's work. We never achieve objectivity perfectly, but we can approach it. The best way for us to improve the objectivity of what we do is to do it within the context of a broader contentious community of truth-seekers (including other scientists) who criticize each other's work. The theories that survive such intense scrutiny are a bit like the species that survive in the evolutionary struggle. (This is sometimes called the *natural selection theory of knowledge* and holds that ideas have 'survival value' and that knowledge evolves through a process of variation, selection and retention). They have adaptive value and are probably as close as our species can come to being objective and understanding reality.

3

The Pragmatism Theory of Truth

Pragmatism is a philosophical movement that includes those who claim that an ideology or proposition is true if it works satisfactorily, that the meaning of a proposition is to be found in the practical consequences of accepting it, and that impractical ideas are to be rejected. Pragmatism, in William James' eyes, was that the truth of an idea needed to be tested to prove its validity. Pragmatism began in the late nineteenth century with Charles Sanders Peirce and his pragmatic maxim. Through the early twentieth-century it was developed further in the works of William James, John Dewey and—in a less orthodox manner—by George Santayana. Other important aspects of pragmatism include, radical empiricism, instrumentalism, verificationism, conceptual relativity, a denial of the fact-value distinction, a high regard for science, and fallibilism.

Pragmatism enjoyed renewed attention from the 1960s on when a new analytic school of philosophy (W. V. O. Quine and Wilfrid Sellars) put forth a revised pragmatism criticizing the logical positivism dominant in the United States and Britain since the 1930s, while a new brand infused with themes from the analytic and other traditions, known sometimes as neopragmatism, gained influence spearheaded by the philosopher Richard Rorty, the most influential of the late 20th-century pragmatists.

Contemporary pragmatism may be, in broad general terms, divided into a strict analytic tradition and "neo-classical" pragmatism (such as Susan Haack) that adheres to the work of Peirce, James, and Dewey.

Origins

Pragmatism as a philosophical movement began in the United States in the 1870s. Its overall direction was determined by the thought and works of Charles Sanders Peirce and William James (both members of The Metaphysical Club) as well as John Dewey, George Herbert Mead, and Chauncey Wright. The first use in print of the name *pragmatism* was in 1898 by James, who credited Peirce with having coined the term during the early 1870s. James regarded as foundational to pragmatism Peirce's 1877–8 "Illustrations of the Logic of Science" series (including "The Fixation of Belief", 1877) — especially the second paper, "How to Make Our Ideas Clear" (1878).

In 1906, Peirce wrote that, in the Metaphysical Club decades earlier, Nicholas St. John Green often urged the importance of applying Bain's definition of belief, as "that upon which a man is prepared to act." From this definition, pragmatism is scarce more than a corollary; so that I am disposed to think of him as the grandfather of pragmatism. James and Peirce, inspired by crucial links among belief, conduct, and disposition, agreed with Green. John Shook has said, "Chauncey Wright also deserves considerable credit, for as both Peirce and James recall, it was Wright who demanded a phenomenalist and fallibilist empiricism as a vital alternative to rationalistic speculation."

Since one may look to practices to distinguish beliefs from thoughts that make no practical difference (even if sometimes a useful formal difference), Peirce developed the idea that inquiry depends on real doubt, not mere verbal or hyperbolic doubt and said, in order to understand a conception in a fruitful way, "Consider what effects that might conceivably have practical bearings you conceive the objects of your conception to have. Then, your conception of those effects is the whole of your conception of the object" — which he later called the pragmatic maxim. It equates any conception of an object to a conception of that object's effects to a general extent of the effects' conceivable implications for informed practice. It is the heart of his pragmatism as a method of experimentational mental reflection arriving at conceptions in terms of conceivable confirmatory and disconfirmatory circumstances — a method hospitable to the generation of explanatory hypotheses, and conducive to the employment and improvement of verification. Typical of Peirce is his concern with inference to explanatory hypotheses as outside the usual foundational alternative between deductivist rationalism and inductivist empiricism, though he himself was a mathematical logician and a founder of statistics.

Prompted by James's making famous of Peirce and his ideas starting in 1897, Peirce lectured and further wrote on pragmatism to make clear his own interpretation. While framing a conception's meaning in terms of conceivable tests, Peirce emphasized that, since a conception is general, its meaning, its intellectual purport, equates to its acceptance's implications for general practice, rather than to any definite set of actual consequences (or test results) themselves; a conception's clarified meaning points toward its conceivable verifications, but actual outcomes are not meanings but individual upshots. Peirce in 1905 coined the new name pragmaticism "for the precise purpose of expressing the original definition", saying that "all went happily" with James's and Schiller's variant uses of the old name "pragmatism" and that he nonetheless coined the new name because of the old name's growing use in "literary journals, where it gets abused". Yet in a 1906 manuscript he cited as causes his differences with James and Schiller. and, in a 1908 publication, his differences with James as well as literary author Giovanni Papini. Peirce in any case regarded his views that truth is immutable and infinity is real, as being opposed by the other pragmatists, but he remained allied with them on other issues.

Inspiration for the various pragmatists included:

- Francis Bacon who coined the saying *ipsa scientia potestas est* ("knowledge itself is power"),
- David Hume for his naturalistic account of knowledge and action,
- Thomas Reid, for his direct realism,
- Immanuel Kant, for his idealism and from whom Peirce derives the name "pragmatism",

- Georg Hegel who introduced temporality into philosophy (Pinkard in Misak 2007), and
- J.S. Mill for his nominalism and empiricism.

CENTRAL PRAGMATIST TENETS

The Primacy of Practice

The pragmatist proceeds from the basic premise that the human capability of theorizing is integral to intelligent practice. Theory and practice are not separate spheres; rather, theories and distinctions are tools or maps for finding our way in the world. As John Dewey put it, there is no question of theory *versus* practice but rather of intelligent practice versus uninformed, stupid practice and noted in a conversation with William Pepperell Montague that "[h]is effort had not been to practicalize intelligence but to intellectualize practice". (Quoted in Eldridge 1998, p. 5) Theory is an abstraction from direct experience and ultimately must return to inform experience in turn. Thus an organism navigating his or her environment is the grounds for pragmatist inquiry.

Anti-reification of Concepts and Theories

Dewey, in *The Quest For Certainty*, criticized what he called "the philosophical fallacy": philosophers often take categories (such as the mental and the physical) for granted because they don't realize that these are merely nominal concepts that were invented to help solve specific problems. This causes metaphysical and conceptual confusion. Various examples are the "ultimate Being" of Hegelian philosophers, the belief in a "realm of value", the idea that logic, because it is an abstraction from concrete thought, has nothing to do with the act of concrete thinking, and so on. David L. Hildebrand sums up the problem: "Perceptual inattention to the specific functions comprising inquiry led realists and idealists alike to formulate accounts of knowledge that project the products of extensive abstraction back onto experience."

Naturalism and Anti-Cartesianism

From the outset, pragmatists wanted to reform philosophy and bring it more in line with the scientific method as they understood it. They argued that idealist and realist philosophy had a tendency to present human knowledge as something beyond what science could grasp. These philosophies then resorted either to a phenomenology inspired by Kant or to correspondence theories of knowledge and truth. Pragmatists criticized the former for its a priorism, and the latter because it takes correspondence as an unanalyzable fact. Pragmatism instead tries to explain, psychologically and biologically, how the relation between knower and known 'works' in the world.

In 1868, C.S. Peirce argued there there is no power of *intuition* in the sense of a cognition unconditioned by inference, and no power of introspection, intuitive or otherwise, and that awareness of an internal world is by hypothetical inference from external facts. Introspection and intuition were staple philosophical tools at least since Descartes. He argued that there is no absolutely first cognition in a cognitive process; such a process has its beginning but can always be analyzed into finer cognitive stages. That which we call introspection does not give privileged access to knowledge about the mind-the self is a concept that is derived from our interaction with the external world and not the other way around. At the same time he held persistently that pragmatism and epistemology in general could not be derived from principles of psychology understood as a special science : what we *do* think is too different from what we *should* think; in his "Illustrations of the Logic of Science" series, Peirce formulated both pragmatism and principles of statistics as aspects of scientific method in general. This is an important point of disagreement with most other pragmatists, who advocate a more thorough naturalism and psychologism.

Richard Rorty expanded on these and other arguments in *Philosophy and the Mirror of Nature* in which he criticized attempts by many philosophers of science to carve out a space for epistemology that is entirely unrelated to-and sometimes thought of as superior to-the empirical sciences. W.V. Quine, instrumental in bringing naturalized epistemology back into favour with his essay *Epistemology Naturalized* (Quine 1969), also criticized 'traditional' epistemology and its "Cartesian dream" of absolute certainty. The dream, he argued, was impossible in practice as well as misguided in theory because it separates epistemology from scientific inquiry.

The Reconciliation of Anti-skepticism and Fallibilism

Hilary Putnam has suggested that the reconciliation of antiskepticism and fallibilism is the central goal of American pragmatism. Although all human knowledge is partial, with no ability to take a 'God's-eye-view,' this does not necessitate a globalized skeptical attitude. Peirce insisted that contrary to Descartes' famous and influential methodology in the Meditations on First Philosophy, doubt cannot be feigned or created for the purpose of conducting philosophical inquiry. Doubt, like belief, requires justification. It arises from confrontation with some specific recalcitrant matter of fact (which Dewey called a 'situation'), which unsettles our belief in some specific proposition. Inquiry is then the rationally self-controlled process of attempting to return to a settled state of belief about the matter. Note that anti-skepticism is a reaction to modern academic skepticism in the wake of Descartes. The pragmatist insistence that all knowledge is tentative is actually quite congenial to the older skeptical tradition.

Pragmatist Theory of Truth and Epistemology

The epistemology of early pragmatism was heavily influenced by Charles Darwin. Pragmatism was not the first to apply evolution to theories of knowledge: Schopenhauer advocated a *biological idealism* as what's useful to an organism to believe might differ wildly from what is true. Here knowledge and action are portrayed as two separate spheres with an absolute or transcendental truth above and beyond any sort of inquiry organisms use to cope with life. Pragmatism challenges this idealism by providing an "ecological" account of knowledge: inquiry is how organisms can get a grip on their environment. *Real* and *true* are functional labels in inquiry and cannot be understood outside of this context. It is not *realist* in a traditionally robust sense of realism (what Hilary Putnam would later call metaphysical realism), but it is realist in how it acknowledges an external world which must be dealt with.

With the tendency of philosophers to group all views as either idealistic or realistic, pragmatism was seen as a form of subjectivism or idealism. Many of James' best-turned phrases—*truth's cash value* and *the true is only the expedient in our way of thinking* — were taken out of context and caricatured in contemporary literature as representing the view where any idea with practical utility is true. William James wrote:

It is high time to urge the use of a little imagination in philosophy. The unwillingness of some of our critics to read any but the silliest of possible meanings into our statements is as discreditable to their imaginations as anything I know in recent philosophic history. Schiller says the truth is that which 'works.' Thereupon he is treated as one who limits verification to the lowest material utilities. Dewey says truth is what gives 'satisfaction'! He is treated as one who believes in calling everything true which, if it were true, would be pleasant.

In reality, James asserts, the theory is a great deal more subtle. The role of belief in representing reality is widely debated in pragmatism. Is a belief valid when it represents reality? *Copying is one (and only one) genuine mode of knowing,*. Are beliefs dispositions which qualify as true or false depending on how helpful they prove in inquiry and in action? Is it only in the struggle of intelligent organisms with the surrounding environment that beliefs acquire meaning? Does a belief only become true when it succeeds in this struggle? In Pragmatism nothing practical or useful is held to be necessarily true, nor is anything which helps to survive merely in the short term. For example, to believe my cheating spouse is faithful may help me feel better now, but it is certainly not useful from a more long-term perspective because it doesn't accord with the facts (and is therefore not true).

PRAGMATISM IN OTHER FIELDS OF PHILOSOPHY

While pragmatism started out simply as a criterion of meaning, it quickly expanded to become a full-fledged epistemology with wide-ranging implications for the entire philosophical field. Pragmatists who work in these fields share a common inspiration, but their work is diverse and there are no received views.

Philosophy of Science

In the philosophy of science, instrumentalism is the view that concepts and theories are merely useful instruments whose worth is measured not by whether the concepts and theories somehow mirror reality, but by how effective they are in explaining and predicting phenomena. Instrumentalism does not state that truth doesn't matter, but rather provides a specific answer to the question of what truth and falsity mean and how they function in science. One of C.I. Lewis' main arguments in *Mind and the World Order: Outline of a Theory of Knowledge* was that science does not merely provide a copy of reality but must work with conceptual systems and that those are chosen for pragmatic reasons, that is, because they aid inquiry. Lewis' own development of multiple modal logics is a case in point. Lewis is sometimes called a 'conceptual pragmatist' because of this.

Another development is the cooperation of logical positivism and pragmatism in the works of Charles W. Morris and Rudolph Carnap. The influence of pragmatism on these writers is mostly limited to the incorporation of the pragmatic maxim into their epistemology. Pragmatists with a broader conception of the movement don't often refer to them. W. V. Quine's paper "Two Dogmas of Empiricism", published 1951, is one of the most celebrated papers of twentieth-century philosophy in the analytic tradition. The paper is an attack on two central tenets of the logical positivists' philosophy. One is the distinction between analytic truths, statements which are true simply in value of the meanings of their words ('all bachelors are unmarried'), and synthetic truths, which are grounded in empirical fact. The other is reductionism, the theory that each meaningful statement gets its meaning from some logical construction of terms which refers exclusively to immediate experience. Quine's argument brings to mind Peirce's insistence that axioms aren't a priori truths but synthetic statements.

Logic

Later in his life Schiller became famous for his attacks on logic in his textbook "Formal Logic." By then, Schiller's pragmatism had become the nearest of any of the classical pragmatists to an ordinary language philosophy. Schiller sought to undermine the very possibility of formal logic, by showing that words only had meaning when used in an actual context. The least famous of Schiller's main works was the constructive sequel to his destructive book "Formal Logic." In this sequel, "Logic for Use," Schiller attempted to construct a new logic to replace the formal logic he had just decimated in "Formal Logic." What he offers is something philosophers would recognize today as a logic covering the context of discovery and the hypothetico-deductive method.

Whereas F.C.S. Schiller actually dismissed the possibility of formal logic, most pragmatists are critical rather of its pretension to ultimate validity and see logic as one logical tool among others-or perhaps, considering the multitude of formal logics, one *set* of tools among others. This is the view of C.I. Lewis. C.S. Peirce developed multiple methods for doing formal logic. Stephen Toulmin's *The Uses of Argument* inspired scholars in informal logic and rhetoric studies (although it is actually an epistemological work).

Metaphysics

James and Dewey were empirical thinkers in the most straightforward fashion: experience is the ultimate test and experience is what needs to be explained. They were dissatisfied with ordinary empiricism because in the tradition dating from Hume, empiricists had a tendency to think of experience as nothing more than individual sensations. To the pragmatists, this went against the spirit of empiricism: we should try to explain all that is given in experience including connections and meaning, instead of explaining them away and positing sense data as the ultimate reality. Radical empiricism, or Immediate Empiricism in Dewey's words, wants to give a place to meaning and value instead of explaining them away as subjective additions to a world of whizzing atoms.

William James gives an interesting example of this philosophical shortcoming: [A young graduate] began by saying that he had always taken for granted that when you entered a philosophic classroom you had to open relations with a universe entirely distinct from the one you left behind you in the street. The two were supposed, he said, to have so little to do with each other, that you could not possibly occupy your mind with them at the same time. The world of concrete personal experiences to which the street belongs is multitudinous beyond imagination, tangled, muddy, painful and perplexed. The world to which your philosophy-professor introduces you is simple, clean and noble. The contradictions of real life are absent from it. [...] In point of fact it is far less an account of this actual world than a clear addition built upon it [...] It is no explanation of our concrete universe

F.C.S. Schiller's first book, "Riddles of the Sphinx", was published before he became aware of the growing pragmatist movement taking place in America. In it, Schiller argues for a middle ground between materialism and absolute metaphysics. The result of the split between these two explanatory schemes that are comparable to what William James called tough-minded empiricism and tender-minded rationalism, Schiller contends, is that mechanistic naturalism cannot make sense of the "higher" aspects of our world (freewill, consciousness, purpose, universals and some would add God), while abstract metaphysics cannot make sense of the "lower" aspects of our world (the imperfect, change, physicality).

While Schiller is vague about the exact sort of middle ground he is trying to establish, he suggests metaphysics as a tool that can aid inquiry and is only valuable insofar as it actually does help in explanation.

In the second half of the twentieth century, Stephen Toulmin argued that the need to distinguish between reality and appearance only arises within an explanatory scheme and therefore that there is no point in asking what 'ultimate reality' consists of. More recently, a similar idea has been suggested by the postanalytical philosopher Daniel Dennett, who argues that anyone who wants to understand the world has to adopt the intentional stance and acknowledge both the 'syntactical' aspects of reality (i.e. whizzing atoms) and its emergent or 'semantic' properties (i.e. meaning and value).

Radical Empiricism gives interesting answers to questions about the limits of science if there are any, the nature of meaning and value and the workability of reductionism. These questions feature prominently in current debates about the relationship between religion and science, where it is often assumed-most pragmatists would disagree-that science degrades everything that is meaningful into 'merely' physical phenomena.

Philosophy of Mind

Both John Dewey in *Nature and Experience* (1929) and half a century later Richard Rorty in his monumental *Philosophy and the Mirror of Nature* (1979) argued that much of the debate about the relation of the mind to the body results from conceptual confusions. They argue instead that there is no need to posit the mind or mindstuff as an ontological category.

Pragmatists disagree over whether philosophers ought to adopt a quietist or a naturalist stance toward the mind-body problem. The former (Rorty among them) want to do away with the problem because they believe it's a pseudo-problem, whereas the latter believe that it is a meaningful empirical question.

Ethics

Pragmatism sees no fundamental difference between practical and theoretical reason, nor any ontological difference between facts and values. Both facts and values have cognitive content: knowledge is what we should believe; values are hypotheses about what is good in action. Pragmatist ethics is broadly humanist because it sees no ultimate test of morality beyond what matters for us as humans. Good values are those for which we have good reasons, viz. the Good Reasons approach. The pragmatist formulation pre-dates those of other philosophers who have stressed important similarities between values and facts such as Jerome Schneewind and John Searle. William James' contribution to ethics, as laid out in his essay *The Will to Believe* has often been misunderstood as a plea for relativism or irrationality. On its own terms it argues that ethics always involves a certain degree of trust or faith and that we cannot always wait for adequate proof when making moral decisions.

Moral questions immediately present themselves as questions whose solution cannot wait for sensible proof. A moral question is a question not of what sensibly exists, but of what is good, or would be good if it did exist. [...] A social organism of any sort whatever, large or small, is what it is because each member proceeds to his own duty with a trust that the other members will simultaneously do theirs. Wherever a desired result is achieved by the co-operation of many independent persons, its existence as a fact is a pure consequence of the precursive faith in one another of those immediately concerned. A government, an army, a commercial system, a ship, a college, an athletic team, all exist on this condition, without which not only is nothing achieved, but nothing is even attempted. (James 1896)

Of the classical pragmatists, John Dewey wrote most extensively about morality and democracy. (Edel 1993) In his classic article *Three Independent Factors in Morals* (Dewey 1930), he tried to integrate three basic philosophical perspectives on morality: the right, the virtuous and the good. He held that while all three provide meaningful ways to think about moral questions, the possibility of conflict among the three elements cannot always be easily solved. (Anderson, SEP)

Dewey also criticized the dichotomy between means and ends which he saw as responsible for the degradation of our everyday working lives and education, both conceived as merely a means to an end. He stressed the need for meaningful labour and a conception of education that viewed it not as a preparation for life but as life itself. Dewey was opposed to other ethical philosophies of his time, notably the emotivism of Alfred Ayer. Dewey envisioned the possibility of ethics as an experimental discipline, and thought values could best be characterized not as feelings or imperatives, but as hypotheses about what actions will lead to satisfactory results or what he termed *consummatory experience*. A further implication of this view is that ethics is a fallible undertaking, since human beings are frequently unable to know what would satisfy them.

A recent pragmatist contribution to meta-ethics is Todd Lekan's "Making Morality". Lekan argues that morality is a fallible but rational practice and that it has traditionally been misconceived as based on theory or principles. Instead, he argues, theory and rules arise as tools to make practice more intelligent.

Aesthetics

John Dewey's *Art as Experience*, based on the William James lectures he delivered at Harvard, was an attempt to show the integrity of art, culture and everyday experience. (Field, IEP) Art, for Dewey, is or should be a part of everyone's creative lives and not just the privilege of a select group of artists. He also emphasizes that the audience is more than a passive recipient. Dewey's treatment of art was a move away from the transcendental approach to aesthetics in the wake of Immanuel Kant who emphasized the unique character of art and the disinterested nature of aesthetic appreciation. A notable contemporary pragmatist aesthetician is Joseph Margolis. He defines a work of art as "a physically embodied, culturally emergent entity", a human "utterance" that isn't an ontological quirk but in line with other human activity and culture in general. He emphasizes that works of art are complex and difficult to fathom, and that no determinate interpretation can be given.

Philosophy of Religion

Both Dewey and James have investigated the role that religion can still play in contemporary society, the former in *A Common Faith* and the latter in *The Varieties of Religious Experience*. It should be noted, from a general point of view, that for William James, something is true *only insofar* as it works. Thus, the statement, for example, that prayer is heard may work on a psychological level but (a) will not actually help to bring about the things you pray for (b) may be better explained by referring to its soothing effect than by claiming prayers are actually heard. As such, pragmatism isn't antithetical to religion but it isn't an apologetic for faith either.

Joseph Margolis, in *Historied Thought, Constructed World*, makes a distinction between "existence" and "reality". He suggests using the term "exists" only for those things which adequately exhibit Peirce's *Secondness*: things which offer brute physical resistance to our movements. In this way, such things which affect us, like numbers, may be said to be "real", though they do not "exist". Margolis suggests that God, in such a linguistic usage, might very well be "real", causing believers to act in such and such a way, but might not "exist".

ANALYTICAL, NEOCLASSICAL AND NEOPRAGMATISM

Neopragmatism is a broad contemporary category used for various thinkers, some of them radically opposed to one another. The name neopragmatist signifies that the thinkers in question incorporate important insights of, and yet significantly diverge from, the classical pragmatists. This divergence may occur either in their philosophical methodology (many of them are loyal to the analytic tradition) or in actual conceptual formation (C.I. Lewis was very critical of Dewey; Richard Rorty dislikes Peirce). Important analytical neopragmatists include the aforementioned Lewis, W.V.O. Quine, Donald Davidson, Hilary Putnam and the early Richard Rorty. Stanley Fish, the later Rorty and Jürgen Habermas are closer to continental thought. Neoclassical pragmatism denotes those thinkers who consider themselves inheritors of the project of the classical pragmatists. Sidney Hook and Susan Haack (known for the theory of foundherentism) are well-known examples.

Not all pragmatists are easily characterized. It is probable, considering the advent of postanalytic philosophy and the diversification of Anglo-American philosophy, that more philosophers will be influenced by pragmatist thought without necessarily publicly committing themselves to that philosophical school. Daniel Dennett, a student of Quine's, falls into this category, as does Stephen Toulmin, who arrived at his philosophical position via Wittgenstein, whom he calls "a pragmatist of a sophisticated kind" (foreword for Dewey 1929 in the 1988 edition, p. xiii). Another example is Mark Johnson whose embodied philosophy (Lakoff and Johnson 1999) shares its psychologism, direct realism and anti-cartesianism with pragmatism. Conceptual pragmatism is a theory of knowledge originating with the work of the philosopher and logician Clarence Irving Lewis. The epistemology of conceptual pragmatism was first formulated in the 1929 book *Mind and the World Order: Outline of a Theory of Knowledge*.

'French Pragmatism' is attended with theorists like Bruno Latour, Michel Crozier and Luc Boltanski and Laurent Thévenot. It is often seen as opposed to structural problems connected to the French Critical Theory of Pierre Bourdieu.

CONTEMPORARY REVERBERATIONS

In the twentieth century, the movements of logical positivism and ordinary language philosophy have similarities with pragmatism. Like pragmatism, logical positivism provides a verification criterion of meaning that is supposed to rid us of nonsense metaphysics. However, logical positivism doesn't stress action like pragmatism does. Furthermore, the pragmatists rarely used their maxim of meaning to rule out all metaphysics as nonsense. Usually, pragmatism was put forth to correct metaphysical doctrines or to construct empirically verifiable ones rather than to provide a wholesale rejection.

Ordinary language philosophy is closer to pragmatism than other philosophy of language because of its nominalist character and because it takes the broader functioning of language in an environment as its focus instead of investigating abstract relations between *language* and *world*. Pragmatism has ties to process philosophy. Much of their work developed in dialogue with process philosophers like Henri Bergson and Alfred North Whitehead, who aren't usually considered pragmatists because they differ so much on other points. (Douglas Browning et al. 1998; Rescher, SEP)

Behaviorism and functionalism in psychology and sociology also have ties to pragmatism, which is not surprising considering that James and Dewey were both scholars of psychology and that Mead became a sociologist. Utilitarianism has some significant parallels to Pragmatism and John Stuart Mill espoused similar values.

Influence of Pragmatism in Social Sciences

Increasing attention is being given to pragmatist epistemology in social sciences, which have struggled with divisive debates over the status of social scientific knowledge. Enthusiasts suggest that pragmatism offers an approach which is both pluralist and practical.

Influence of Pragmatism in Public Administration

The classical pragmatism of John Dewey, William James and Charles Sanders Peirce has influenced research in the field of Public Administration. Scholars claim classical pragmatism had a profound influence on the origin of the field of Public Administration. At the most basic level, public administrators are responsible for making programs "work" in a pluralistic, problems oriented environment. Public administrators are also responsible for the day to day work with citizens. Dewey's participatory democracy can be applied in this environment. Dewey and James notion of theory as a tool, helps administrators craft theories to resolve policy and administrative problems. Further, the birth of American public administration coincides closely with the period of greatest influence of the classical pragmatists.

Which pragmatism (classical pragmatism or neo-pragmatism) makes the most sense in public administration has been the source of debate. The debate began when Patricia Shields introduced Dewey's notion of the Community of Inquiry. Hugh Miller objected to one element of the community of inquiry (problematic situation, scientific attitude, participatory democracy)-Scientific attitude. A debate that included responses from a practitioner, an economist, a planner, other Public Administration Scholars, and noted philosophers followed. Miller and Shields also responded. In addition, applied scholarship of public administration that assesses charter schools, contracting out or outsourcing, financial management, performance measurement, urban quality of life initiatives, and urban planning explicitly draws on the ideas of classical pragmatism in the development of the conceptual framework and focus of analysis.

Pragmatism and Feminism

Since the mid 1990s, feminist philosophers have re-discovered classical pragmatism as a source of feminist theories. Works by Seigfried, Duran, Keith, and Whipps explore the historic and philosophic links between feminism and pragmatism. The connection between pragmatism and feminism took so long to be rediscovered because pragmatism itself was eclipsed by logical positivism during the middle decades of the 20th century. As a result it was lost from feminine discourse. The very features of pragmatism that led to its decline are the characteristics that feminists now consider its greatest strength. These are "persistent and early criticisms of positivist interpretations of scientific methodology; disclosure of value dimension of factual claims"; viewing aesthetics as informing everyday experience; subordinating logical analysis to political, cultural and social issues; linking the dominant discourses with domination; "realigning theory with praxis; and resisting the turn to epistemology and instead emphasizing concrete experience". These feminist philosophers point to Jane Addams as a founder of classical pragmatism. In addition, the ideas of Dewey, Mead and James are consistent with many feminist tenets. Jane Addams, John Dewey & George Herbert Mead developed their philosophies as all three became friends, influenced each other and were engaged in the Hull-House experience and women's rights causes.

Criticism

Although many later pragmatists such as W.V.O. Quine were actually analytic philosophers, the most vehement criticisms of classical pragmatism came from within the analytic school. Bertrand Russell was especially known for his vituperative attacks on what he considered little more than epistemological relativism and short-sighted practicalism. Realists in general often could not fathom how pragmatists could seriously call themselves empirical or realist thinkers and thought pragmatist epistemology was only a disguised manifestation of idealism. (Hildebrand 2003) Louis Menand argues that during the Cold War, the intellectual life of the United States became dominated by ideologies. Since pragmatism seeks "to avoid the violence inherent in abstraction," it was not very popular at the time.

Neopragmatism as represented by Richard Rorty has been criticized as relativistic both by neoclassical pragmatists such as Susan Haack (Haack 1997) and by many analytic philosophers. Rorty's early analytical work, however, differs notably from his later work which some, including Rorty himself, consider to be closer to literary criticism than to philosophy-most criticism is aimed at this latter phase of Rorty's thought.

PRAGMATIC THEORY OF TRUTH

Pragmatic theory of truth refers to those accounts, definitions, and theories of the concept *truth* that distinguish the philosophies of pragmatism and pragmaticism. The conception of truth in question varies along lines that reflect the influence of several thinkers, initially and notably, Charles Sanders Peirce, William James, and John Dewey, but a number of common features can be identified. The most characteristic features are (1) a reliance on the *pragmatic maxim* as a means of clarifying the meanings of difficult concepts, *truth* in particular, and (2) an emphasis on the fact that the *product* variously branded as *belief*, *certainty*, *knowledge*, or *truth* is the result of a *process*, namely, *inquiry*.

Background

Pragmatic theories of truth enter on a stage that was set by the philosophies of former ages, with special reference to the Golden Age, the Scholastics, and Immanuel Kant. Recalling a few elements of this background as the great scholar Ignacio said it can provide invaluable insight into the play of ideas that developed into modern times. And because pragmatic ideas about truth are often confused with a number of quite distinct notions, it is useful to say a few words about these other theories, and to highlight the points of significant contrast.

In one classical formulation, truth is defined as the good of logic, where logic is a normative science, that is, an inquiry into a *good* or a *value* that seeks knowledge of it and the means to achieve it. In this view, truth cannot be discussed to much effect outside the context of inquiry, knowledge, and logic, all very broadly considered. Most inquiries into the character of truth begin with a notion of an informative, meaningful, or significant element, the truth of whose information, meaning, or significance may be put into question and needs to be evaluated. Depending on the context, this element might be called an *artefact*, *expression*, *image*, *impression*, *lyric*, *mark*, *performance*, *picture*, *sentence*, *sign*, *string*, *symbol*, *text*, *thought*, *token*, *utterance*, *word*, *work*, and so on. Whatever the case, one has the task of judging whether the bearers of information, meaning, or significance are indeed truth-bearers. This judgment is typically expressed in the form of a specific *truth predicate*, whose positive application to a sign, or so on, asserts that the sign is true.

Considered within the broadest horizon, there is little reason to imagine that the process of judging a *work*, that leads to a predication of false or true, is necessarily amenable to formalization, and it may always remain what is commonly called a *judgment call*. But there are indeed many well-circumscribed domains where it is useful to consider disciplined forms of evaluation, and the observation of these limits allows for the institution of what is called a *method* of judging truth and falsity. One of the first questions that can be asked in this setting is about the relationship between the significant performance and its reflective critique. If one expresses oneself in a particular fashion, and someone says "that's true", is there anything useful at all that can be said in general terms about the relationship between these two acts? For instance, does the critique add value to the expression criticized, does it say something significant in its own right, or is it just an insubstantial echo of the original sign?

Theories of truth may be described according to several dimensions of description that affect the character of the predicate "true". The truth predicates that are used in different theories may be classified by the number of things that have to be mentioned in order to assess the truth of a sign, counting the sign itself as the first thing. In formal logic, this number is called the *arity* of the predicate. The kinds of truth predicates may then be subdivided according to any number of more specific characters that various theorists recognize as important.

1. A *monadic* truth predicate is one that applies to its main subject — typically a concrete representation or its abstract content — independently of reference to anything else. In this case one can say that a truthbearer is true in and of itself.
2. A *dyadic* truth predicate is one that applies to its main subject only in reference to something else, a second subject. Most commonly, the auxiliary subject is either an *object*, an *interpreter*, or a *language* to which the representation bears some relation.
3. A *triadic* truth predicate is one that applies to its main subject only in reference to a second and a third subject. For example, in a pragmatic theory of truth, one has to specify both the object of the sign, and either its interpreter or another sign called the *interpretant* before one can say that the sign is true *of* its object *to* its interpreting agent or sign.

Several qualifications must be kept in mind with respect to any such radically simple scheme of classification, as real practice seldom presents any pure types, and there are settings in which it is useful to speak of a theory of truth that is "almost" *k*-adic, or that "would be" *k*-adic if certain details can be abstracted away and neglected in a particular context of discussion. That said, given the generic division of truth predicates according to their rarity, further species can be differentiated within each genus according to a number of more refined features.

The truth predicate of interest in a typical correspondence theory of truth tells of a relation between representations and objective states of affairs, and is therefore expressed, for the most part, by a dyadic predicate. In general terms, one says that a representation is *true of* an objective situation, more briefly, that a sign is true of an object. The nature of the correspondence may vary from theory to theory in this family. The correspondence can be fairly arbitrary or it can take on the character of an *analogy*, an *icon*, or a *morphism*, whereby a representation is rendered true of its object by the existence of corresponding elements and a similar structure.

PEIRCE

Very little in Peirce's thought can be understood in its proper light without understanding that he thinks all thoughts are signs, and thus, according to his theory of thought, no thought is understandable outside the context of a sign relation. Sign relations taken collectively are the subject matter of a theory of signs. So Peirce's *semiotic*, his theory of sign relations, is key to understanding his entire philosophy of pragmatic thinking and thought. In his contribution to the article "Truth and Falsity and Error" for Baldwin's *Dictionary of Philosophy and Psychology* (1901), Peirce defines truth in the following way: Truth is that concordance of an abstract statement with the ideal limit towards which endless investigation would tend to bring scientific belief, which concordance the abstract statement may possess by virtue of the confession of its inaccuracy and one-sidedness, and this confession is an essential ingredient of truth.

This statement emphasizes Peirce's view that ideas of approximation, incompleteness, and partiality, what he describes elsewhere as *fallibilism* and "reference to the future", are essential to a proper conception of truth. Although Peirce occasionally uses words like *concordance* and *correspondence* to describe one aspect of the pragmatic sign relation, he is also quite explicit in saying that definitions of truth based on mere correspondence are no more than *nominal* definitions, which he follows long tradition in relegating to a lower status than *real* definitions.

> That truth is the correspondence of a representation with its object is, as Kant says, merely the nominal definition of it. Truth belongs exclusively to propositions. A proposition has a subject (or set of subjects) and a predicate. The subject is a sign; the predicate is a sign; and the proposition is a sign that the predicate is a sign of that of which the subject is a sign. If it be so, it is true. But what does this correspondence or reference of the sign, to its object, consist in? (Peirce 1906, CP 5.553).

Here Peirce makes a statement that is decisive for understanding the relationship between his pragmatic definition of truth and any theory of truth that leaves it solely and simply a matter of representations corresponding with their objects. Peirce, like Kant before him, recognizes Aristotle's distinction between a *nominal definition*, a definition in name only, and a *real definition*, one that states the function of the concept, the reason for conceiving it, and so indicates the *essence*, the underlying *substance* of its object. This tells us the sense in which Peirce entertained a *correspondence theory of truth*, namely, a purely nominal sense. To get beneath the superficiality of the nominal definition it is necessary to analyze the notion of correspondence in greater depth.

In preparing for this task, Peirce makes use of an allegorical story, omitted here, the moral of which is that there is no use seeking a conception of truth that we cannot conceive ourselves being able to capture in a humanly conceivable concept. So we might as well proceed on the assumption that we have a real hope of comprehending the answer, of being able to "handle the truth" when the time comes. Bearing that in mind, the problem of defining truth reduces to the following form:

> Now thought is of the nature of a sign. In that case, then, if we can find out the right method of thinking and can follow it out — the right method of transforming signs — then truth can be nothing more nor less than the last result to which the following out of this method would ultimately carry us. In that

case, that to which the representation should conform, is itself something in the nature of a representation, or sign — something noumenal, intelligible, conceivable, and utterly unlike a thing-in-itself.

Peirce's theory of truth depends on two other, intimately related subject matters, his theory of *sign relations* and his theory of *inquiry*. Inquiry is a special case of *semiosis*, a process that transforms signs into signs while maintaining a specific relationship to an object, which object may be located outside the trajectory of signs or else be found at the end of it. Inquiry includes all forms of belief revision and logical inference, including *scientific method*, what Peirce here means by "the right method of transforming signs". A sign-to-sign transaction relating to an object is a transaction that involves three parties, or a relation that involves three roles. This is called a *ternary or triadic relation* in logic. Consequently, pragmatic theories of truth are largely expressed in terms of triadic truth predicates.

The statement above tells us one more thing: Peirce, having started out in accord with Kant, is here giving notice that he is parting ways with the Kantian idea that the ultimate object of a representation is an unknowable *thing-in-itself*. Peirce would say that the object is knowable, in fact, it is known in the form of its representation, however imperfectly or partially.

Reality and *truth* are coordinate concepts in pragmatic thinking, each being defined in relation to the other, and both together as they participate in the time evolution of inquiry. Inquiry is not a disembodied process, nor the occupation of a singular individual, but the common life of an unbounded community.

The real, then, is that which, sooner or later, information and reasoning would finally result in, and which is therefore independent of the vagaries of me and you. Thus, the very origin of the conception of reality shows that this conception essentially involves the notion of a COMMUNITY, without definite limits, and capable of an indefinite increase of knowledge.

Different minds may set out with the most antagonistic views, but the progress of investigation carries them by a force outside of themselves to one and the same conclusion. This activity of thought by which we are carried, not where we wish, but to a foreordained goal, is like the operation of destiny. No modification of the point of view taken, no selection of other facts for study, no natural bent of mind even, can enable a man to escape the predestinate opinion. This great law is embodied in the conception of truth and reality. The opinion which is fated to be ultimately agreed to by all who investigate, is what we mean by the truth, and the object represented in this opinion is the real.

JAMES

William James's version of the pragmatic theory is often summarized by his statement that "the 'true' is only the expedient in our way of thinking, just as the 'right' is only the expedient in our way of behaving." By this, James meant that truth is a quality the value of which is confirmed by its effectiveness when applying concepts to actual practice (thus, "pragmatic"). James's pragmatic theory is a synthesis of correspondence theory of truth and coherence theory of truth, with an added dimension. Truth is verifiable to the extent that thoughts and statements correspond with actual things, as well as "hangs together," or coheres, fits as pieces of a puzzle might fit together, and these are in turn verified by the observed results of the application of an idea to actual practice. James said that "all true processes must lead to the face of directly verifying sensible experiences somewhere." He also extended his pragmatic theory well beyond the scope of scientific verifiability, and even into the realm of the mystical: "On pragmatic principles, if the hypothesis of God works satisfactorily in the widest sense of the word, then it is 'true.'"

Truth, as any dictionary will tell you, is a property of certain of our ideas. It means their 'agreement', as falsity means their disagreement, with 'reality'. Pragmatists and intellectualists both accept this definition as a matter of course. They begin to quarrel only after the question is raised as to what may precisely be meant by the term 'agreement', and what by the term 'reality', when reality is taken as something for our ideas to agree with.

William James (1907) begins his chapter on "Pragmatism's Conception of Truth" in much the same letter and spirit as the above selection from Peirce (1906), noting the nominal definition of truth as a plausible point of departure, but immediately observing that the pragmatist's quest for the meaning of truth can only begin, not end there.

The popular notion is that a true idea must copy its reality. Like other popular views, this one follows the analogy of the most usual experience. Our true ideas of sensible things do indeed copy them. Shut your eyes and think of yonder clock on the wall, and you get just such a true picture or copy of its dial. But your idea of its 'works' (unless you are a clockmaker) is much less of a copy, yet it passes muster, for it in no way clashes with reality. Even though it should shrink to the mere word 'works', that word still serves you truly; and when you speak of the 'time-keeping function' of the clock, or of its spring's 'elasticity', it is hard to see exactly what your ideas can copy.

James exhibits a knack for popular expression that Peirce seldom sought, and here his analysis of correspondence by way of a simple thought experiment cuts right to the quick of the first major question to ask about it, namely: To what extent is the notion of correspondence involved in truth covered by the ideas of analogues, copies, or iconic images of the thing represented? The answer is that the iconic aspect of correspondence can be taken literally only in regard to sensory experiences of the more precisely eidetic sort. When it comes to the kind of correspondence that might be said to exist between a symbol, a word like "works", and its object, the springs and catches of the clock on the wall, then the pragmatist recognizes that a more than nominal account of the matter still has a lot more explaining to do.

MAKING TRUTH

Instead of truth being ready-made for us, James asserts we and reality jointly "make" truth. This idea has two senses: (1) truth is mutable, (often attributed to William James and F.C.S. Schiller); and (2) truth is relative to a conceptual scheme (more widely accepted in Pragmatism).

Mutability of Truth

"Truth" is not readily defined in Pragmatism. Can beliefs pass from being *true* to being *untrue* and back? For James, beliefs are not true until they have been made true by verification. James believed propositions become true over the long term through proving their utility in a person's specific situation. The opposite of this process is not falsification, but rather the belief ceases to be a "live option." F.C.S. Schiller, on the other hand, clearly asserted beliefs could pass into and out of truth on a situational basis. Schiller held that truth was relative to specific problems. If I want to know how to return home safely, the true answer will be whatever is useful to solving that problem. Later on, when faced with a different problem, what I came to believe with the earlier problem may now be false. As my problems change, and as the most useful way to solve a problem shifts, so does the property of truth.

C.S. Peirce considered the idea that beliefs are true at one time but false at another (or true for one person but false for another) to be one of the "seeds of death" by which James allowed his pragmatism to become "infected." For Peirce the pragmatic view implies theoretical claims should be tied to verification processes (i.e. they should be subject to test). They shouldn't be tied to our specific problems or life needs. Truth is defined, for Peirce, as what *would* be the ultimate outcome (not any outcome in real time) of inquiry by a (usually scientific) community of investigators. John Dewey, while agreeing with this definition, also characterized truthfulness as a species of the good: if something is true it is trustworthy and reliable and will remain so in every conceivable situation. Both Peirce and Dewey connect the definitions of truth and warranted assertability. Hilary Putnam also developed his internal realism around the idea a belief is true if it is ideally justified in epistemic terms. About James' and Schiller's view, Putnam says: Truth cannot simply *be* rational acceptability for one fundamental reason; truth is supposed to be a property of a statement that cannot be lost, whereas justification can be lost. The statement 'The earth is flat' was, very likely, rationally acceptable 3000 years ago; but it is not rationally acceptable today. Yet it would be wrong to say that 'the earth is flat' was true 3,000 years ago; for that would mean that the earth has changed its shape.

Rorty has also weighed in against James and Schiller: Truth is, to be sure, an absolute notion, in the following sense:

"true for me but not for you" and "true in my culture but not in yours" are weird, pointless locutions. So is "true then, but not now." [...] James would, indeed, have done better to say that phrases like "the good in the way of belief" and "what it is better for us to believe" are interchangeable with "justified" rather than with "true."

Conceptual Relativity

With James and Schiller we make things true by verifying them—a view rejected by most pragmatists. However, nearly all pragmatists do accept the idea there can be no truths without a conceptual scheme to express those truths. That is, Unless we decide upon how we are going to use concepts like 'object', 'existence' etc., the question 'how many objects exist' does not really make any sense. But once we decide the use of these concepts, the answer to the above-mentioned question within that use or 'version', to put in Nelson Goodman's phrase, is no more a matter of 'convention'. F.C.S. Schiller used the analogy of a chair to make clear what he meant by the phrase that truth is made: just as a carpenter *makes* a chair out of existing materials and doesn't *create* it out of nothing, truth is a transformation of our experience—but this doesn't imply reality is something we're free to construct or imagine as we please.

Dewey

John Dewey, less broadly than William James but much more broadly than Charles Peirce, held that inquiry, whether scientific, technical, sociological, philosophical or cultural, is self-corrective over time *if* openly submitted for testing by a community of inquirers in order to clarify, justify, refine and/ or refute proposed truths. In his *Logic: The Theory of Inquiry* (1938), Dewey gave the following definition of inquiry:

Inquiry is the controlled or directed transformation of an indeterminate situation into one that is so determinate in its constituent distinctions and relations as to convert the elements of the original situation into a unified whole. The index of the same book has exactly one entry under the heading *truth*, and it refers to the following footnote: The best definition of *truth* from the logical standpoint which is known to me is that by

Peirce: "The opinion which is fated to be ultimately agreed to by all who investigate is what we mean by the truth, and the object represented in this opinion is the real. Dewey says more of what he understands by *truth* in terms of his preferred concept of *warranted assertibility* as the end-in-view and conclusion of inquiry.

Mead

Criticism

Several objections are commonly made to pragmatist account of truth, of either sort. First, due originally to Bertrand Russell (1907) in a discussion of James's theory, is that pragmatism mixes up the notion of truth with *epistemology*. Pragmatism describes an *indicator* or a *sign* of truth. It really cannot be regarded as a theory of the *meaning* of the word "true". There's a difference between *stating an indicator* and *giving the meaning*. For example, when the streetlights turn at the end of a day, that's an indicator, a sign, that evening is coming on. It would be an obvious mistake to say that the word "evening" just means "the time that the streetlights turn on". In the same way, while it might be an *indicator* of truth, that a proposition is part of that perfect science at the ideal limit of inquiry, that just isn't what "truth" *means*.

Russell's objection isn't so much an argument against pragmatism, so much as it is a request — that we make sure that we aren't confusing an *indicator* of truth with the *meaning* of the concept truth. There is a difference between the two and pragmatism confuses them.

Other objections to pragmatism include how we define what it means to say a belief "works", or that it is "useful to believe". The vague usage of these terms, first popularized by James, has led to much debate.

A final objection is that pragmatism of James's variety entails relativism. What is useful for *you* to believe might not be useful for *me* to believe. It follows that "truth" for you is different from "truth" for me (and that the relevant facts don't matter). This is relativism. A viable, more sophisticated consensus theory of truth, a mixture of Peircean theory with speech-act theory and social theory, is that presented and defended by Jürgen Habermas, which sets out the universal pragmatic conditions of ideal consensus and responds to many objections to earlier versions of a pragmatic, consensus theory of truth. Habermas distinguishes explicitly between factual consensus, i.e. the beliefs that happen to hold in a particular community, and rational consensus, i.e. consensus attained in conditions approximating an "ideal speech situation", in which inquirers or members of a community suspend or bracket prevailing beliefs and engage in rational discourse aimed at truth and governed by the force of the better argument, under conditions in which all participants in discourse have equal opportunities to engage in constative (assertions of fact), normative, and expressive speech acts, and in which discourse is not distorted by the intervention of power or the internalization of systematic blocks to communication.

Functionalism : Philosophy of Mind

Functionalism is a theory of the mind in contemporary philosophy, developed largely as an alternative to both the identity theory of mind and behaviourism. Its core idea is that mental states (beliefs, desires, being in pain, etc.) are constituted solely by their functional role — that is, they are causal relations to other mental states, sensory inputs, and behavioural outputs. Functionalism is a theoretical level between the physical implementation and behavioural output.

Therefore, it is different from its predecessors of Cartesian dualism (advocating discrete mental and physical substances) and Skinnerian behaviourism and physicalism (declaring only physical substances) because it is only concerned with the effective functions of the brain, through its organization or its 'software programs'.

Since mental states are identified by a functional role, they are said to be realized on multiple levels; in other words, they are able to be manifested in various systems, even perhaps computers, so long as the system performs the appropriate functions. While computers are physical devices with electronic substrate that perform computations on inputs to give outputs, so brains are physical devices with neural substrate that perform computations on inputs which produce behaviours. While functionalism has its advantages, there have been several arguments against it, claiming that it is an insufficient account of the mind.

MULTIPLE REALIZABILITY

An important part of some accounts of functionalism is the idea of multiple realizability. Since, according to standard functionalist theories, mental states are the corresponding functional role, mental states can be sufficiently explained without taking into account the underlying physical medium (e.g. the brain, neurons, etc.) that realizes such states; one need only take into account the higher-level functions in the cognitive system. Since mental states are not limited to a particular medium, they can be realized in multiple ways, including, theoretically, within non-biological systems, such as computers. In other words, a silicon-based machine could, in principle, have the same sort of mental life that a human being has, provided that its cognitive system realized the proper functional roles. Thus, mental states are individuated much like a valve; a valve can be made of plastic or metal or whatever material, as long as it performs the proper function (say, controlling the flow of liquid through a tube by blocking and unblocking its pathway).

However, there have been some functionalist theories that combine with the identity theory of mind, which deny multiple realizability. Such *Functional Specification Theories* (FSTs), as they are called, were most notably developed by David Lewis (1980) and David Malet Armstrong (1968). According to FSTs, mental states are the particular "realizers" of the functional role, not the functional role itself. The mental state of belief, for example, just is whatever brain or neurological process that realizes the appropriate belief function. Thus, unlike standard versions of functionalism (often called *Functional State Identity Theories*), FSTs do not allow for the multiple realizability of mental states, because the fact that mental states are realized by brain states is essential. What often drives this view is the belief that if we were to encounter an alien race with a cognitive system composed of significantly different material from humans' (e.g., silicon-based) but performed the same functions as human mental states (e.g., they tend to yell "Yowzas!" when poked with sharp objects, etc.) then we would say that their type of mental state is perhaps similar to ours, but too different to say it's the same. For some, this may be a disadvantage to FSTs. Indeed, one of Hilary Putnam's (1960, 1967) arguments for his version of functionalism relied on the intuition that such alien creatures would have the same mental states as humans do, and that the multiple realizability of standard functionalism makes it a better theory of mind.

TYPES OF FUNCTIONALISM

Machine-state functionalism

The broad position of "functionalism" can be articulated in many different varieties. The first formulation of a functionalist theory of mind was put forth by Hilary Putnam (1960, 1967). This formulation, which is now called machine-state functionalism, or just machine functionalism, was inspired by the analogies which Putnam and others noted between the mind and the theoretical "machines" or computers capable of computing any given algorithm which were developed by Alan Turing (called universal Turing machines).

In non-technical terms, a Turing machine can be visualized as an indefinitely and infinitely long tape divided into rectangles (the memory) with a box-shaped scanning device that sits over and scans one component of the memory at a time. Each unit is either blank (*B*) or has a *1* written on it. These are the inputs to the machine. The possible outputs are:

- Halt: Do nothing.
- *R*: move one square to the right.
- *L*: move one square to the left.
- *B*: erase whatever is on the square.
- *1*: erase whatever is on the square and print a '1.

The essential point to consider here is the *nature of the states* of the Turing machine. Each state can be defined exclusively in terms of its relations to the other states as well as inputs and outputs. State one, for example, is simply the state in which the machine, if it reads a *B*, writes a *1* and stays in that state, and in which, if it reads a *1*, it moves one square to the right and goes into a different state. This is the functional definition of state one; it is its causal role in the overall system. The details of how it accomplishes what it accomplishes and of its material constitution are completely irrelevant. According to machine-state functionalism, the nature of a mental state is just like the nature of the automaton states described above.

Just as *state one* simply is the state in which, given an input *B*, such and such happens, so being in pain is the state which disposes one to cry "ouch", become distracted, wonder what the cause is, and so forth.

Psychofunctionalism

A second form of functionalism is based on the rejection of behaviourist theories in psychology and their replacement with empirical cognitive models of the mind. This view is most closely associated with Jerry Fodor and Zenon Pylyshyn and has been labelled psychofunctionalism.

The fundamental idea of psychofunctionalism is that psychology is an irreducibly complex science and that the terms that we use to describe the entities and properties of the mind in our best psychological theories cannot be redefined in terms of simple behavioural dispositions, and further, that such a redefinition would not be desirable or salient were it achievable. Psychofunctionalists view psychology as employing the same sorts of irreducibly teleological or purposive explanations as the biological sciences. Thus, for example, the function or role of the heart is to pump blood, that of the kidney is to filter it and to maintain certain chemical balances and so on—this is what accounts for the purposes of scientific explanation and taxonomy. There may be an infinite variety of physical realizations for all of the mechanisms, but what is important is only their role in the overall biological theory. In an analogous manner, the role of mental states, such as belief and desire, is determined by the functional or causal role that is designated for them within our best *scientific* psychological theory. If some mental state which is postulated by folk psychology (e.g. hysteria) is determined not to have any fundamental role in cognitive psychological explanation, then that particular state may be considered not to exist. On the other hand, if it turns out that there are states which theoretical cognitive psychology posits as necessary for explanation of human behaviour but which are not foreseen by ordinary folk psychological language, then these entities or states exist.

Analytic Functionalism

A third form of functionalism is concerned with the meanings of theoretical terms in general. This view is most closely associated with David Lewis and is often referred to as analytic functionalism. The basic idea of analytic functionalism is that theoretical terms are implicitly defined by the theories in whose formulation they occur and not by intrinsic properties of the phonemes they comprise. In the case of ordinary language terms, such as "belief", "desire", or "hunger", the idea is that such terms get their meanings from our common-sense "folk psychological" theories about them, but that such conceptualizations are not sufficient to withstand the rigor imposed by materialistic theories of reality and causality. Such terms are subject to conceptual analyses which take something like the following form:

Mental state M is the state that is preconceived by P and causes Q. For example, the state of pain is *caused* by sitting on a tack and *causes* loud cries, and higher order mental states of anger and resentment directed at the careless person who left a tack lying around. These sorts of functional definitions in terms of causal roles are claimed to be *analytic* and *a priori* truths about the submental states and the (largely fictitious) propositional attitudes they describe. Hence, its proponents are known as *analytic* or *conceptual* functionalists. The essential difference between analytic and psychofunctionalism is that the latter emphasizes the importance of laboratory observation and experimentation in the determination of which mental state terms and concepts are genuine and which functional identifications may be considered to be genuinely contingent and *a posteriori* identities. The former, on the other hand, claims that such identities are necessary and not subject to empirical scientific investigation.

Homuncular Functionalism

Homuncular functionalism was developed largely by Daniel Dennett and has been advocated by William Lycan. It arose in response to the challenges that Ned Block's China Brain (a.k.a. Chinese nation) and John Searle's Chinese Room thought experiments presented for the more traditional forms of functionalism. In attempting to overcome the conceptual difficulties that arose from the idea of a nation full of Chinese people wired together with each one carrying out the functional or causal role that would normally be ascribed to the mental states of an individual mind, for example, many functionalists simply bit the bullet, so to speak, and argued that such a Chinese nation would indeed possess all of the qualitative and intentional properties of a mind; i.e. it would become a sort of systemic or collective mind with propositional attitudes and other mental characteristics. Whatever the worth of this latter hypothesis, it was immediately objected that it entailed an unacceptable sort of mind-mind supervenience: the *systemic* mind which somehow emerged at the higher-level must necessarily supervene on the individual minds of each individual member of the Chinese nation, to stick to Block's formulation. But this would seem to put into serious doubt, if not directly contradict, the fundamental idea of the supervenience thesis: there can be no change in the mental realm without some change in the underlying physical substratum. This can be easily seen if we label the set of mental facts that occur at the higher-level *M* and the set of mental facts that occur at the lower-level *M1*. Given the transitivity of supervenience, if *M* supervenes on *M1* and *M1* supervenes on *P* (physical base), then *M* and *M1* both supervene on *P*, even though they are (allegedly) totally different sets of mental facts.

Since mind-mind supervenience seemed to have become acceptable in functionalist circles, it seemed to some that the only way to resolve the puzzle was to postulate the existence of an entire hierarchical series of mind levels (analogous to homunculi) which became less and less sophisticated in terms of functional organization and physical composition all the way down to the level of the physico-mechanical neuron or group of neurons. The homunculi at each level, on this view, have authentic mental properties but become simpler and less intelligent as one works one's way down the hierarchy.

FUNCTIONALISM AND PHYSICALISM

There is much confusion about the sort of relationship that is claimed to exist (or not exist) between the general thesis of functionalism and physicalism. It has often been claimed that functionalism somehow "disproves" or falsifies physicalism *tout court* (i.e. without further explanation or description). On the other hand, most philosophers of mind who are functionalists claim to be physicalists—indeed, some of them, such as David

Lewis, have claimed to be strict reductionist-type physicalists. Functionalism is fundamentally what Ned Block has called a broadly metaphysical thesis as opposed to a narrowly ontological one. That is, functionalism is not so much concerned with *what there is* as with what it is that characterizes a certain type of mental state, e.g. pain, as the type of state that it is. Previous attempts to answer the mind-body problem have all tried to resolve it by answering *both* questions: dualism says there are two substances and that mental states are characterized by their immateriality; behaviorism claimed that there was one substance and that mental states were behavioural disposition; physicalism asserted the existence of just one substance and characterized the mental states as physical states (as in "pain = C-fiber firings").

On this understanding, type physicalism can be seen as incompatible with functionalism, since it claims that what characterizes mental states (e.g. pain) is that they are physical in nature, while functionalism says that what characterizes pain is its functional/causal role and its relationship with yelling "ouch", etc. However, any weaker sort of physicalism which makes the simple ontological claim that everything that exists is made up of inorganic matter is perfectly compatible with functionalism. Moreover, most functionalists who are physicalists require that the properties that are quantified over in functional definitions be physical properties. Hence, they *are* physicalists, even though the general thesis of functionalism itself does not commit them to being so.

In the case of David Lewis, there is a distinction in the concepts of "having pain" (a rigid designator true in all possible worlds) and just "pain" (a non-rigid designator). Pain, for Lewis, stands for something like the definite description "the state with the causal role x". The referent of the description in humans is a type of brain state to be determined by science. The referent among silicon-based life forms is something else. The referent of the description among angels is some immaterial, non-physical state. For Lewis, therefore, *local* type-physical reductions are possible and compatible with conceptual functionalism. There seems to be some confusion between types and tokens that needs to be cleared up in the functionalist analysis.

CRITICISM

China Brain

Ned Block (1980b) argues against the functionalist proposal of multiple realizability, where hardware implementation is irrelevant because only the functional level is important. The "China brain" or "Chinese nation" thought experiment involves supposing that the entire nation of China systematically organizes itself to operate just like a brain, with each individual acting as a neuron (forming what has come to be called a "Blockhead"). According to functionalism, so long as the people are performing the proper functional roles, with the proper causal relations between inputs and outputs, the system will be a real mind, with mental states, consciousness, and so on. However, Block argues, this is patently absurd, so there must be something wrong with the thesis of functionalism since it would allow this to be a legitimate description of a mind.

Some functionalists believe China would have qualia but that due to the size it is impossible to imagine China being conscious (Lycan, 1987). Indeed, it may be the case that we are constrained by our theory of mind and will never be able to understand what Chinese consciousness is like. Therefore, if functionalism is true either qualia will exist across all hardware or will not exist at all but are illusory (Dennett, 1990).

The Chinese Room

The Chinese room argument by John Searle (1980) is a direct attack on the claim that thought can be represented as a set of functions. The thought experiment asserts that it is possible to mimic intelligent action without any interpretation or understanding through the use of a purely functional system. In short, Searle describes a person who only speaks English who is in a room with only Chinese symbols in baskets and a rule book in English for moving the symbols around. The person is then ordered by people outside of the room to follow the rule book for sending certain symbols out of the room when given certain symbols. Further suppose that the people outside of the room are Chinese speakers and are communicating with the person inside via the Chinese symbols. According to Searle, it would be absurd to claim that the English speaker inside knows Chinese simply based on these syntactic processes. This thought experiment attempts to show that systems which operate merely on syntactic processes (inputs and outputs, based on algorithms) cannot realize any semantics (meaning) or intentionality (aboutness). Thus, Searle attacks the idea that thought can be equated with following a set of syntactic rules; that is, functionalism is an insufficient theory of the mind.

As noted above, in connection with Block's Chinese nation, many functionalists responded to Searle's thought experiment by suggesting that there was a form of mental activity going on at a higher level than the man in the Chinese room could comprehend (the so-called "system reply"); that is, the system does know Chinese. Of course, Searle responds that there is nothing more than syntax going on at the higher-level as well, so this reply is subject to the same initial problems. Furthermore, Searle suggests the man in the room could simply memorize the rules and symbol relations. Again, though he would convincingly mimic communication, he would be aware only of the symbols and rules, not of the meaning behind them.

Inverted Spectrum

Another main criticism of functionalism is the inverted spectrum or inverted qualia scenario, most specifically proposed as an objection to functionalism by Ned Block. This thought experiment involves supposing that there is a person, call her Jane, that is born with a condition which makes her see the opposite spectrum of light that is normally perceived. Unlike "normal" people, Jane sees the colour violet as yellow, orange as blue, and so forth.

So, suppose, for example, that you and Jane are looking at the same orange. While you perceive the fruit as colored orange, Jane sees it as colored blue. However, when asked what colour the piece of fruit is, both you and Jane will report "orange". In fact, one can see that all of your behavioural as well as functional relations to colors will be the same. Jane will, for example, properly obey traffic signs just as any other person would, even though this involves the colour perception. Therefore, the argument goes, since there can be two people who are functionally identical, yet have different mental states (differing in their qualitative or phenomenological aspects), functionalism is not robust enough to explain individual differences in qualia.

Chalmers (1996) tries to show that even though mental content cannot be fully accounted for in functional terms, there is nevertheless a *nomological correlation* between mental states and functional states in this world. A silicon-based robot, for example, whose functional profile matched our own, would *have* to be fully conscious.

His argument for this claim takes the form of a *reductio ad absurdum*. The general idea is that since it would be very unlikely for a conscious human being to experience a change in its qualia which it utterly fails to notice, mental content and functional profile appear to be inextricably bound together, at least in the human case.

If the subject's qualia were to change, we would expect the subject to notice, and therefore his functional profile to follow suit. A similar argument is applied to the notion of *absent* qualia. In this case, Chalmers argues that it would be very unlikely for a subject to experience a fading of his qualia which he fails to notice and respond to. This, coupled with the independent assertion that a conscious being's functional profile just could be maintained, irrespective of its experiential state, leads to the conclusion that the subject of these experiments would remain fully conscious.

The problem with this argument, however, as Brian G. Crabb (2005) has observed, is that it begs the central question: How could Chalmers *know* that functional profile can be preserved, for example while the conscious subject's brain is being supplanted with a silicon substitute, unless he already assumes that the subject's possibly changing qualia would not be a determining factor? And while changing or fading qualia in a conscious subject might force changes in its functional profile, this tells us nothing about the case of a permanently inverted or unconscious robot.

A subject with inverted qualia from birth would have nothing to notice or adjust to. Similarly, an unconscious functional simulacrum of ourselves (a zombie) would have no experiential changes to notice or adjust to. Consequently, Crabb argues, Chalmers' 'fading qualia' and 'dancing qualia' arguments fail to establish that cases of permanently inverted or absent qualia are nomologically impossible.

A related critique of the inverted spectrum argument is that it assumes that mental states (differing in their qualitative or phenomenological aspects) can be independent of the functional relations in the brain. Thus, it begs the question of functional mental states: its assumption denies the possibility of functionalism itself, without offering any independent justification for doing so. (Functionalism says that mental states are produced by the functional relations in the brain.) This same type of problem—that there is no argument, just an antithetical assumption at their base—can also be said of both the Chinese room and the Chinese nation arguments. Notice, however, that Crabb's response to Chalmers does not commit this fallacy: His point is the more restricted observation that *even if* inverted or absent qualia turn out to be nomologically impossible, and it is perfectly possible that we might subsequently discover this fact by other means, Chalmers' argument fails to demonstrate that they are impossible.

Twin Earth

The Twin Earth thought experiment, introduced by Hilary Putnam (1975b), is responsible for one of the main arguments used against functionalism, although it was originally intended as an argument against semantic internalism.

The thought experiment is simple and runs as follows. Imagine a Twin Earth which is identical to Earth in every way but one: water does not have the chemical structure H, O, but rather some other structure, say XYZ. It is critical, however, to note that XYZ on Twin Earth is still called 'water' and exhibits all the same macro-level properties that H, O exhibits on Earth (i.e., XYZ is also a clear drinkable liquid that is in lakes, rivers, and so on).

Since these worlds are identical in every way except in the underlying chemical structure of water, you and your Twin Earth doppelgänger see exactly the same things, meet exactly the same people, have exactly the same jobs, behave exactly the same way, and so on. In other words, since you share the same inputs, outputs, and relations between other mental states, you are functional duplicates. So, for example, you both believe that water is wet. However, the content of your mental state of believing that water is wet differs from your duplicate's because your belief is of H, O, while your duplicate's is of XYZ. Therefore, so the argument goes, since two people can be functionally identical, yet have different mental states, functionalism cannot sufficiently account for all mental states.

Most defenders of functionalism initially responded to this argument by attempting to maintain a sharp distinction between internal and external content. The internal contents of propositional attitudes, for example, would consist exclusively in those aspects of them which have no relation with the external world *and* which bear the necessary functional/causal properties that allow for relations with other internal mental states. Since no one has yet been able to formulate a clear basis or justification for the existence of such a distinction in mental contents, however, this idea has generally been abandoned in favour of externalist *causal theories of mental contents* (also known as informational semantics). Such a position is represented, for example, by Jerry Fodor's account of an "asymmetric causal theory" of mental content. This view simply entails the modification of functionalism to include within its scope a very broad interpretation of input and outputs to include the objects that are the causes of mental representations in the external world.

The twin earth argument hinges on the assumption that experience with an imitation water would cause a different mental state than experience with natural water. However, since no one would notice the difference between the two waters, this assumption seems hard to swallow. Further, this basic assumption is directly antithetical to functionalism; and, thereby, the twin earth argument does not constitute a genuine argument: as this assumption entails a flat denial of functionalism itself (which would say that the two waters would not produce different mental states, because the functional relationships would remain unchanged).

Meaning Holism

Another common criticism of functionalism is that it implies a radical form of semantic holism. Block and Fodor (1972) referred to this as the *damn/darn problem*. The difference between saying "damn" or "darn" when one smashes one's finger with a hammer can be mentally significant. But since these outputs are, according to functionalism, related to many (if not all) internal mental states, two people who experience the same pain and react with different outputs must share little (perhaps nothing) in common in any of their mental states. But this is counter-intuitive; it seems clear that two people share something significant in their mental states of being in pain if they both smash their finger with a hammer, whether or not they utter the same word when they cry out in pain.

Another possible solution to this problem is to adopt a moderate (or molecularist) form of holism. But even if this succeeds in the case of pain, in the case of beliefs and meaning, it faces the difficulty of formulating a distinction between relevant and non-relevant contents (which can be difficult to do without invoking an analytic-synthetic distinction, as many seek to avoid).

STRUCTURALISM AND FUNCTIONALISM

Early Schools of Thought

When psychology was first established as a science separate from biology and philosophy, the debate over how to describe and explain the human mind and behaviour began. Structuralism emerged as the first school of thought and some of the ideas associated with the structuralist school were advocated by the founder of the first psychology lab, Wilhelm Wundt.

One of Wundt's students, an man named Edward B. Tichener, would later go on to formally establish and name structuralism, although he broke away from many of Wundt's ideas. Almost immediately other theories surfaced to vie for dominance in psychology. In response to structuralism, an American perspective emerged under the influence of thinkers such as Charles Darwin and William James.

In 1906, Mary Whiton Calkins published an article in *Psychological Review* asking for a reconciliation between these two schools of thought. Structuralism and functionalism were not so different, she argued, since both are principally concerned with the conscious self. Despite this, aspersions continued to be cast by both sides. William James wrote that structuralism had "plenty of school, but no thought" (James, 1904), while Wilhelm Wundt dismissed functionalism as "literature." Eventually both of these schools of thought lost dominance in psychology, replaced by the rise of behaviorism, psychoanalysis, and humanism.

Structuralism

Structuralism was the first school of psychology and focused on breaking down mental processes into the most basic components. Researchers tried to understand the basic elements of consciousness using a method known as introspection. Wilhelm Wundt, founder of the first psychology lab, was an advocate of this position and is often considered the founder of structuralism, despite the fact that it was his student, Edward B. Titchener who first coined the term to describe this school of thought.

While Wundt's work helped to establish psychology as a separate science and contributed methods to experimental psychology and Titchener development of structuralism helped establish the very first "school" of psychology, the structuralism did not last long beyond Titchener's death.

Major Structuralist Thinkers:

- Wilhelm Wundt
- Edward B. Titchner.

Criticisms of Structuralism:

- By today's scientific standards, the experimental methods used to study the structures of the mind were too subjective—the use of introspection led to a lack of reliability in results.
- Other critics argue that structuralism was too concerned with internal behaviour, which is not directly observable and cannot be accurately measured.

Strengths of Structuralism:

- Structuralism is important because it is the first major school of thought in psychology.
- Structuralism also influenced experimental psychology.

Functionalism

Functionalism formed as a reaction to the structuralism and was heavily influenced by the work of William James and the evolutionary theory of Charles Darwin. Functionalists sought to explain the mental processes in a more systematic and accurate manner. Rather than focusing on the elements of consciousness, functionalists focused on the *purpose* of consciousness and behaviour. Functionalism also emphasized individual differences, which had a profound impact on education.

5

A Phenomenology of Lifeworld and Place

A key to a phenomenology of community and locality is, the lifeworld–the taken-for-granted pattern and context of everyday living through which the person conducts his or her day-to-day life without having to make it an object of conscious attention. Immersed in their daily world of cares and concerns, people normally do not consider the lifeworld; it is concealed as a phenomenon. A phenomenological approach works to unmask the lifeworld's concealment, bringing its aspects and qualities to explicit scholarly attention.

The geographer and architect, working phenomenologically, are concerned with the geographical, environmental, and architectural dimensions of the lifeworld and focus on such themes as sense of place, at-homeness, and environmental experience and behaviour. Two key phenomenological notions important here are outsideness and insideness, which are especially significant because they set up an immediate relationship of fusion between person and world.

Buttimer (1977) emphasizes that much conventional work on locality and place emphasizes the perspective of outsider–i.e., the researcher assumes "the role of detached observer encouraged by conventional definitions of scientific method to take a so-called 'objective' stance on the data which he perceives". In this perspective, the researcher views region and place largely in terms of tangible artifacts and flows: for example, land use, housing types, activity patterns, political linkages, or number of services. For planning and policy, the assumption is that manipulation of the material environment will lead to a more livable place or region. This point of view dominates much of the so-called "applied" environmental architectural and planning research today. The weakness of the outsider's view is that the researcher interprets region in his or her own presupposed terms and "is therefore inevitably drawn toward finding in places what he or she intends to find in them ".

Buttimer argues that the need is to understand locality and region in terms of the insider, the person who normally lives in and uses the place or region. The insider's world is grounded in the everyday experience of living in a particular environment; it involves processes and events normally unnoticed and unquestioned. The insider generally takes his or her place and region for granted, rarely conceiving of them as explicit entities that might be made objects of directed attention. In relation to planning and policy, says Buttimer, the trap for the insider is that "one lives in places and may be so immersed in the particulars of everyday life and action that he or she may see no point in questioning the taken-for-granted or in seeing home in its wider spatial or social context".

Buttimer concludes that a major need in terms of community and locality is to promote a reflexive understanding for both insider and outsider. This self-conscious awareness would serve two functions: first, help the insider to see his place as an explicit entity with links to a larger socio-economic milieu; second, help the outsider to supplement his language of material patterns and processes with the experiential dynamics of place. The main task, in other words, is pedagogical and involves "a calling to conscious awareness those taken-for-granted ideas and practices within one's own personal world and then to reach beyond them toward a more reasonable and mutually respectful dialogue between those who wish to live in places and those who wish to plan for them".

The difficult question is how such sensitization and dialogue can proceed practically. The idea of congruence between insider and outsider is attractive theoretically, but practically it often seems impossible. The first need is a framework of understanding that portrays outsideness and insideness, especially the latter, in terms that individuals, both experts and laypersons, can readily grasp. Work in conventional environmental psychology and behavioural geography has, of course, attempted to clarify the nature of the insider's world. The phenomenological criticism of this work is its grounding in a conventional positivist approach. The result has often been concepts and theories–for example, cognitive mapping, territoriality, environmental preferences–which more often appear to be contrived intellectual constructs than genuine behavioural and experimental structures residing in the lifeworld. In contrast, a phenomenological approach to insideness and outsideness attempts to illuminate these worlds as they are in their own fashion in a way that will help insiders and outsiders to understand patterns and dynamics which otherwise might go unnoticed.

One important author in this regard is Relph (1976), who explores the nature of space and place phenomenologically and extends Buttimer's presentation of outsideness and insideness by viewing them as ends of a continuum along which can be identified various modes of place experience. Relph's key argument is that places have meaning in direct proportion to the degree that one feels inside that place–i.e., "here" rather than "there," enclosed rather than exposed, secure rather than threatened. Next, one can speak of varying degrees of insideness: for example, existential insideness, the deepest experience of place and involving an unself-conscious immersion in place; or empathetic insideness, a situation where a person who is an outsider in terms of place works through concern, interest, and empathy to understand that place and comes to know its essential meaning and structure. On the other hand, one can feel outside place: for example, existential outsideness, a sense of alienation and homelessness; or objective outsideness, the intentional separating of person from place in order to study it selectively in terms of one particular attribute or activity.

Though clearly incipient and not inclusive, Relph's inside-outsideness continuum is an important beginning for providing a self-consciousness presentation of place experience which applies to particular places yet extends beyond them to help people understand their environmental dealings in more general, reflexive terms. Relph's continuum sensitizes researchers to different modes of place experience, helping them to realize that the same place may foster considerably different modes of insideness and outsideness for different individuals and groups. Consider, for example, the use of this continuum in the classroom. Students are asked to select a mode of insideness and outsideness with which they feel familiar and to describe it in writing. A Nigerian student depicts the strong existential outsideness he felt when first arriving in America, while a woman who grew up in a small Kansas town pictures the intense sense of existential insideness she knew there. Yet another student, formerly a travelling salesman, speaks about the incidental outsideness he felt passing through places that were little more than backgrounds for his primary aim of selling. Next, students are asked to assemble in small groups and describe to each other their various accounts. The result is a self-conscious awareness of experiences and places which before were unreflected upon and therefore unnoticed.

Buttimer suggests that ultimately it is the empathetic insider who is best able to mediate between people who live in places and people who wish to plan for those places. The empathetic insider attempts to understand place and region as they are in their own fashion and therefore takes the time and effort to grasp the insider's life and to render an accurate account. An important contribution that the phenomenological perspective can offer the student wishing to become an empathetic insider is a set of concepts authentically portraying essential structures of place and lifeworld. Relph's inside-outside continuum is successful in this regard, and other reflexive research offers valuable additional themes. For example, my research, drawing in part from Merleau-Ponty, has explored the role of body as subject in place experience and details such extended bodily behaviors as "body ballets" and "time-space routines." Further, I have argued that individual bodily behaviors can interact in a supportive physical environment to create "place ballets"–a regularity of individual habits and routines in terms of space, as in an outdoor marketplace, local diner, or street neighborhood. Crucial real-world studies here include Jacobs' (1961) examination of urban street life and diversity, Whyte's (1980) analysis of successful city parks and plazas, Newman's (1980) architectural efforts to create urban residential designs that promote a sense of community consciousness and responsibility, and Fathy's (1973) attempt to construct housing and villages for displaced Egyptian peasants. Though not directly phenomenological, these works show an insightful ability to see and understand environment and community experientially. They give clues as to what, in practical, day-to-day terms, an authentic phenomenology of the person-world relationship must be.

A PHENOMENOLOGY OF PHYSICAL ENVIRONMENT AND LANDSCAPE

Phenomenology also offers valuable insight into the physical, ecological, and energy dimensions of locality, community, and place. An ecological phenomenology of physical environment and landscape asks how people-in-places work experientially and behaviorally as ecological units. A major concern is whether stability and rootedness in place promote a more efficient use of energy, space, and environment than today's predominant-place relationship emphasizing spatial mobility and the frequent disruption and destruction of unique places. An existential phenomenology of physical environment and landscape asks a complementary question: what are the existential advantages of place-bound lifeworlds? Do they, for example, facilitate in better measure than a physically dispersed lifeworld such qualities as at-homeness, community participation, or care and concern for the environment?

The overriding questions for both the ecological and existential dimensions of a phenomenological focus are what, ecologically and existentially, is a suitable balance between home and surrounding places, between one's own region and the larger world? Has Western society presently extended itself too far at the expense of home? Are Western people presently too mobile at the expense of community stability and continuity? How can technological devices such as transportation, cybernetics, and mass communication be used to serve home and local region as well as places beyond them? What technologies promote dwelling and a sense of region rather than placelessness, homelessness, and the destruction of regional identity?

It is in relation to questions like these that a phenomenology of landscape becomes significant, for a major question is how the physical environment contributes to a sense of region and place. The ancient Romans held that all natural places possessed a genius loci, a spirit of place. This spirit, it was believed, gave life to people and places and determined their character or essence. A phenomenology of landscape gives the notion of genius loci renewed academic attention. It asks how the qualities of the natural environment meet together in place to create the place's special character and style. One important first attempt here is Norberg-Schulz's (1980), which establishes phenomenologically a four-fold typology of natural places grounded in such qualities as spatial character, light, and daily and seasonal rhythms.

First, Norberg-Schulz describes the romantic landscape, an environment of change, variety, and detail best illustrated by the forests of Scandinavia; second, the cosmic landscape, an environment of monotony and massive expanse, best exemplified by the desert; third, the classical landscape, an environment balancing variety and continuity, best illustrated by the Greek landscape; and, fourth, the complex landscape, a blend of the first three and ultimately best representing most actual places, which generally are never pure but mixed in their natural expression. In short, Norberg-Schulz's aim is to identify how atmosphere, water, land, and life meet in location to generate a particular style of physical environment, natural place, and region. If asked to summarize the underlying thrust in the work just described, one might respond that it is the creative effort to reunite person and world through the existential structure of place grounded spatially and environmentally. People are not separate from their worlds; rather, they are immersed through an invisible net of bodily, emotional, and environmental ties. Place, of course, is only one phenomenological vantage point from which to clarify the person-world relationship, but it is a crucial starting point for the human sciences, since people are physical, bodily beings who must establish and identify themselves spatially and environmentally. At the same time, this physical grounding probably has links with other dimensions of human existence–take, for example, the social lifeworld. The phenomenological Schutz (1962) writes that "all the other manifold social relationships are derived from the originary experiencing of the totality of the other's self in the community of time and space. Any theoretical analysis of the notion of environment... would have to start from the face-to-face relations as a basic structure of the world of daily life". This statement suggests that the geographical lifeworld, especially its spatial dimension of informal, face-to-face interaction housed in body-subject, provides the foundation for the social lifeworld. More than likely, a focus on this theme is where themes in social geography, environmental psychology, sociology, and communications studies meet.

PHENOMENOLOGY (PHILOSOPHY)

Phenomenology is a philosophical movement. It was founded in the early years of the 20th century by Edmund Husserl, expanded together with a circle of his followers at the universities of Göttingen and Munich in Germany, and spread across to France, the United States, and elsewhere, often in contexts far removed from Husserl's early work.

Phenomenology, in Husserl's conception, is primarily concerned with the systematic reflection on and analysis of the structures of consciousness, and the phenomena which appear in acts of consciousness. Such reflection was to take place from a highly modified "first person" viewpoint, studying phenomena not as they appear to "my" consciousness, but to any consciousness whatsoever. Husserl believed that phenomenology could thus provide a firm basis for all human knowledge, including scientific knowledge, and could establish philosophy as a "rigorous science" of measurable perception.. Husserl's conception of phenomenology has been criticised and developed not only by himself, but also by his students Edith Stein and Martin Heidegger, by existentialists, such as Max Scheler, Nicolai Hartmann, Maurice Merleau-Ponty, Jean-Paul Sartre, and by other philosophers, such as Paul Ricoeur, Emmanuel Levinas, and sociologists Alfred Schütz and Eric Voegelin.

THE IDEA OF PHENOMENOLOGY

In its most basic form, phenomenology attempts to create conditions for the objective study of topics usually regarded as subjective: consciousness and the content of conscious experiences such as judgments, perceptions, and emotions. Although phenomenology seeks to be scientific, it does not attempt to study consciousness from the perspective of clinical psychology or neurology. Instead, it seeks through systematic reflection to determine the essential properties and structures of consciousness and conscious experience.

Husserl derived many important concepts central to phenomenology from the works and lectures of his teachers, the philosophers and psychologists Franz Brentano and Carl Stumpf. An important element of phenomenology that Husserl borrowed from Brentano was intentionality (often described as "aboutness"), the notion that consciousness is always consciousness *of* something. The object of consciousness is called the *intentional object*, and this object is constituted for consciousness in many different ways, through for instance perception, memory, retention and protention, signification, etc. Throughout these different intentionalities, though they have different structures and different ways of being "about" the object, an object is still constituted as the same identical object; consciousness is directed at the same intentional object in direct perception as it is in the immediately following retention of this object and the eventual remembering of it.

Though many of the phenomenological methods involve various reductions, phenomenology is essentially anti-reductionistic; the reductions are mere tools to better understand and describe the workings of consciousness, not to reduce any phenomenon to these descriptions. In other words, when a reference is made to a thing's *essence* or *idea*, or when one details the constitution of an identical coherent thing by describing what one "really" sees as being only these sides and aspects, these surfaces, it does not mean that the thing is only and exclusively what is described here: The ultimate goal of these reductions is to understand *how* these different aspects are constituted into the actual thing as experienced by the person experiencing it. Phenomenology is a direct reaction to the psychologism and physicalism of Husserl's time.

Although previously employed by Hegel, it was Husserl's adoption of this term (circa 1900) that propelled it into becoming the designation of a philosophical school. As a philosophical perspective, phenomenology is its method, though the specific meaning of the term varies according to how it is conceived by a given philosopher. As envisioned by Husserl, phenomenology is a method of philosophical inquiry that rejects the rationalist bias that has dominated Western thought since Plato in favour of a method of reflective attentiveness that discloses the individual's "lived experience." Loosely rooted in an epistemological device, with Sceptic roots, called epoché, Husserl's method entails the suspension of judgment while relying on the intuitive grasp of knowledge, free of presuppositions and intellectualizing. Sometimes depicted as the "science of experience," the phenomenological method is rooted in intentionality, Husserl's theory of consciousness (developed from Brentano). Intentionality represents an alternative to the representational theory of consciousness which holds that reality cannot be grasped directly because it is available only through perceptions of reality which are representations of it in the mind. Husserl countered that consciousness is not "in" the mind but rather conscious of something other than itself (the intentional object), whether the object is a substance or a figment of imagination (i.e. the real processes associated with and underlying the figment). Hence the phenomenological method relies on the description of phenomena as they are given to consciousness, in their immediacy.

According to Maurice Natanson (1973), *"The radicality of the phenomenological method is both continuous and discontinuous with philosophy's general effort to subject experience to fundamental, critical scrutiny: to take nothing for granted and to show the warranty for what we claim to know."*

In practice, it entails an unusual combination of discipline and detachment to suspend, or bracket, theoretical explanations and second-hand information while determining one's "naive" experience of the matter. The phenomenological method serves to momentarily erase the world of speculation by returning the subject to his or her primordial experience of the matter, whether the object of inquiry is a feeling, an idea, or a perception. According to Husserl the suspension of belief in what we ordinarily take for granted or infer by conjecture diminishes the power of what we customarily embrace as objective reality. According to Safranski (1998, 72), "[Husserl and his followers'] great ambition was to disregard anything that had until then been thought or said about consciousness or the world [while] on the lookout for a new way of letting the things [they investigated] approach them, without covering them up with what they already knew."

Heidegger modified Husserl's conception of phenomenology because of (what he perceived as) his subjectivist tendencies. Whereas Husserl conceived humans as having been constituted by states of consciousness, Heidegger countered that consciousness is peripheral to the primacy of one's existence (i.e., the mode of being of Dasein) which cannot be reduced to one's consciousness of it. From this angle, one's state of mind is an "effect" rather than a determinant of existence, including those aspects of existence that one is not conscious of. By shifting the centre of gravity from consciousness (psychology) to existence (ontology), Heidegger altered the subsequent direction of phenomenology, making it at once both personal and mysterious. One of the consequences of Heidegger's modification of Husserl's conception of phenomenology was its increased relevance to psychoanalysis. Whereas Husserl gave priority to a depiction of consciousness that was fundamentally alien to the psychoanalytic conception of the unconscious, Heidegger offered a way to conceptualize experience that could accommodate those aspects of one's existence that lie on the periphery of sentient awareness.

SPECIAL TERMINOLOGY

Intentionality

Intentionality refers to the notion that consciousness is always consciousness *of* something. The word itself should not be confused with the "ordinary" use of the word intentional, but should rather be taken as playing on the etymological roots of the word. Originally, intention referred to a "stretching out" ("in tension," lat. *intendere*), and in this context it refers to consciousness "*stretching out*" towards its object (although one should be careful with this image, seeing as there is not some consciousness first that, subsequently, stretches out to its object. Rather, consciousness *occurs as* the simultaneity of a conscious act and its object.) Intentionality is often summed up as "aboutness."

Whether this *something* that consciousness is about is in direct perception or in fantasy is inconsequential to the concept of intentionality itself; whatever consciousness is directed at, *that* is what consciousness is consciousness of. This means that the object of consciousness doesn't *have* to be a *physical* object apprehended in perception: it can just as well be a fantasy or a memory. Consequently, these "structures" of consciousness, i.e., perception, memory, fantasy, etc., are called *intentionalities*.

The cardinal principle of phenomenology, the term intentionality originated with the Scholastics in the medieval period and was resurrected by Brentano who in turn influenced Husserl's conception of phenomenology, who refined the term and made it the cornerstone of his theory of consciousness. The meaning of the term is complex and depends entirely on how it is conceived by a given philosopher. The term should not be confused with "intention" or the psychoanalytic conception of unconscious "motive" or "gain."

Intuition

Intuition in phenomenology refers to those cases where the intentional object is directly present to the intentionality at play; if the intention is "filled" by the direct apprehension of the object, you have an intuited object. Having a cup of coffee in front of you, for instance, seeing it, feeling it, or even imagining it-these are all filled intentions, and the object is then *intuited*. The same goes for the apprehension of mathematical formulae or a number.

If you do not have the object as referred to directly, the object is not intuited, but still intended, but then *emptily*. Examples of empty intentions can be signitive intentions-intentions that only *imply* or *refer to* their objects.

Evidence

In everyday language, we use the word evidence to signify a special sort of relation between a state of affairs and a proposition: State A is evidence for the proposition "A is true." In phenomenology, however, the concept of evidence is meant to signify the "subjective achievement of truth." This is not an attempt to reduce the objective sort of evidence to subjective "opinion," but rather an attempt to describe the structure of having something present in intuition with the addition of having it present as *intelligible*: "Evidence is the successful presentation of an intelligible object, the successful presentation of something whose truth becomes manifest in the evidencing itself."

Noesis and Noema

In Husserl's phenomenology, this pair of terms, derived from the Greek *nous* (mind), designate respectively the real content, noesis, and the ideal content, noema, of an intentional act (an act of consciousness). The Noesis is the part of the act which gives it a particular sense or character (as in judging or perceiving something, loving or hating it, accepting or rejecting it, and so on). This is real in the sense that it is actually part of what takes place in the consciousness (or psyche) of the subject of the act. The Noesis is always correlated with a Noema; for Husserl the full Noema is a complex ideal structure comprising at least a noematic sense and a noematic core. The correct interpretation of what Husserl meant by the Noema has long been controversial, but the noematic sense is generally understood as the ideal meaning of the act and the noematic core as the act's referent or object *as it is meant in the act.* One element of controversy is whether this noematic object is the same as the actual object of the act (assuming it exists) or is some kind of ideal object.

Empathy and Intersubjectivity

In phenomenology, empathy refers to the experience of another human body as another. to think of this part of the phenomenology we have to refer all of our experience as and respect it independendly. subjectivity: In one sense, you see another body, but what you immediately perceive or experience is another subject. In Husserl's original account, this was done by a sort of apperception built on the experiences of your own lived-body. The lived body is your own body as experienced by yourself, *as* yourself. Your own body manifests itself to you mainly as your possibilities of acting in the world. It is what lets you reach out and grab something, for instance, but it also, and more importantly, allows for the possibility of changing your point of view. This helps you differentiate one thing from another by the experience of moving around it, seeing new aspects of it (often referred to as making the absent present and the present absent), and still retaining the notion that this is the same thing that you saw other aspects of just a moment ago (it is identical). Your body is also experienced as a duality, both as object (you can touch your own hand) and as your own subjectivity (you are being touched).

The experience of your own body as your own subjectivity is then applied to the experience of another's body, which, through apperception, is constituted as another subjectivity. You can thus recognise the Other's intentions, emotions, etc. This experience of empathy is important in the phenomenological account of intersubjectivity. In phenomenology, intersubjectivity is what constitutes objectivity (i.e., what you experience as objective is experienced as being intersubjectively available-available to all other subjects. This does not imply that objectivity is reduced to subjectivity nor does it imply a relativist position, cf. for instance intersubjective verifiability).

In the experience of intersubjectivity, one also experiences oneself as being a subject among other subjects, and one experiences oneself as existing objectively *for* these Others; one experiences oneself as the noema of Others' noeses, or as a subject in another's empathic experience. As such, one experiences oneself as objectively existing subjectivity. Intersubjectivity is also a part in the constitution of one's lifeworld, especially as "homeworld."

Lifeworld

The lifeworld is the "world" each one of us *lives* in. One could call it the "background" or "horizon" of all experience, and it is that on which each object stands out as itself (as different) and with the meaning it can only hold for us. The lifeworld is both personal and intersubjective (it is then called a "homeworld," and it is shared by "homecomrades"), and, as such, it does not enclose each one of us in a solus ipse.

HUSSERL'S *LOGISCHE UNTERSUCHUNGEN* (1900/1901)

In the first edition of the *Logical Investigations*, still under the influence of Brentano, Husserl describes his position as "descriptive psychology." Husserl analyzes the intentional structures of mental acts and how they are directed at both real and ideal objects. The first volume of the *Logical Investigations*, the *Prolegomena to Pure Logic*, begins with a devastating critique of psychologism, i.e., the attempt to subsume the *a priori* validity of the laws of logic under psychology. Husserl establishes a separate field for research in logic, philosophy, and phenomenology, independently from the empirical sciences.

Transcendental Phenomenology after the *Ideen* (1913)

Some years after the publication of the *Logical Investigations*, Husserl made some key elaborations which led him to the distinction between the act of consciousness (*noesis*) and the phenomena at which it is directed (the *noemata*).

- "noetic" refers to the intentional act of consciousness (believing, willing, etc.)
- "noematic" refers to the object or content (noema) which appears in the noetic acts (the believed, wanted, hated, and loved...).

What we observe is not the object as it is in itself, but how and inasmuch it is given in the intentional acts. Knowledge of essences would only be possible by "bracketing" all assumptions about the existence of an external world and the inessential (subjective) aspects of how the object is concretely given to us. This procedure Husserl called *epoché*.

Husserl in a later period concentrated more on the ideal, essential structures of consciousness. As he wanted to exclude any hypothesis on the existence of external objects, he introduced the method of phenomenological reduction to eliminate them. What was left over was the pure transcendental ego, as opposed to the concrete empirical ego. Now (transcendental) phenomenology is the study of the essential structures that are left in pure consciousness: this amounts in practice to the study of the noemata and the relations among them. The philosopher Theodor Adorno criticised Husserl's concept of phenomenological epistemology in his metacritique *Against Epistemology*, which is anti-foundationalist in its stance.

Transcendental phenomenologists include Oskar Becker, Aron Gurwitsch, and Alfred Schutz.

Realist Phenomenology

After Husserl's publication of the *Ideen* in 1913, many phenomenologists took a critical stance towards his new theories. Especially the members of the Munich group distanced themselves from his new transcendental phenomenology and preferred the earlier realist phenomenology of the first edition of the *Logical Investigations*. Realist phenomenologists include Adolf Reinach, Alexander Pfänder, Johannes Daubert, Max Scheler, Roman Ingarden, Nicolai Hartmann, Dietrich von Hildebrand.

EXISTENTIAL PHENOMENOLOGY

Existential phenomenology differs from transcendental phenomenology by its rejection of the transcendental ego. Merleau-Ponty objects to the ego's transcendence of the world, which for Husserl leaves the world spread out and completely transparent before the conscious. Heidegger thinks of a conscious being as always already in the world. Transcendence is maintained in existential phenomenology to the extent that the method of phenomenology must take a presuppositionless starting point-transcending claims about the world arising from, for example, natural or scientific attitudes or theories of the ontological nature of the world.

While Husserl thought of philosophy as a scientific discipline that had to be founded on a phenomenology understood as epistemology, Heidegger held a radically different view. Heidegger himself states their differences this way:

For Husserl, the phenomenological reduction is the method of leading phenomenological vision from the natural attitude of the human being whose life is involved in the world of things and persons back to the transcendental life of consciousness and its noetic-noematic experiences, in which objects are constituted as correlates of consciousness. For us, phenomenological reduction means leading phenomenological vision back from the apprehension of a being, whatever may be the character of that apprehension, to the understanding of the Being of this being (projecting upon the way it is unconcealed).

According to Heidegger, philosophy was not at all a scientific discipline, but more fundamental than science itself. According to him science is only one way of knowing the world with no special access to truth. Furthermore, the scientific mindset itself is built on a much more "primordial" foundation of practical, everyday knowledge. Husserl was skeptical of this approach, which he regarded as quasi-mystical, and it contributed to the divergence in their thinking.

Instead of taking phenomenology as *prima philosophia* or a foundational discipline, Heidegger took it as a metaphysical ontology: *"being is the proper and sole theme of philosophy...* this means that philosophy is not a science of beings but of being.". Yet to confuse phenomenology and ontology is an obvious error. Phenomena are not the foundation or Ground of Being. Neither are they appearances, for as Heidegger argues in *Being and Time*, an appearance is "that which shows itself in something else," while a phenomenon is "that which shows itself in itself."

While for Husserl, in the epochè, being appeared only as a correlate of consciousness, for Heidegger being is the starting point. While for Husserl we would have to abstract from all concrete determinations of our empirical ego, to be able to turn to the field of pure consciousness, Heidegger claims that "the possibilities and destinies of philosophy are bound up with man's existence, and thus with temporality and with historicality."

However, ontological being and existential being are different categories, so Heidegger's conflation of these categories is, according to Husserl's view, the root of Heidegger's error. Husserl charged Heidegger with raising the question of ontology but failing to answer it, instead switching the topic to the Dasein, the only being for whom Being is an issue. That is neither ontology nor phenomenology, according to Husserl, but merely abstract anthropology.

To clarify, perhaps, by abstract anthropology, as a non-existentialist searching for essences, Husserl rejected the existentialism implicit in Heidegger's distinction between being (sein) as things in reality and Being (Da-sein) as the encounter with being, as when being becomes present to us, that is, is unconcealed.

Existential phenomenologists include: Martin Heidegger (1889–1976), Hannah Arendt (1906–1975), Emmanuel Levinas (1906–1995), Gabriel Marcel (1889–1973), Jean-Paul Sartre (1905–1980), Paul Ricoeur (1913–2005) and Maurice Merleau-Ponty (1908–1961).

Phenomenology and Eastern Thought

Some researchers in phenomenology (particularly in reference to Heidegger's legacy) see possibilities of establishing dialogues with traditions of thought outside of the so-called Western philosophy, particularly with respect to East-Asian thinking, and despite perceived differences between "Eastern" and "Western". Furthermore, it has been claimed that a number of elements within phenomenology (mainly Heidegger's thought) have some resonance with Eastern philosophical ideas, particularly with Zen Buddhism and Taoism. According to Tomonubu Imamichi, the concept of *Dasein* was inspired — although Heidegger remains silent on this — by Okakura Kakuzo's concept of *das-in-der-Welt-sein* (being in the world) expressed in *The Book of Tea* to describe Zhuangzi's philosophy, which Imamichi's teacher had offered to Heidegger in 1919, after having studied with him the year before.

There are also recent signs of the reception of phenomenology (and Heidegger's thought in particular) within scholarly circles focused on studying the impetus of metaphysics in the history of ideas in Islam and Early Islamic philosophy; perhaps under the indirect influence of the tradition of the French Orientalist and philosopher Henri Corbin.

In addition, the work of Jim Ruddy in the field of comparative philosophy, combined the concept of Transcendental Ego in Husserl's phenomenology with the concept of the primacy of self-consciousness in the work of Sankaracharya. In the course of this work, Ruddy uncovered a wholly new eidetic phenomenological science which he called "convergent phenomenology." This new phenomenology takes over where Husserl left off, and deals with the constitution of relation-like, rather than merely thing-like, or "intentional" objectivity.

Historical Overview of the use of the Term

Phenomenology has at least three main meanings in philosophical history: one in the writings of G.W.F. Hegel, another in the writings of Edmund Husserl in 1920, and a third, deriving from Husserl's work, in the writings of his former research assistant Martin Heidegger in 1927.

- For G.W.F. Hegel, phenomenology is an approach to philosophy that begins with an exploration of phenomena (what presents itself to us in conscious experience) as a means to finally grasp the absolute, logical, ontological and metaphysical Spirit that is behind phenomena. This has been called a *"dialectical phenomenology"*.

- For Edmund Husserl, phenomenology is "the reflective study of the essence of consciousness as experienced from the first-person point of view." Phenomenology takes the intuitive experience of phenomena (what presents itself to us in phenomenological reflexion) as its starting point and tries to extract from it the essential features of experiences and the essence of what we experience. When generalized to the essential features of any possible experience, this has been called *"transcendental phenomenology"*. Husserl's view was based on aspects of the work of Franz Brentano and was developed further by philosophers such as Maurice Merleau-Ponty, Max Scheler, Edith Stein, Dietrich von Hildebrand and Emmanuel Levinas.
- Martin Heidegger believed that Husserl's approach overlooked basic structural features of both the subject and object of experience (what he called their "being"), and expanded phenomenological enquiry to encompass our understanding and experience of Being itself, thus making phenomenology the method (in the first phase of his career at least) of the study of being, ontology.

The difference in approach between Husserl and Heidegger influenced the development of existential phenomenology and existentialism in France, as is seen in the work of Jean-Paul Sartre and Simone de Beauvoir. Munich phenomenologists (Johannes Daubert, Adolf Reinach, Alexander Pfänder in Germany and Alfred Schütz in Austria), and Paul Ricoeur have all been influenced. Readings of Husserl and Heidegger have also been crucial elements of the philosophies of Jacques Derrida and Bernard Stiegler.

Although the term "phenomenology" was used occasionally in the history of philosophy before Husserl, modern use ties it more explicitly to his particular method. Following is a list of thinkers in rough chronological order who used the term "phenomenology" in a variety of ways, with brief comments on their contributions:

- Friedrich Christoph Oetinger (1702–1782) German pietist, for the study of the "divine system of relations"
- David Hume (1711–1776) Scottish philosopher, called variably a skeptic or a common sense advocate. While this connection is somewhat tenuous, Hume, in A Treatise of Human Nature, does seem to take a phenomenological or psychological approach by describing the process of reasoning causality in psychological terms. This is also the inspiration for the Kantian distinction between phenomenal and noumenal reality.
- Johann Heinrich Lambert (1728–1777) (mathematician, physician and philosopher) known for the theory of appearances underlying empirical knowledge.
- Immanuel Kant (1724–1804), in the Critique of Pure Reason, distinguished between objects as phenomena, which are objects as shaped and grasped by human sensibility and understanding, and objects as *things-in-themselves* or noumena, which do not appear to us in space and time and about which we can make no legitimate judgments.
- G.W.F. Hegel (1770–1831) challenged Kant's doctrine of the unknowable thing-in-itself, and declared that by knowing phenomena more fully we can gradually arrive at a consciousness of the absolute and spiritual truth of Divinity. Hegel's *Phenomenology of Spirit*, published in 1807, prompted many opposing views, including the existential work of Søren Kierkegaard, Martin Heidegger, and Jean-Paul Sartre, as well as the materialist work of Marx and his many followers.
- Franz Brentano (1838–1917) seems to have used the term in some of his lectures at Vienna, where Edmund Husserl studied with him and came under his influence.
- Carl Stumpf (1848–1936), student of Brentano and mentor to Husserl, used "phenomenology" to refer to an ontology of sensory contents.
- Edmund Husserl (1859–1938) established phenomenology at first as a kind of "descriptive psychology" and later as a transcendental and eidetic

science of consciousness. He is considered to be the founder of contemporary phenomenology.

- Max Scheler (1874–1928) developed further the phenomenological method of Edmund Husserl and extended it to include also a reduction of the scientific method. He influenced the thinking of Pope John Paul II, Dietrich von Hildebrand, and Edith Stein.
- Martin Heidegger (1889–1976) criticized Husserl's theory of phenomenology and attempted to develop a theory of ontology that led him to his original theory of Dasein, the non-dualistic human being.
- Alfred Schütz (1899–1959) developed a phenomenology of the social world on the basis of everyday experience which has influenced major sociologists such as Harold Garfinkel, Peter Berger, and Thomas Luckmann.
- Graham Harman (1968-) Although working from within phenomenology, Harman finds the broad history of phenomenology to be deficient in that it constantly subordinates the independent life of objects to our (human) access to them. His radical break with the traditional use of terms such as intentionality as well as a fresh approach to metaphysics, stems from his greatest influences by such as the great phenomenologists Alphonso Lingis, Husserl, Ortega y Gasset, Zubiri, and Heidegger. Harman's thought is perhaps the first to combine phenomenology with speculative philosophers such as Whitehead, Leibniz, and the sort of radical thinking typified by Speculative Realism.

Later usage is mostly based on or (critically) related to Husserl's introduction and use of the term. This branch of philosophy differs from others in that it tends to be more "descriptive" than "prescriptive".

6

Geography and Cyberspace

REFLECTIONS OF ITS RELATION IN THE 21ST CENTURY

The present text shows a synthesis of the investigations realized from 1998 and that have been synthesized in two recent publications: Buzai (1998, 2001) and Toudert-Buzai (2004, in press). The objective is to analyze the bonds between Geography like science and the present digital technologies, as far as the geographic treatment of the information and the conformation of new realities through Cyberspace. Next three main lines are developed. First it corresponds to a route that today turns one decade and in which one has struggled with respect to the impact of the digital automatization in our discipline. The sprouting of the *Geography Automated* like specialty that revalues geographic developments of previous years and the incorporated planning of a *Global Geography* like scientific discipline of ample transdisciplinario impact through the concepts and geographic methodologies in the computer systems.

Second it corresponds to an advance towards the *Cybergeography*, which is arising from the use from the alert networks and communication, mainly from the real and virtual spaces that are physics and conceptually between the screens of the computers. It corresponds to the impact that the *Cyberspace* is having in our vision of the world and the sprouting of the new specialty with its different lines of boarding.

Third it discusses how a modelística vision will both have superiority before previous sustenances. It begins with the relation between technical and theoretical contents to arrive at the digital modelling of different methodologic procedures in the field from Geography: from that they have a qualitative base and they are possible to be incoporar to the computer atmosphere from numerical identifications, until worlds of digital simulation like new spaces of the perception. *The Geoinformática* and the *GIS* include everything an intermediate space.

Finally it is our intention to clarify that both works mentioned initially are the unique ones mentioned in the final bibliography. They concentrate more than one hundred appointments bibliographical, impossible to brief themselves here, therefore the last name of each author in each case between parenthesis has been mentioned solely and it is recommended to go to the mentioned bibliography to obtain the complete appointments in each case.

THE PARADIGM GEOTECHNOLOGICAL

Initial Visions

In the Sixties the first contributions regarding the subject of the automatization of procedures in the geographic investigation can be verified (*Tobler, Kao, Hägerstrand and Haggett*), nevertheless just in the Eighties (Debate in the magazine *Professional The Geographer*, vol.35 n° 3, 1983) from the initial work of *Dobson* takes place the first formal debate about the possibility of application of the computer science technologies integrated and its impact in the procedures within the framework of our discipline.

The remarkable advances in the field of computer science, according to *Dobson* perimitieron to automate the majority of the procedures of space analysis and glimpses the sprouting of a new specialization: *the Geography Automated*, which is defined as a particular discipline that uses cybernetic systems, human and electronic for the physical and social system analysis.

Although their conclusions are very optimistic as far as the irreversible way that will take towards the automatization, it does not stop recognizing two disadvantages: (a) the strictly speaking theoretical possibility of loss to the detriment of the technology, and (b) the limitations that can arise when the investigations are oriented towards the automatization. The first disadvantage already was well-known in the period dominated by the quantitative paradigm in the middle of twenty century and the second-arisen directly from the automatization a flexible integration of the computer systems could be surpassed by means of the technical advance and.

Although at the beginning the integral components of *Automated Geography* (Computer Cartography, Graphical Computation, Digital Processing of Images of Remote Sensors, Digital Models of Elevation and GIS) were compartment rigid at present the different possibilities from integration have been fulfilled under the concept of *GeoInformática* (*Buzai*). The critics towards the planning of this specialty have been diverse; from simple terminological questions with respect to the use of *Geography Automated* (*Marble, Moellering, Peuquet, Poiker, Stetzer*) to the incorporation of theoretical aspects of relevance when considering a lack of ideological neutrality in the computer systems at the time of its application (*Cromley*).

It is clear that the majority of the authors does not consider that the automatization can form a new paradigm (*Cromley, Moellering, Poiker, Stetzer* and the same *Dobson*), but it is alerted on the remarkable impact that the geographic automatization will have in other fields of the knowledge and the possibilities that the geographers will have to participate with greater superiority in interdisciplinary equipment (*Kellerman, Monmonier*).

One decade later, the same magazine (vol.45, n° 4, 1993) retakes retakes the debate through a *Open* titled *Forum Automated Geography in 1993*, in order to analyze its evolution in the development of the discipline.

Of this debate it is clear that the integration of the systems began to be a reality from the innovating force of the Systems of Información Geográfica (SIG) and that began to delineate a theoretical advance from the construction of a field of greater amplitude: *sciences of the Geographic Information*. In this *Dobson* sense it advances when considering that beyond a "technological revolution" it is being arrived at a "scientific revolution". This last one supported by the theory of "multiple intelligences" (*Gardner*) which allows conceptualizar that *space* intelligence will begin to occupy an outstanding place next to the traditionally valorized intellectual abilities. Therefore, with this level of development in diverse scales, Geography will hit of remarkable form not only in diverse disciplines, but mainly in the human thought and in this way an outstanding place in the intellectual revolution will be contributor when occupying that glimpses.

The Definitive Integration of the Systems

The integration of the systems is framed in the geographic data processing. A data obtained through the conceptualizadas tangible manifestations in a double level: (a) attributes as a result of the measurement of diverse aspects regarding the objects of real existence and (b) its particular geometries. First they are associate to the use of text editors, database administrators, lists of calculation, software of statistic analysis and systems of global positioning (*GPS*), whereas second they are associated to the CAD (*CAD*), the cartography computer-assisted through graphical design, the digital processing of satelite images, modeled digital of elevation for works in the three dimensions and software of graphical conversion.

The GeoInformática represents a field of great amplitude within which technology SIG occupies the central place when tying the alphanumeric and graphical data bases, but it is not defined through type of software composes that it, but through the information that handles: geographic information or *geoinformación*, whose basic condition is its space referencing to a coordinate system.

Finally, all this computer science conjunction can be used so much in the surroundings of the personal computers like integral systems or in the surroundings of the computer networks from where it can advance towards worlds of digital simulation of the virtual reality (RV) in the *Cyberspace* aspects that are providing a great impact in the investigation and the present geographic thought.

Diverse Waves

From the sprouting of Geography as human science (final of century XIX) until today considers the existence of two revolutionary paradigmatic changes: (a) in the Fifties, the appearance of the *quantitative paradigm* (*Schaefer*, *Bunge*) like critical position to the *regional paradigm* that its greater update with the *rational paradigm* (*Hartshorne*) of end of the Thirties had had, and in the Seventies the appearance of the radical positions of the *critical paradigm* (*Peet, Harvey*) and of the *paradigm humanist* (*Yi-Fu Tuan, Buttimer, Relph*) like positions opposed to the *quantitative paradigm*.

The paradigm concept (*Kuhn* we have taken) it in its vision from greater amplitude as "vision of the world" and in this case could think a Geography of the short waves when analyzing the paradigmatic succession during century XX: Paradigms *regional* (decade of ´10), *rational* (decade of ´30), *quantitative* (decade of ´50), *critical radical and radical humanist* (decade of ´70). With this logic, the decade of ´90 would have to present/ display a new breakthrough point and in this sense we have verified a evolution towards a tripartite field of knowledge formed by the *Ecology of the Landscape* (*Naveh, Lieberman, Form, Godron*), *Postmoderna Geography* (*Soybean, Harvey*) and *Automated Geography*, field defined by *Dobson*.

Entering in the particular characteristics of each one of the mentioned paradigms and the three geographic perspective of end of century XX we can verify that the historical pendulum of succession between the historicismo and positivism (*Capel*) are joined when concentrating both perspective at a same moment, and at the same time it is possible to be advanced in the discovery of parallel cycles in this evolution.

An intermediate cycle with waves of 50 years of duration corresponds to which they have analyzed for the partner-space evolution world-wide general (*Berry, Taylor*) or of the technological diffusion from a geographic point of view (*Hall, Preston*), both based on the economic cycles of Capitalism.

In this sense "positivist" exists a wave who makes evolve to the geographic analysis towards the digital automatization: (a) Birth of Human Geography-positivism related to Biology (*Ratzel*) at the end of century XIX (b) Quantitative Revolution-positivism related to the Physics in the middle of century XX and (c) Paradigm Geotechnological-positivism bound to Computer science at the end of century XX and principles of the XXI. Finally a long wave of 100 years already deciphers in a series of works would mark two moments of disciplinary explosion that takes the ends of the previous cycles, first when Geography offers objects from study to many "geographic" disciplines that separated of their science mother and the second when Geography offers a "space vision" necessary for the rest of the disciplines from to have incorporated its concepts and methodologies in the computer systems widely spread; it is what we have defined as *Global Geography* (*Buzai*).

Global Geography

Geography explodes towards the rest of the disciplines through *Global Geography* and their concepts including inside the Geotecnología cause a new vision of the world, not like a paradigm of Geography but like a geographic paradigm, perspective that Geography offers to the rest of the disciplines and human practices. In this sense, which has been to define in a series of works: that we went "towards a new paradigm of the Geography based on the Geotecnología", has been verified.

But it was not verified in the short cycle of 20-25 years, in which *Automated Geography* only appears like perspective that revalues aspects of the *rational paradigm* and the *quantitative paradigm* (*Buzai*) but arises with splendor in the cycle of greater amplitude, because there it appears like "vision of the world" that Geography offers the rest of sciences. It is not a paradigm of Geography, is a geographic paradigm that our science provides to other fields and along with it begins to occupy an outstanding place in the culture of the 21st century.

TOWARDS THE CYBERGEOGRAPHY

Cyberspace

In 1984 the writer *William Gibson* in his novel of science *Neuromancer* fiction proposed the concept of *Cyberspace* daily, defining it like "a undergone consensual hallucination by trillions of legitimate operators, in all the nations, by children to those who he teaches to stops mathematical concepts to them... A graphical representation of the abstarída information of the data banks of all the computers of the human system. An unimaginable complexity. Classified blackout lines in the not-space of the mind, conglomerates and constellations of information. Like lights of a city that moves away". From this perspective, the *Cyberspace* is considered as an electronic matrix of interconnection enters digital data bases through the connected computer systems network. A new space that every time superposes with greater force to real geography of the empirical landscapes and in which can interact subsequent to (*Gibson, Barlow, Dery, Dertouzos, Echeverria*) to be dominated like stage the terrestrial occupation (*Nora, Capel*).

Cybergeography

To explore has to do with the company to know unknown places, the use of average materials to locate to the new world and the conservation of the findings for its diffusion. The relational space that today we found between the screens of the computers has abierto new you rule for the exploration and some geographers interested in the study of the *Cyberspace* have sent to this adventure, changing the labyrinth of the forest by leaves of the hypertext and the machete that lays ways by *mouse* in a man-machine relation of important anthropological sense (*Levy, Piscitelli, Reinghold, Mayans*).

In this sense, the new century appears to us with novel perspective for the analysis of the relations that within the framework settle down between the real world and the digital world in diverse scales of the *Cibercultura* (*Dery, Dertouzos*) and aspects of the digital simulation through the *RV* that will become of current use like exploratory means, today only visible in the video games (*Levis*).

The Cybergeography appears then, as the existing study of the space nature of the present communications networks and spaces between the screens of the computers. The possible studies include an ample variety of phenomena, from the purely material ones as the study of the space distribution of physical infrastructures of communication to most abstract like the human perception of the new digital spaces.

CiberCartografía

One of the most attractive points of the *Cybergeography* is the cartographic representation of the *Cyberspace*, aspect that has been demonstrated when the prestigious magazine *National Geographic* in its first number of the 2000 presented/displayed a map of this new reality, realized by *Cheswick and Burch* of the Bell labs (*Carroll*) and in the following years they would leave published the majors systematic works on the subject: *Mapping Ciberespace* and *Atlas of Ciberespace*, both products of the work of geographers *Dodge* and *Kitchin*.

The equipment maps represent the basic modelling being obtained in the level of thematic cartography, and in Argentina first realized they have been possible from the data at departmental level of the National Census of Population and House 2001. This cartographic sequence corresponds to the work of Vela'zquez and Go'mez Lende (2004).

In them the deficit of computer equipment and family connections can be seen in red colour Internet. While for the first east case colour includes the regions with greater level of poverty in the country, the second long ago amplest one, and considering the categories underneath the average interval, practically all the country is place setting. That is to say, that at national level still is due to hope that many more population sectors accede these technologies.

On the other hand, the called maps "topológicos" are those that present/display the linear connections in the relational space, the bonds between places, their relative positions and the measured ciberespaciales distances in times. Using this technical possibility the first map of the *Cyberspace* has been realized from Buenos Aires (*Buzai*) by means of the use of *software VisualRoute 5.0b* (*Pickard*) possible of being obtained in version in time limited of use in www.visualroute.com.

The experience was realized from a computer in the University of Buenos Aires and its connection to at least a page Web of each country integrated to the Internet network. By means of the use of mentioned *software the* data corresponding to the amount of *routers* have been obtained that the connection was journeying, their name, identification number (IP), their geographic location in latitude and length, hour zone and time of the trip of the connection in thousandth of second (*ms*).

The Myth of the Wcrld-wide Network without Centre

The map of the *Cyberspace* shows a remarkable centralization (*Buzai*) and its simple vision immediately shows the existence of diverse centers in its configuration. Our position in Buenos Aires is evidently peripheral. It is possible to mention that of all the realized connections no crossed a direct way between the point of origen and destination. All of them have happened first through some point that finally was transformed into which we called “control post”.

Of all the asked for connections 27.27% happened first through Pennsauken (New Jersey, the USA), 25.75% by Tysons Corner (Virginia, the USA) 15.91% by Italy (Europe), 15.15% by Middletown (New Jersey, the USA), 11.36% by Miami (Florida, the USA) and 4.56% rest enter the Cyberspace by Boston (Massachussets, the USA), Bagnolet (France, Europe) and Vienna (Virgina, the USA). All the trips confirm the high ciberespacial hierarchy, for example New York (480 ms.) is close more than Uruguay (713 ms), since the trip towards our bordering country did not cross by the River of the Silver, but happened previously through Miami, Atlanta, New York, Newark, Baltimore, Fairfax, to arrive at Montevideo.

Some data confirm that from Buenos Aires our nearer point is Middletown (380 ms.) and the most distant point is Armenia (2852 ms.), whereas our second more distant country is a bordering country in real the geographic space: Paraguay (2765 ms.), rather more far than Sri Lanka (1219 ms.), Mongolia (1373 ms.), Zambia (1285 ms.) or Kuwait (1409 ms.).

The centre of the Cyberspace appears us to the means distance second: Boston (552 ms.), London (555 ms.), Italy (559 ms.) and Montreal (583 ms.), some places of Western Europe are just more far: Paris (620 ms.), Madrid (635 ms.), Portugal (637 ms.), Luxembourg (637 ms.), Switzerland (646 ms.) and Stockholm (668 ms.), while they follow the cities of Eastern Europe: Moscow (690 ms.), Bratislava (704 ms.), Budapest (786 ms.) and Warsaw (800 ms.). The region of the Pacific Ocean, in main lines extends the distances still more: Auckland (753 ms.), Sydney (865 ms.), Canberra (994 ms.), Hong Kong (981 ms.) and Peking (1192 ms.). The configuration of the ciberespaciales distances and its determination at cartographic level sample that the connections from Buenos Aires must happen through certain certain and located points in the central countries. Control posts that allow to have a certain dominion on the new space.

In synthesis, both previous points show a vision centered in Argentina, an analysis of local configuration and another one of contextual relations. Of both space analyzes it is clear that still we must cross a long way so that the connection in network and its benefits widely is used by our society.

The Fight by the New Space

In a series of works the control mechanisms in the cyberspace have appeared (*Virilio, Goodspeed Graham, Buzai, Garci'a Mostazo*), mainly through system ECHELON that as much discussion has generated in the scientific community and international the public opinion from the year 2000. This system, although in the days of the "cold war" it was oriented to cut the communications of exURSS and the countries of the communist block, today its millionaire cost justifies as far as driving official against the terrorism (more justified than ever from the 11/9/01). The lack of privacy in the communications never so was affected as at present and of this form they have recovered interest metaphors like the one of the Panóptico (*Bentham*) or the Great Brother (*Orwel*). This allows us to think that not even in the *Cyberspace* we can be separated of the centralidad of the power.

The Cyberspace as already it has been mentioned, is a new space to explore and to dominate. In this sense, as the Romans dominated the ways, English the seas, the United States the air and the deep space, today a new space of dominion appears: *the Cyberspace* (*Nora*) and the fight by its control will be a constant in the new century.

TOWARDS SUPERIORITY MODELÍSTICA

The technologies of the information and the communications based on the digital developments are significantly different from traditional massive means of communication. While these maintain a passive hearing through a linear communication (*TV, radio*) the average digitalizes promote the interactivity, and this way, a user will influence in the development of the sequence through his intervention. To interact through the annexation of the new technologies requires a certain degree (not very elevated) of qualification and here one double possibility takes place; the dichotomy between the education of the tools and the education of thematic contents through her. In our case the procedures of geographic automatization are from particular interest, positions in an outstanding place for two decades (*Dobson*).

This sense, the learning of the technology can become an aim in itself and also it can become means to approach, in a later stage, concepts and own procedures of the scientific activity. The learning of a SIG in itself implies, among others aspects, to know procedures transformation of a map in paper (*analogical model*) digital format (technical knowledge), whereas its use for the learning of geographic concepts as the one of scale will imply in use of "filters" that allow to hide or to make different geographic organizations in different levels from space resolution visible (theoretical knowledge).

On the other hand, the technology is not neutral, and in the case of the SIG, by means of its "neutral" use will unfailingly revalue certain paradigmatic perspective with its associated methodologic procedures. Mainly tie to *rationalist* and *quantitative* aspects (*Buzai*), although we considered that the capacity of the present geographer must be direccionada to look for the best paradigmatic conjunctions and in this way to enrich the interpretation of all study of application.

An advance sets out on the procedural capacities to obtain a transmission of contents humanists and the support to studies critics. Aspects in which interdisciplinary Geography as science acquires an outstanding position by its amplitude in its paradigmatic perspective, possibilities and their nexus between physical-natural and human aspects in the space differentiation and the understanding of the reality. In synthesis, the technology can be seen in two planes: like content in itself and means to accede to other contents. To conjugate these differences becomes extremely necessary in order that the new digital technologies are used in their total dimension and to the service of socialemente significant applications.

Space Intelligence

Intelligence is not prisoner to the brain of a person, but she is much more ample. It also includes the tools, documents available and the network of personal relations (*Gardner*), that is to say, that in the geographic scope we will be able to say that a SIG, books and information, and the colleagues comprise of the present intelligence of an investigator.

Intelligence has been extended through the application tools, the digital technologies are provided materials that go from the simple text editors to the present GPS (Systems of Global Positioning) within the field of the *Geoinformática*. All this, when working under the same digital conditions, contributes to the development of global intelligence at the time of advancing towards the atmosphere of Internet: "Of the same form that the wheel is an extension of the foot, the telescope an extension of the eye, therefore the communications network is an extension of the nervous system" (*McLuhan* apud *Ianni*)

Through the processes of digitalization and this new nervous system, Geography becomes global and hits in different scopes, since we have indicated, from the scientific activity through the interdiscipline to the daily life in the most varied empirical aspects. At personal level all these aspects are related strongly to the sprouting, in recent years, of a "space intelligence" that begins to occupy a place of importance in the planning of the reality.

The Theory of multiple intelligences (*Gardner*) proposal at the beginning of the eighty aims to exile the belief that the individual has a unique intelligence that is due to develop of global form, considers that the human beings have developed to different types from intelligence and not the unique flexible intelligence. It establishes that seven types of intelligence exist: 1. Linguistic, 2. Logico-mathematical, 3. Musical comedy, 4. Space, 5. Cinésticocorporal, 6. Personnel who go towards the others, and 7. Personnel who aims at the own person. The two first according to the author are those that more privileges have in the general education of the present time.

Space intelligence is based mainly on the visual aspects (so important in the post modern culture) and on the way to perceive forms and objects in a relative space. From a general point of view it also serves so that a person also orients and for the interpretation of different graphical aspects like maps and diagrams, but works as art, consequently can be considered that this *code of images* next to a *linguistic code* forms great systems of representation both.

Therefore, we considered that through the geographic information dissemination, *Global Geography*, the elements for the training of "space intelligence" appear and the impact of the geographic space is so great in all type of investigation that we considered that it begins to occupy an outstanding place next to the linguistic capacities and logic-mathematics that traditionally education privileged.

Particularly as far as the geodigital education, we can perceive that another moment of transition occurs, traditional Geography tied mainly to the linguistic one (trips and space description of landscapes and combinations) whereas *Automated Geography* ties mainly with the logic-mathematical one (digitalization and modelling of the space through the digital technologies).

By all means, although we considered the existence of special intelligences important, we did not consider that the components are isolated and again, the right combination of the diverse degrees of intellectual developments, will allow to accede to a global understanding of the reality.

Perception and Logic through the Digital Models

In the present society the use of computers is naturally motivating as far as its use with multiple intentions, and that already represents a great cleared way so that Geography appears like global in the network. To learn and to apply geoinformáticos procedures become a dynamic task and of discovery a felt double, as far as the use of the tool-in certain opportunities novel and as far as the thematic content in certain fields of the knowledge-incorporated concepts and geographic methods to the digital atmosphere and the rest of the disciplines, therefore a challenge for the geographers will be to be able to mainly use the technology like means that through the scientific activity generate concrete solutions to the problems of the population.

Technology SIG (*desktop* or *online*), in their stage of operation, motivates the search of results through established procedures, as the space correlation (alphanumeric or graphical) but previous to it shows to their utility when demanding procedures regarding the observation and description of landscapes (method of the *regional* paradigm) for the purposes of primary data summary, like thus also the indirect interpretation through maps, satelite aerial photography and images from a visual point of view (method of the *rational* paradigm). Therefore, in this sense a clear way can be seen that it goes from the *real world* to the *digital model* of the reality, representation that will be incorporated to the system (*Buzai*) for its treatment and analysis.

In all process, the perception is far from being objective, has to do with the previous experiences that it has had the individual (*Piaget* apud *Serious*), the acquired concepts are fundamental so that the individual can incorporate new learnings to its structure of knowledge, in an intellectual process invigorated by the structuring-*accomodation* within its conceptual scheme.

It is possible to name here the studies realized as far as the accomplishment of *Mental Maps* (cartographic representation of the space perception) in two great lines: (a) a generalizable physics from certain identifiable urban elements: *footpaths, edges, nodes, areas* and *landmarks* (*Lynch, Kepes*) and another one from the quantitative generalization of the spaces of preference at regional level (*Gould, White*). In both cases it is recommended to accede to the works of *Constancio de Castro.*

Finally the conceptual applicability like fundamental task for the development of the scientific activity will be mentioned, since it appears as it forms to structure, to classify and to order the elements of the reality. The majority of the concepts arises from the empirical observation and their description. In this sense the application of methodologic procedures through technology SIG implies to take a tie series from pertaining concepts, according to the procedure, to certain paradigms of Geography. For example, if after to apply a procedure of thematic superposition we obtain the conclusion that the variable To and B have a high space correspondence, this means to recognize the existence of two *systematic regions* and the generation of a *homogenous region* like valid procedure (*rational paradigm*). Although the concept of "region" is always debatable the application of the method establishes that an agreement as far as its meaning exists and if is considered to the result as "objective" its paradigm of origin is used to explain it, because it is generated a result not directly observable and therefore a concept of greater complexity.

In synthesis, perception and planning are central aspects in the process of application of the new *Geoinformáticas* technologies then in their interior produce a series of relations between the basic paradigms and the interpretation of the results. It is essential to have knowledge of these relations in order to be able to use the triggering technologies as for the interdisciplinary and multiparadigmatic boarding without entering contradictions in the concrete application.

Study Regional Geo-digitalis

The present *geoinformáticas* technologies revalue clearly, through the procedures of used analyzes, certain mentioned paradigmatic positions in this work. Perspective of space analysis that shows to different degrees from utility when realizing regional boardings as geographic approach to the study of the reality.

The evolution of the region concept, an element that has offered certain unit to our discipline underwent important changes from its appearance as *object of study* at the beginning of century XX to its present revaluation. We can consider that regions like digital models can be generated in order to act on the real world. For example, from a qualitative point of view, the methodology of construction of regions by thematic superposition by means of a SIG becomes when incorporating each variable in a layer (*to layer*) within the data base of the study area possible. Its numerical identification is only that, an identification, of no way represents a quantification process.

The boolean procedures can be included in this line that will allow to determine regions with "aptitude" by means of the combination of different factors. In this case, each individual variable will have two defined areas: value 0 (without aptitude) and value 1 (with aptitude), those that through a multiplication using the totality of the thematic layers will show the following result: value 0 (where a variable without aptitude exists at least) and value 1 (where only is the combined aptitude of all the variables).

These procedures can extend through the quantification in an average linear combination (*WLC*) in which determines a value of consideration according to the importance of each variable within the problematic total that represents a 100%.

This way variables will be compensated on others in an average risk in the location decision. On the other hand, from a quantitative point of view, nevertheless, the greater contribution for the construction of regions takes place by means of the application of statistical procedures through use of *software* of statistic analysis for the matrix transformation of data: original, index, standardized and of correlations, as much in variables as in space units.

It must consider that the unique procedures that they generate unique results are both first, the following present/display an important flexibility for the determination of macrovariables, amount of regions on the geographic space or factors of the partner-space structure. The solution appears in the decision of theoretical level in which the subjectivity of the methods has been called "objectives" (*Johnston*).

Arrived at this point, it is important to advance beyond the procedures previous when showing that at present we were before the existence of own digital regions of the digital world, since the digital simulation allows the parallel world generation in the scope of the *Cyberspace*. Several examples can be considered. On world-wide or national scales through the maps of the cyberspace functional regions of flows of digital communication with the support of Internet (*Dodge* can be determined, *Kitchin* to see for some countries of Latin America: *Toudert, Buzai*). A quantitative geography from the use of graphs and until the application of potential models of interactional simulation will imagine.

They can also consider the world virtual arisen from the *Chats* in three dimensions (3d), which can be crossed through a *transformation* (virtual body) that will realize the movements indicated from a remote location. A qualitative geography from the empirical perception of the digital world (traditional and humanist) will imagine, which will present/display landscapes and a space friction between reality and magical realism.

Many of the new virtual spaces today within reach of all, take traditional models that from Geography considered in their initial postulates the use of an *isotropic space*. Some virtual world creators as Bios present/display own concepts of the classic geographic models (*Bon Thünen, Weber, Christaller*) during the search of Web sites. Although others as It activates Worlds try to represent the same frictional impedimientos of the real world (the didactic capacity of these systems from the route by the *Arles* is seen de *Vincent van Gogh)*. At the moment some developments of the virtual reality are arriving at the public through the videojuegos, since many technological developments must take this step, because only thus they begin to be profitable (*Levis*). Some of these worlds can personally be visited through the models 2000SD, 2000SU, 1000SD and 1000CS of the English company Virtuality which can take to the user to digital landscapes of inmersivo realism.

CONCLUSIONS

The consideration of an historical evolution of Geography by regular cycles, bound to its contextual bonds, has been of extreme utility to analyze its paradigmatic changes and to arrive at the discovery of parallel cycles in its evolution. The Geography of beginnings of the 21st century shows a remarkable fragmentation, own of the development than it has been called *postindustrial society* and *postmodern culture*. A fragmentation that is broken the pendulum of succession between positivism and historicismo to concentrate at a unique moment a tripartite field of knowledge.

Of this crystallization it is *Automated Geography* the one that occupies our interest, because it is the specialty that leans more back in new computer science means and going in the *rationalist* and *quantitative* developments of half-full of century XX. The incorporation of the concepts and methodologies developed by fifty years have entered in the computer systems to distribute themselves in the most varied scopes and this standardized Geography generates *Geography Global*. At present, by cause to *Global Geography* our discipline has had the greater impact in other sciences and a cultural recognition of importance. Although it is a geography that works through simplifying digital models of the reality is the one that could have been used in numerous applications from the massive use of computer science means.

In this sense, all standardized geographic knowledge at the level of the *byte* has possibilities of entering, of being distributed or to be used/processed through the alert networks and communication. But this situation much more goes there, since the *Cyberspace*, an almost immaterial place that is between the computer monitors generating new visions and perceptions from the digital simulation. Perhaps in the future it will be normal to walk by the interior of the maps that we have created. Today the studies in the field of the *Cybergeography* have to do with the intervention that any user can realize from the keyboard and *mouse* of their computer. In the future surely the studies corresponding to the field of the perception of the spaces virtual, but mentally real will be extended.

The results presented/displayed in the field of the accomplishment of ciberespaciales maps show that this zone is a new space of fight by the dominion of the new activities in a planetary level and that already arises like priority on the part of the great world-wide powers. Therefore it is not a space free of dangers as far as the logics of the power. Finally, both sustenances technician-conceptua them: (a) *Global Geotecnología-Geography* and, (b) Network-Cyberspace-*Cybergeography* privileges a superiority of the modelística vision of the reality, in which the efforts will be destined to a resolution in the tension of the dichotomy between qualitative and the quantitative thing in the purpose of representing the real world in their better approach.

Geography will have new challenges. To the relation society-nature him the plane of the virtual thing will be due to add and in this sense they will appear a great variety of relations. *And-I hardly deal*, and-*work*, and-*magazines*, and-*government* are initial steps that at the moment need many resolutions. By the seen speeds, I consider that before half-full of the 21st century we will have a concrete answer about the true paper that our science will carry out and have to carry out in the *digital society*. Although the moment to try to construct one more a more egalitarian society, than soon moves to the virtual relations, is today.

7

Paradigms of Geography

EXPLORATORY PARADIGM

The exploratory paradigm includes from greco-roman Period to century approximately XIX. Geography was born about 2,000 years ago in the Greek school from Alexandria. At this time the questions of the geographers were the referring ones to the location of the places, " dónde". In this sense can be considered to Eratóstones the founder of geography. I devise a method of Location of places with certain precision and profit to measure Length of Dazzling. The knowledge of the Greek thought arrives through Roman to us, and especially from Estrabón, whose Geography constitutes one encyclopedic Description of inhabited world or " Ecumene ". In the Greeks they appear two tendencies that are going to be essential in geography; general Geography and descriptive Geography. First Eratóstones incarnates, second appears in writings of Heródoto, that although Historian, owns a geographic sense, since he has the preoccupation to locate the historical facts in a geographic context.

In the Roman world geography is conceived of utilitarian form and the function is assigned of responds to him to the questions of type " dónde" and " qué". was Ptolomeo that greater contribution did at this time.

In Average Age, can be distinguished two scopes, Christian and Muslim. In the Christian scope a backward movement, explained by the configuration of Europe and the strong Censorious presence takes place of Church. Europe was constituted by small states with small relation and society was not urgent to respond it to the question of " donde". Therefore, geography was supplanted by Bible. The cartographic production more important at this time arrives from the hand of San Isidoro, that marked rules in the Christian scope during several centuries. However, the representation of Land of San Isidoro represents a backward movement with respect to the cartographic productions of the Roman world. The great transformation of geography began with the discovery of the classic thought around Century XIII. Within Low Average Age emphasizes the work of Great Alberto. Generally and in spite of some exceptional Spyings is precise to recognize that during this period the geographic innovations are almost null and the absence of critical Spirit incapacitated discerning the scientist and the monk. Nevertheless when finalizing the Average Age occurs to clear symptoms of renovation on the part of some authors with Guillermo de Occam or Nominalistas that they induce to a renovation of geography.

As far as the Muslim scope, it is possible to emphasize that he is rather less shadier. The possession of a vast empire, and the obligation of the good believer to peregrinate to Mecca once in the life causes that in this one scope geography is developed of way superior to the Christian scope. is possible to emphasize the trips of Ibn Baton, the climatic divisions of the Idrisi and the study of the different ways of life from Ibn Jaldum. From centuries XV, Europe recovers the supremacy and the interest by the trips, and so occurs to the period of Discoveries. This historical moment, also known like " Iberian Period " it supposes a height in geography, because before the society had never resorted as much to geography. This fact was harnessed essentially by the trips of Columbus with the discovery of New World, and so Portugal, and mainly Spain, acquires an absolute protagonism in this matter.

At the end of Century XVI, and during the century following, Holland happened to Spain in the hegemonic paper of the geographic studies, agreeing with the naval weakening of Spain., Apiano, Ortelius, Mercator, Münster or Varenio arise at this time the names from Tasmán. This one last one indicates Dualism between physical Geography and human Geography that in essence arrives until us.

Century XVII is also the century of Bacon, René Descartes, Boyle, Galileo, Blaise Pascal or Isaac Newton. That is to say, an essential century in History of science in which the classic knowledge consolidates and insinuates the new scientific system supported in Observation.

In Century XVIII is of great Importance in geographic Thought the ideas of Immanuel Kant and Buffon. First provided the philosophical foundation of geography. Kant indicated that three forms exist to organize the knowledge, one of them is based on the way of how organizing the things, ordering them as they are associated in Space. This it is the dominion of geographic sciences. As far as Buffon, Half emphasizes the impact of on Man and the one of this one on Half natural. In this one century sciences of the Nature experience a great advance, ligatures to geography, as Meteorology is the case of, with names like Dampier, Halley and Hadley, of Geology with authors like Werner and Hutton, of Botanical with Ray and Carl von Linné, etc.

Century XIX is going to be decisive to include/understand the development of the geographic thought, since during this century geography is going away to constitute in a discipline with contents and a community of professional scientists. The presence of geographers like Wilhelm is vital for this task von Humboldt and Karl Ritter, that consolidates geography like an independent branch of the knowledge. Humboldt is considered the father of physical geography. He tries to provide explanatory descriptions of regions and to compare them with others of terrestrial Surface, which contrasts with the usual geography that provided a chaotic catalog of facts and names of places referred to political-administrative units. Ritter has one more a more philosophical and historical formation. Its objective is to study the relations between the natural frame and the man with an Anthropocentric approach. It can say that the work of these two authors forms the base of traditional Geography, in such a way that the later works are going away to send to these authors to accept them or to reject them. In spite of their important contribution to the geographic thought, the Humboldts and Ritter do not leave school, but they leave a legacy that will be used by all the schools, constituting traditional geography.

After the death of Humboldt and Ritter general geography is not developed, but advances in the field of take place

Systematization of special studies, like Penck with Geomorphology or Köppen in Climatology. During this century also of geography is going away to attend Institutionalization, consequently of the development of educative System. This institutionalization impels the creation of Chairs of geography and geographic societies.

ENVIRONMENTALIST DETERMINIST PARADIGM

From second half of century XIX, with the legacy of Humboldt and Ritter and of the institutionalization of him geography, national schools take place theoretical that translate the conceptual weakness and of the discipline. They are the schools German and French those that emphasize more. Germany really does not form a state, but it forms a conglomerate of kingdoms, duchies and principalities, without more union than a cultural base. Soon it begins to be developed to a common economic base and a political development that in 1870 culminates with National Unification. Therefore, the absence of a centre of space organization does that the geographic debate copper interest.

The ideas of Ratzel have a great repercussion at this time, since their expositions constitute a tool that legitimate German Expansionism. Ratzel, is seen directly influenced by evolucionistas ideas of Charles Darwin. On the other hand, Ratzel takes as of Auguste Comte bases philosophical Positivismo, supported in the observation and doing without the purpose and the origin of the phenomena study object, thus breaking with the theological approach of Ritter. In this way, Ratzel combines Evolucionismo and the positivismo to support Imperialism. Ratzel defines the geographic thing as the study of the influences that the conditions of natural means exert on the man. Also, Nature will act in the expansion possibility of a town, well favoring it or preventing it. Generally, geographic Determinism is taken to Ratzel like the foundation from, that supposes that the freedom of the man is conditional by the factors of physical means. Consequently, the progress means a greater use of the nature, therefore, the increase of Territory and with this, a greater use of the same, can suppose the progress of a society. vital Space, or Lebensraum, represents therefore the balance between a population of a certain society and the resources available to do against the needs. The disciples of Ratzel radicalize their positions constituting a clearly determinist approach. They get to consider that the natural conditions determine History or that the man is a simple product of means.

Besides in Germany, the ratzelianas ideas also acquire protagonism in the United States, with the foundation of the first colonies on the part of the European puritanos, that were based on the legitimation of imperialism and the unionismo of Ratzel to constitute the United States of America. Taking as it bases the fundamental ideas of Ratzel, the school that arises from him is geopolitics. This considers the consequences space of the policy of a state, and has like maximum exponents to MacKinder and Swedish Kjellen in Great Britain, and mainly, by its ominous consequences, to the general Haushofer, friend of Hitler, in Germany.

On the other hand, the Keyneses, understands what is the vital space and criticism the measures of the Treaty of Versailles that ended the I World war. After II the World war, the ideas of the Keyneses consider. Between these they are the international collaboration that it includes the establishment of a unique currency (in principle the gold and later the dollar), the common financial system, the creation of United Nations and the expansion of the international trade. To sum up, the paper of Ratzel in the development of geography resides in consolidating human geography, when introducing in the geographic debate the political and economic subjects, locating to the man in centre of the geographic analysis, although with a biologizante and justificadora vision of expansionism.

REGIONAL POSITIVE PARADIGM

It mainly has his origin in the French school and in the ideas of Paul Vidal of the Blache. This school is against to the geographic principles set out by Ratzel and the positivistas ideas of Comte. For Vidal, human sciences are sciences different from the natural ones and they talk about to the scope of the freedom of the man, understanding the time like a Cultural value

In order to include/understand the thought of Vidal it is necessary to before know the context historical the French society of end of century XIX. In 1870, France is the loser of the war with Prusia, losing therefore the territories of Alsace and Lorraine, vital for Industrialization. At this time chairs and university institutes of geography are created. The war had shown the necessity to reflect and to think about the space, to make a geography opposed to the German and that deslegitimase Germanic expansionism, at the same time as it defended the territorial interests and it justified French Expansionism. Therefore, Vidal of the Blache tries to create an opposite to the one of Ratzel and suitable geographic speech to the interests defended by dominant French Bourgeoisie of Third Republic. Thus, while Ratzel power legitimate state Authoritarianism and, Vidal indicates a Liberal tone more to it. Vidal indicates the necessity of " neutrality of the speech científico". Thus, criticism the idea of vital space, but at the same time is based on France a specialization in colonial Geography. Vidal criticized the character ratzeliano Naturalist, since the man appears like a being passive and dominated by means, although without completely doing without the naturalistic load then for Vidal geography is the science of Places not of the men. For Vidal the object of geography was Relation man-nature, from the point of view of Landscape, of the study of Region. To the man a being considers active, who undergoes the influence of means, acting on this and transforming it. Under this perspective the nature is considered like a set of possibilities for the action of the man.

Vidal thinks that one Community is developed on a region, that supposes the infrastructure offered by the nature. The man adapts to this region by means of a set of techniques, habits, customs, that Vidal denominates sorts of life, a situation of balance between the man and the means constructed historically by the societies. The territory affected by these sorts of life is the dominion of Civilization. For Vidal, geography must be in charge of the study of the regions, thus to include/ understand the sorts of life, the causes of its permanence and the formation of civilization dominions. Therefore, criticism the ratzeliano approach, but supports French expansionism being based on history. Not to respect Opposite of an European state supposes an aggression to a long process of civilization, nevertheless, the American, African towns and Asian they represent suspended societies, reason why he is positive to break that process to make them enter the progress, that legitimizing a subtle way, French colonialism.

Finally we can summarize Posibilismo like a set of options that the means offer to the man and that freely this it is become accustomed forming societies that are developed on that means.

Paradigm of Geography like Technical Space Science

In the middle of Century XX, appears a tendency clear to extend the objective and the reach of geography to include the study of the man and the places. was Ackerman first that proposed like objective of geography constructing experimental laws and theories in the regional scopes. But it was the article of Schaefer (1953), the one that originated quantitative Revolution and theoretics in geography. Schaefer esteem that the central objective of geography is the search of Laws that govern the distribution of certain characteristics on terrestrial Surface. The objective of the geography is not in studying what there is and why in a place, but the reasons for which happen a phenomenon in a certain site and not in another one.

Other important landmarks in the quantitative revolution will be the publication in 1962 of the work Theoretical Geography of William Bunge. For this date the new geography had been developed enough in the United States from the universities of Wisconsin and Washington. From the United States the movement was transmitted soon to Great Britain and Sweden. In countries like France and Spain, where Regionalism had a great influence, the reception of this current was more delayed. In summary, the reaction against the regional paradigm began in the United States in the middle of century XX. To the objectives nor the definition of geography are not discussed, but laws and theories by means of the application of social and physical sciences look for that favour the generalizing process. But these changes did not have an application on a coherent field to geography, for that reason it was tried to look for a specific field in which this new geography worked. In spite of this, the point of view that prevailed went the one to consider to geography like a space science, considering the space analysis like the centre and essential object of the geographic investigation. But quantitative Geography not only incorporated new Methods and new Object of study (the explanation of the distribution of phenomena on the terrestrial surface) but also influenced in the reformulation of the ecological tradition and the regional tradition that followed, therefore, being present in the geographic work from these new positions and the traditional conceptions.

Therefore, unlike the classic or regional geography that were boarded joint studies on concrete areas, quantitative geography, will direct to a preferred attention to the problems of Socioeconomic order; the systems and urban hierarchies, the factors of the industrial location, Accessibility of market areas, the landlords of use of Suelo, you rule of Population and the communications networks will be among others, the most frequent subjects of investigation of the geographers who follow the approach quantitative. From this point of view, the region would have to serve like laboratory to resist the theories and laws of general type.

Generally, the mathematics represent a quite frequent resource for the formation of new theories as well as for the data processing in this new geography. The development of computer science and the computers allows to deal with agility the voluminous statistical series with which the geographer works, and also to realize simulations of complex systems in which they must consider great number of variables.

PARADIGM OF THE GEOGRAPHY OF THE PERCEPTION

Before the insufficiency of a space or technical model like, with premises moved away of the reality, it was tried not only to discover the certain aspect that would take the world under supposed from economic rationality in the decision making, but to see and to try to include/understand and to discover the exceptions and the limits. In fact Conductistas did not break totally with the paradigm of the positivistas of space science, but normative Axioms try to modify by means of inductive procedures that they look for to find the rules of the behaviour to soon use them in the prediction and the explanation of space forms. Also the conductistas operate with data different from the employees by those in favour of space science. The conductistas create their own data, and so they need techniques like the survey, and many of their profits were applied to the historical and cultural geography, that was obstinate to get up itself to the quantitative revolution.

It intends to study the compression of how it interacts the man and means, but by means of the knowledge of the psychological processes, through which the man learns of the means in which he lives, examining the way in which these processes influence in the resulting behaviour. This current is based on the principle of the existence of an own and specific scale of each individual. The inclusion of praxis individual, implies an approach to Psychology, the psychological anthropology and other approaches opposed to quantitative geography.

Geography concentrates on the space man, with the aim of finding in him, decisions. One sets out to value the conduct of the man, like brake to Dehumanization that underwent geography. This current has two phases of development:

- *First stage (beginning of the 60):* One is going away to define as a renovadora current of the positivismo, being adapted the instruments of analysis to the definition that introduces the decisions of the free individual will, without still resigning to deductive Method. The main subjects are: The discovery of you rule of the space behaviour, the formula of the model of decision making, and the definition of structures of mental maps.
- *Second phase:* A direction consolidates that identifies more with a geography of the perception, under one more a more humanistic and more subjective perspective actually. The contributions of psychology and are integrated Ethology. The essential bases of the work of the geography of the perception are two: · The individual behaviors are the result of the wills and personal decisions. · Those are the individual behaviors that lead to model the space.

PARADIGM OF RADICAL GEOGRAPHY

In the decade of the Seventies of Century XX appears a critical movement between the social scientists in the capitalist industrial countries. The disappointment lead to a rupture of liberalism and a critical tendency that is going to also pronounce themselves in all the social sciences and in geography. This necessity to approach a geographic revolution emphasizing the social thing causes that different groups within the radical movement arise. · Humanists like Zelinsky, Wolf, Yi-Fu Tuan, Law or Buttimer, alarmed by the march of the world. In 1970, Zelinsky indicates its frustration and his I disillusion proposing that the geographer dedicates to his activity to the geodemográfica cartography, of Contamination, of Stress, that is to say, that plays a role " diagnosticador". In addition, he recommends a effort to devise new world and that the geographer is " architect of utopías".

Liberal radicals like Smith, Johnston or Brookfield, that combines science in the western democracy with a strong commitment in better the executive and legislative action for the evils social. Its main contribution is the cartography of goods and the evils in order to correct the territorial inequalities. The exposition of these is rather reformist that radical, since they bet by a change in the thematic one that contributes to the social welfare.

Marxist radicals like Richard Peet, David Harvey, Milton Holy, Edward Soybean or Walter. They base his investigation on the analysis of the social processes, always put in front to the space ones, although they do not deny these last ones. They lean in the historical materialism, method that stops its followers solves to the antinomy naturalismo and historicismo, denying the geographic and economic determinism. The essential object of these geographers is to show the contradictions of the capitalist system, causes of the space imbalances and the social operation. The unique way to correct those partner-space misalignments is overthrowing the capitalist system and introducing the socialism. As far as the legacy of the Marxist radical geographers, it mainly emphasizes his contribution to urban geography with the study of the institutions or agents of the urban space.

HISTORY OF GEOGRAPHY

BABYLON

The oldest known world maps date back to ancient Babylon from the 9th century BC. The best known Babylonian world map, however, is the *Imago Mundi* of 600 BC. The map as reconstructed by Eckhard Unger shows Babylon on the Euphrates, surrounded by a circular landmass showing Assyria, Urartu and several cities, in turn surrounded by a "bitter river" (Oceanus), with seven islands arranged around it so as to form a seven-pointed star. The accompanying text mentions seven outer regions beyond the encircling ocean. The descriptions of five of them have survived. In contrast to the *Imago Mundi*, an earlier Babylonian world map dating back to the 9th century BC depicted Babylon as being further north from the centre of the world, though it is not certain what that centre was supposed to represent.

GRECO-ROMAN WORLD

The ancient Greeks saw the poet Homer as the founder of geography. His works the *Iliad* and the *Odyssey* are works of literature, but both contain a great deal of geographical information. Homer describes a circular world ringed by a single massive ocean. The works show that the Greeks by the 8th century BC had considerable knowledge of the geography of the eastern Mediterranean. The poems contain a large number of place names and descriptions, but for many of these it is uncertain what real location, if any, is actually being referred to.

Thales of Miletus is one of the first known philosophers known to have wondered about the shape of the world. He proposed that the world was based on water, and that all things grew out of it. He also laid down many of the astronomical and mathematical rules that would allow geography to be studied scientifically. His successor Anaximander is the first person known to have attempted to create a scale map of the known world and to have introduced the gnomon to Ancient Greece.

Hecataeus of Miletus initiated a different form of geography, avoiding the mathematical calculations of Thales and Anaximander he learnt about the world by gathering previous works and speaking to the sailors who came through the busy port of Miletus. From these accounts he wrote a detailed prose account of what was known of the world. A similar work, and one that mostly survives today, is Herodotus' *Histories*. While primarily a work of history, the book contains a wealth of geographic descriptions covering much of the known world.

Egypt, Scythia, Persia, and Asia Minor are all described in great detail. Little is known about areas further a field, and descriptions of areas such as India are almost wholly fanciful. Herodotus also made important observations about geography. He is the first to have noted the process by which large rivers, such as the Nile, build up deltas, and is also the first recorded as observing that winds tend to blow from colder regions to warmer ones.

Pythagoras was perhaps the first to propose a spherical world, arguing that the sphere was the most perfect form. This idea was embraced by Plato and Aristotle presented empirical evidence to verify this. He noted that the Earth's shadow during an eclipse is curved, and also that stars increase in height as one moves north. Eudoxus of Cnidus used the idea of a sphere to explain how the sun created differing climatic zones based on latitude. This led the Greeks to believe in a division of the world into five regions. At each of the poles was an uncharitably cold region. While extrapolating from the heat of the Sahara it was deduced that the area around the equator was unbearably hot. Between these extreme regions both the northern and southern hemispheres had a temperate belt suitable for human habitation.

Hellenistic Period

These theories clashed with the evidence of explorers, however. Hanno the Navigator had traveled as far south as Sierra Leone, and it is possible other Phoenicians had circumnavigated Africa. In the 4th century BC the Greek explorer Pytheas traveled through northwest Europe, and circled the British Isles. He found that the region was considerably more habitable than theory expected, but his discoveries were largely dismissed as fanciful by his contemporaries because of this. Conquerors also carried out exploration, for example, Caesar's invasions of Britain and Germany, expeditions/ invasions sent by Augustus to Arabia Felix and Ethiopia (Res Gestae 26), and perhaps the greatest Ancient Greek explorer of all, Alexander the Great, who deliberately set out to learn more about the east through his military expeditions and so took a large number of geographers and writers with his army who recorded their observations as they moved east.

The ancient Greeks divided the world into three continents, Europe, Asia, and Libya (Africa). The Hellespont formed the border between Europe and Asia. The border between Asia and Libya was generally considered to be the Nile river, but some geographers, such as Herodotus objected to this. Herodotus argued that there was no difference between the people on the east and west sides of the Nile, and that the Red Sea was a better border. The relatively narrow habitable band was considered to run from the Atlantic Ocean in the west to an unknown sea somewhere east of India in the east. The southern portion of Africa was unknown, as was the northern portion of Europe and Asia, so it was believed that they were circled by a sea. These areas were generally considered uninhabitable.

The size of the Earth was an important question to the Ancient Greeks. Eratosthenes attempted to calculate its circumference by measuring the angle of the sun at two different locations. While his numbers were problematic, most of the errors cancelled themselves out and he got quite an accurate figure. Since the distance from the Atlantic to India was roughly known, this raised the important question of what was in the vast region east of Asia and to the west of Europe. Crates of Mallus proposed that there were in fact four inhabitable land masses, two in each hemisphere. In Rome a large globe was created depicting this world. That some of the figures Eratosthenes had used in his calculation were considerably in error became known, and Posidonius set out to get a more accurate measurement. This number actually was considerably smaller than the real one, but it became accepted that the eastern part of Asia was not a huge distance from Europe.

Roman Period

While the works of almost all earlier geographers have been lost, many of them are partially known through quotations found in Strabo. Strabo's seventeen volume work of geography is almost completely extant, and is one of the most important sources of information on classical geography. Strabo accepted the narrow band of habitation theory, and rejected the accounts of Hanno and Pytheas as fables. None of Strabo's maps survive, but his detailed descriptions give a clear picture of the status of geographical knowledge of the time. A century after Strabo

Ptolemy launched a similar undertaking. By this time the Roman Empire had expanded through much of Europe, and previously unknown areas such as the British Isles had been explored. The Silk Road was also in operation, and for the first time knowledge of the far east began to be known. Ptolemy's *Geographia* opens with a theoretical discussion about the nature and techniques of geographical inquiry, and then moves to detailed descriptions of much the known world. Ptolemy lists a huge number of cities, tribes, and sites and places them in the world. It is uncertain what Ptolemy's names correspond to in the modern world, and a vast amount of scholarship has gone into trying to link Ptolemaic descriptions to know locations.

Pliny the Elder's Natural History also has sections on geography. For the most part Ancient Greek geography was an academic field. There is little evidence that maps or charts were used for navigation. It does, however, seem that at least in Athens the people were acquainted with maps and that several were on public display. It was the Romans who made far more extensive practical use of geography and maps.

CHINA

In China, the earliest known geographical Chinese writing dates back to the 5th century BC, during the beginning of the Warring States (481 BC-221 BC). This was the 'Yu Gong' ('Tribute of Yu') chapter of the book *Shu Jing* (*Classic of History*). The book describes the traditional nine provinces, their kinds of soil, their characteristic products and economic goods, their tributary goods, their trades and vocations, their state revenues and agricultural systems, and the various rivers and lakes listed and placed accordingly. The nine provinces in the time of this geographical work was very small in terrain size compared to what modern China occupies today. In fact, its description pertained to areas of the Yellow River, the lower valleys of the Yangtze, with the plain between them and the Shandong peninsula, and to the west the most northern parts of the Wei River and the Han River were known (along with the southern parts of modern day Shanxi province).

In this ancient geographical treatise (which would greatly influence later Chinese geographers and cartographers), the Chinese used the mythological figure of Yu the Great to describe the known earth (of the Chinese). Apart from the appearance of Yu, however, the work was devoid of magic, fantasy, Chinese folklore, or legend. Although the Chinese geographical writing in the time of Herodotus and Strabo were of lesser quality and contained less systematic approach, this would change from the 3rd century onwards, as Chinese methods of documenting geography became more complex than found in Europe (until the 13th century).

The earliest extant maps found in archeological sites of China date to the 4th century BC and were made in the ancient State of Qin. The earliest known reference to the application of a geometric grid and mathematically graduated scale to a map was contained in the writings of the cartographer Pei Xiu (224–271). From the 1st century AD onwards, official Chinese historical texts contained a geographical section, which was often an enormous compilation of changes in place-names and local administrative divisions controlled by the ruling dynasty, descriptions of mountain ranges, river systems, taxable products, etc. The ancient Chinese historian Ban Gu (32–92) most likely started the trend of the gazeteer in China, which became prominent in the Southern and Northern Dynasties period and Sui Dynasty. Local gazeteers would feature a wealth of geographic information, although its cartographic aspects were not as highly professional as the maps created by professional cartographers.

From the time of the 5th century BC *Shu Jing* forward, Chinese geographical writing provided more concrete information and less legendary element. This example can be seen in the 4th chapter of the *Huainanzi* (Book of the Master of Huainan), compiled under the editorship of Prince Liu An in 139 BC during the Han Dynasty (202 BC-202 AD). The chapter gave general descriptions of topography in a systematic fashion, given visual aids by the use of maps (di tu) due to the efforts of Liu An and his associate Zuo Wu. In Chang Chu's *Hua Yang Guo Chi* (*Historical Geography of Szechuan*) of 347 AD, not only rivers, trade routes, and various tribes were described, but it also wrote of a 'Ba Jun Tu Jing' ('Map of Szechuan'), which had been made much earlier in 150 AD. The *Shui Jing* (*Waterways Classic*) was written anonymously in the 3rd century during the Three Kingdoms era (attributed often to Guo Pu), and gave a description of some 137 rivers found throughout China. In the 6th century AD, the book was expanded to forty times its original size by the geographers Li Daoyuan, given the new title of *Shui Jing Zhu* (*The Waterways Classic Commented*).

In later periods of the Song Dynasty (960-1279 AD) and Ming Dynasty (1368-1644 AD) there were much more systematic and professional approaches to geographic literature. The Song Dynasty poet, scholar, and government official Fan Chengda (1126–1193) wrote the geographical treatise known as the *Gui Hai Yu Heng Chi*. It focused primarily on the topography of the land, along with the agricultural, economic and commercial products of each region in China's southern provinces. The polymath Chinese scientist Shen Kuo (1031–1095) devoted a significant amount of his written work to geography, as well as a hypothesis of land formation (geomorphology) due to the evidence of marine fossils found far inland, along with bamboo fossils found underground in a region far from where bamboo was suitable to grow. The 14th century Yuan Dynasty geographer Na-xin wrote a treatise of archeological topography of all the regions north of the Yellow River, in his book *He Shuo Fang Gu Ji*. The Ming Dynasty geographer Xu Xiake (1587–1641) traveled throughout the provinces of China (often on foot) to write his enormous geographical and topographical treatise, documenting various details of his travels, such as the locations of small gorges, or mineral beds such as mica schists. Xu's work was largely systematic, providing accurate details of measurement, and his work (translated later by Ding Wenjiang) read more like a 20th century field surveyor than an early 17th century scholar.

The Chinese were also concerned with documenting geographical information of foreign regions far outside of China. Although Chinese had been writing of civilizations of the Middle East, India, and Central Asia since the traveller Zhang Qian (2nd century BC), later Chinese would provide more concrete and valid information on the topography and geographical aspects of foreign regions. The Tang Dynasty (618-907 AD) Chinese diplomat Wang Xuance traveled to Magadha (modern northeastern India) during the 7th century AD. Afterwards he wrote the book *Zhang Tian-zhu Guo Tu* (Illustrated Accounts of Central India), which included a wealth of geographical information. Chinese geographers such as Jia Dan (730–805) wrote accurate descriptions of places far abroad. In his work written between 785 and 805 AD, he described the sea route going into the mouth of the Persian Gulf, and that the medieval Iranians (whom he called the people of the Luo-He-Yi country, i.e. Persia) had erected 'ornamental pillars' in the sea that acted as lighthouse beacons for ships that might go astray. Confirming Jia's reports about lighthouses in the Persian Gulf, Arabic writers a century after Jia wrote of the same structures, writers such as al-Mas'udi and al-Muqaddasi. The later Song Dynasty ambassador Xu Jing wrote his accounts of voyage and travel throughout Korea in his work of 1124 AD, the *Xuan-He Feng Shi Gao Li Tu Jing* (*Illustrated Record of an Embassy to Korea in the Xuan-He Reign Period*). The geography of medieval Cambodia (the Khmer Empire) was documented in the book *Zhen-La Feng Tu Ji* of 1297 AD, written by Zhou Daguan.

MEDIEVAL ISLAMIC WORLD

In the Middle East, Muslim geographers such as al-Idrisi, al-Yaqubi, al-Masudi, Ibn Khurdadhbih, Ibn al-Faqih, al-Istakhri, Ibn Battuta, Ibn Khaldun, etc. maintained the Greek and Roman techniques and developed new ones. The Islamic empire stretched from Spain to India, and Arab and Jewish traders (known as Radhanites) travelled throughout Eurasia, Africa and the Indian Ocean. The Arabs added a great deal of knowledge to expand and correct the classical sources. There were some representatives of the West that produced geographical works of quality, such as the Syrian bishop Jacob of Edessa (633-708), but this paled in comparison to the virtual mountain of work published by Islamic writers of the Middle Ages (who were largely responsible for the foundations of knowledge present in later Western geography).

During the Muslim conquests of the seventh and early 8th centuries, Arab armies established the Islamic Arab Empire, reaching from Central Asia to the Iberian Peninsula. An early form of globalization began emerging during the Islamic Golden Age, when the knowledge, trade and economies from many previously isolated regions and civilizations began integrating due to contacts with Muslim explorers, sailors, scholars, traders, and travellers. Subhi Y. Labib has called this period the *Pax Islamica*, and John M. Hobson has called it the *Afro-Asiatic age of discovery*, in reference to the Muslim Southwest Asian and North African traders and explorers who travelled most of the Old World, and established an early global economy across most of Asia, Africa, and Europe, with their trade networks extending from the Atlantic Ocean and Mediterranean Sea in the west to the Indian Ocean and China Seas in the east, and even as far as Japan, Korea and the Bering Strait. Arabic silver *dirham* coins were also being circulated throughout the Afro-Eurasian landmass, as far as sub-Saharan Africa in the south and northern Europe in the north, often in exchange for goods and slaves. In England, for example, the Anglo-Saxon king Offa of Mercia (r. 757-796) had coins minted with the Shahadah in Arabic. These factors helped establish the Arab Empire (including the Rashidun, Umayyad, Abbasid and Fatimid caliphates) as the world's leading extensive economic power throughout the 7th–13th centuries.

In the 9th century, Alkindus was the first to introduce experimentation into the Earth sciences. An early adherent of environmental determinism was the medieval Afro-Arab writer al-Jahiz, who explained how the environment can determine the physical characteristics of the inhabitants of a certain community. He used his early theory of evolution to explain the origins of different human skin colors, particularly black skin, which he believed to be the result of the environment. He cited a stony region of black basalt in the northern Najd as evidence for his theory. In the early 10th century, Abû Zayd al-Balkhî, originally from Balkh, founded the "Balkhî school" of terrestrial mapping in Baghdad. The geographers of this school also wrote extensively of the peoples, products, and customs of areas in the Muslim world, with little interest in the non-Muslim realms. Suhrâb, a late 10th century Muslim geographer, accompanied a book of geographical coordinates with instructions for making a rectangular world map, with equirectangular projection or cylindrical cylindrical equidistant projection. In the early 11th century, Avicenna hypothesized on the geological causes of mountains in *The Book of Healing* (1027).

In mathematical geography, Abû Rayhân al-Bîrûnî, around 1025, was the first to describe a polar equi-azimuthal equidistant projection of the celestial sphere. He was also regarded as the most skilled when it came to mapping cities and measuring the distances between them, which he did for many cities in the Middle East and western Indian subcontinent. He often combined astronomical readings and mathematical equations, in order to develop methods of pin-pointing locations by recording degrees of latitude and longitude. He also developed similar techniques when it came to measuring the heights of mountains, depths of valleys, and expanse of the horizon, in *The Chronology of the Ancient Nations*. He also discussed human geography and the planetary habitability of the Earth. He hypothesized that roughly a quarter of the Earth's surface is habitable by humans, and also argued that the shores of Asia and Europe were "separated by a vast sea, too dark and dense to navigate and too risky to try" in reference to the Atlantic Ocean and Pacific Ocean.

At the age of 17, al-Biruni calculated the latitude of Kath, Khwarazm, using the maximum altitude of the Sun. Al-Biruni also solved a complex geodesic equation in order to accurately compute the Earth's circumference, which were close to modern values of the Earth's circumference. His estimate of 6,339.9 km for the Earth radius was only 16.8 km less than the modern value of 6,356.7 km. In contrast to his predecessors who measured the Earth's circumference by sighting the Sun simultaneously from two different locations, al-Biruni developed a new method of using trigonometric calculations based on the angle between a plain and mountain top which yielded more accurate measurements of the Earth's circumference and made it possible for it to be measured by a single person from a single location. By the age of 22, al-Biruni had written several short works, including a study of map projections, *Cartography*, which included a method for projecting a hemisphere on a plane.

John J. O'Connor and Edmund F. Robertson write in the *MacTutor History of Mathematics archive*:

"Important contributions to geodesy and geography were also made by al-Biruni. He introduced techniques to measure the earth and distances on it using triangulation. He found the radius of the earth to be 6339.6 km, a value not obtained in the West until the 16th century. His *Masudic canon* contains a table giving the coordinates of six hundred places, almost all of which he had direct knowledge."

The Arab geographer Al-Idrisi's Mappa Mundi incorporated the knowledge of Africa, the Indian Ocean and the Far East gathered by Arab merchants and explorers with the information inherited from the classical geographers to create one of the most accurate maps of the world to date. The Tabula Rogeriana was drawn by Al-Idrisi in 1154 for the Norman King Roger II of Sicily, after a stay of eighteen years at his court, where he worked on the commentaries and illustrations of the map. The map, written in Arabic, shows the Eurasian continent in its entirety, but only shows the northern part of the African continent.

In the 14th century, Ibn Bammûmah, a Moroccan, began his travels. He started as a pilgrim to Mecca, but continued his journeys for the next 30 years, covering some 73,000 miles (117,000 km). Before returning home, he had visited most of the Muslim world and beyond, from Europe and southern Africa in the west to eastern Asia in the east. The universal use of Arabic in the Muslim world and his status as judge trained in law gave him access to royal courts at most locations he visited.

Ibn Battuta (1304–1368) was a traveller and explorer, whose account documents his travels and excursions over a period of almost thirty years, covering some 73,000 miles (117,000 km). These journeys covered most of the known Old World, extending from North Africa, West Africa, Southern Europe and Eastern Europe in the west, to the Middle East, Indian subcontinent, Central Asia, Southeast Asia and China in the east, a distance readily surpassing that of his predecessors and his near-contemporary Marco Polo.

Medieval Europe

During the Early Middle Ages, geographical knowledge in Europe regressed (though it is a popular misconception that they thought the world was flat), and the simple T and O map became the standard depiction of the world.

The trips of Venetian explorer Marco Polo in the 13th century, the Christian Crusades of the 12th and 13th centuries, and the Portuguese and Spanish voyages of exploration during the 15th and 16th centuries opened up new horizons and stimulated geographic writings. The Mongols also learned much about the geography of Asia. During the 15th century, Henry the Navigator of Portugal supported explorations of the African coast and became a leader in the promotion of geographic studies. Among the most notable accounts of voyages and discoveries published during the 16th century were those by Giambattista Ramusio in Venice, by Richard Hakluyt in England, and by Theodore de Bry in what is now Belgium.

Early Modern Period

Following the journeys of Marco Polo, interest in geography spread throughout Europe. From around *circa* 1400, the writings of Ptolemy and his Islamic successors provided a systematic framework to tie together and portray geographical information. The great voyages of exploration in 16th and 17th centuries revived a desire for both accurate geographic detail, and more solid theoretical foundations. The *Geographia Generalis* by Bernhardus Varenius and Gerardus Mercator's world map are prime examples of the new breed of scientific geography.

The Muslim Ottoman cartographer Piri Reis drawn navigational maps in his *Kitab-ý Bahriye*. The work includes an atlas of charts for small segments of the Mediterranean, accompanied by sailing instructions covering the sea. In the second version of the work, he included a map of the Americas. The Piri Reis map drawn by the Ottoman cartographer Piri Reis in 1513 is an early surviving map to show the Americas.

19TH CENTURY

By the 18th century, geography had become recognized as a discrete discipline and became part of a typical university curriculum in Europe (especially Paris and Berlin), although not in the United Kingdom where geography was generally taught as a sub-discipline of other subjects.

One of the great works of this time was *Kosmos: a sketch of a physical description of the Universe*, by Alexander von Humboldt, the first volume of which was published in German in 1845. Such was the power of this work that Dr Mary Somerville, of Cambridge University intended to scrap publication of her own *Physical Geography* on reading *Kosmos*. Von Humboldt himself persuaded her to publish (after the publisher sent him a copy).

In 1877, Thomas Henry Huxley published his Physiography with the philosophy of universality presented as an integrated approach in the study of the natural environment. The philosophy of universality in geography was not a new one but can be seen as evolving from the works of Alexander von Humboldt and Immanuel Kant.

The publication of Huxley physiography presented a new form of geography that analysed and classified cause and effect at the micro-level and then applied these to the macro-scale (due to the view that the micro was part of the macro and thus an understanding of all the micro-scales was need to understand the macro level). This approach emphasized the empirical collection of data over the theoretical. The same approach was also used by Halford John Mackinder in 1887. However, the integration of the Geosphere, Atmosphere and Biosphere under physiography was soon over taken by Davisian geomorphology.

Over the past two centuries the quantity of knowledge and the number of tools has exploded. There are strong links between geography and the sciences of geology and botany, as well as economics, sociology and demographics.

The Royal Geographical Society was founded in England in 1830, although the United Kingdom did not get its first full Chair of geography until 1917. The first real geographical intellect to emerge in United Kingdom geography was Halford John Mackinder, appointed reader at Oxford University in 1887. The National Geographic Society was founded in the USA in 1888 and began publication of the *National Geographic* magazine which became and continues to be a great popularizer of geographic information. The society has long supported geographic research and education.

20TH CENTURY

In the West during the second half of the 19th and the 20th century, the discipline of geography went through four major phases: environmental determinism, regional geography, the quantitative revolution, and critical geography.

Environmental Determinism

Environmental determinism is the theory that a people's physical, mental and moral habits are directly due to the influence of their natural environment. Prominent environmental determinists included Carl Ritter, Ellen Churchill Semple, and Ellsworth Huntington.

Popular hypotheses included "heat makes inhabitants of the tropics lazy" and "frequent changes in barometric pressure make inhabitants of temperate latitudes more intellectually agile." Environmental determinist geographers attempted to make the study of such influences scientific.

Around the 1930s, this school of thought was widely repudiated as lacking any basis and being prone to (often bigoted) generalizations. Environmental determinism remains an embarrassment to many contemporary geographers, and leads to skepticism among many of them of claims of environmental influence on culture (such as the theories of Jared Diamond).

Regional Geography

Regional geography was coined by a group of geographers known as possibilists and represented a reaffirmation that the proper topic of geography was study of places (regions). Regional geographers focused on the collection of descriptive information about places, as well as the proper methods for dividing the earth up into regions.

Well-known names from these period are Alfred Hettner in Germany and Paul Vidal de la Blache in France. The philosophical basis of this field in United States was laid out by Richard Hartshorne, who defined geography as a study of areal differentiation, which later led to criticism of this approach as overly descriptive and unscientific.

The Quantitative Revolution

The quantitative revolution in geography began in the 1950s. Geographers formulated geographical theories and subjected the theories to empirical tests, usually using statistical methods (especially hypothesis testing). This quantitative revolution laid the groundwork for the development of geographic information systems. Well-known geographers from this period are Fred K. Schaefer, Waldo Tobler, William Garrison, Peter Haggett, Richard J. Chorley, William Bunge, and Torsten Hägerstrand.

Critical Geography

Though positivist approaches remain important in geography, critical geography arose as a critique of positivism. The first strain of critical geography to emerge was humanistic geography. Drawing on the philosophies of existentialism and phenomenology, humanistic geographers (such as Yi-Fu Tuan) focused on people's sense of, and relationship with, places. More influential was Marxist geography, which applied the social theories of Karl Marx and his followers to geographic phenomena. David Harvey and Richard Peet are well-known Marxist geographers. Feminist geography is, as the name suggests, the use of ideas from feminism in geographic contexts. The most recent strain of critical geography is postmodernist geography, which employs the ideas of postmodernist and poststructuralist theorists to explore the social construction of spatial relations.

Existentialism and Existential Geography

Existential geography refers to a range of geographic approaches that insist human experience, awareness, and meaning must be incorporated into any study of peoples' relationships with space, place, and environment. Existential geography is most closely related to the larger movement of humanistic geography, which arose in the 1970s as a critical response to positivist research that, at the time, dominated the discipline. In emphasizing the conceptual and applied need for understanding the lived relationship between people and their geographical worlds, humanistic geographers argued that positivist geography reduced environmental and place experience and meaning to tangible, measurable, quantitative units and relationships expressed spatially and materially—for example, symbols on maps, points on graphs, physical linkages in flow diagrams, or figures in equations.

Today the term "existential geography" is rarely used because the point of view and subject matter are subsumed in different ways by more specific topical and conceptual labels that include phenomenological geography, phenomenological ecology, environmental hermeneutics, ecopsychology, environmental philosophy, and place studies. Geographers of postmodernist, poststructuralist, and critical-theory persuasions claim that their approaches reinterpret, improve upon, and supplant earlier existential-geographical work, though geographers and other environmental researchers who continue to work in the existential tradition strongly disagree.

EXISTENTIALISM AND PHENOMENOLOGY

Philosophically, existential geography is most closely related to the continental traditions of existentialism and phenomenology. Associated especially with 20th-century philosophers Jean-Paul Sartre, Simone de Beauvoir, Albert Camus, Karl Jaspers, Martin Buber, and Gabriel Marcel, existentialism is a way of philosophy that works to understand the basic structures of human existence so that individuals can create useful meaning in their lives through free and informed action. Existentialism insists that philosophy must arise from a person's own life and from his or her own particular individual, historical, and societal situation. "Existence precedes essence," proclaimed Sartre, meaning that human beings experience their world first and only then endow it with self-conscious meaning, whether personal, cultural, ideological, or scholarly.

Existentialists claim that earlier Western philosophy was too much concerned with reason, ideas, and abstract theory. Instead, philosophy must start with one's own experience and personal understanding, which can be studied, clarified, and thus enriched. Reason can contribute to this effort, but all other aspects of human being—e.g., bodily, sensual, sexual, emotional, interpersonal, cultural, societal, and transpersonal dimensions—must also be considered and given a place. The philosophical tradition of phenomenology became important to some existentialists because it offered a practical method for probing and understanding the nature and quality of human existence, though this was not the original aim of phenomenology's founder, philosopher Edmund Husserl, who instead had developed the phenomenological method as a means to identify invariant structures of cognitive consciousness.

Because Husserl viewed consciousness and its essential structures as a pure "region" separate from the flux of specific experiences and thoughts, his style of phenomenology came to be known as "constitutive" or "transcendental." Eventually, however, other phenomenological philosophers such as Martin Heidegger and Maurice Merleau-Ponty reacted against Husserl's transcendental structures of consciousness. These "existential phenomenologists," as they came to be called, argued that such transcendental structures are questionable because Husserl based their reality on speculative, cerebral reflection rather than on actual human experience taking place within the world of everyday life.

In 1927 in his *Being and Time*, Heidegger argued that consciousness was not separate from the world and human existence. He called for an existential correction to Husserl that would interpret essential structures as basic categories of human experience rather than as pure, cerebral consciousness. In 1945 in his *Phenomenology of Perception*, Maurice Merleau-Ponty broadened Heidegger's correction to include the active role of the body in human experience. Merleau-Ponty sought to reinterpret the division between body and mind common in traditional Western philosophy and psychology. This "existential turn" of Heidegger and Merleau-Ponty shifted away from Husserl's focus on pure intellectual consciousness and toward a reflexive understanding of everyday human life and its lived meanings.

CENTRAL EXISTENTIAL CLAIMS

As the preceding account suggests, there are great range and variation in the approaches and conclusions of existential and phenomenological philosophers. Both Camus and Heidegger, for example, repudiated the "existentialist" label, while Sartre would eventually attempt to reconcile his existentialism with Marxism. These contrasting understandings of existentialism have led to different uses and points of view on the part of geographers claiming some degree of existential perspective in their work, thus, for example, Tim Cresswell, in his 2004 *Place: A Short Introduction,* finds a continuation of earlier existential perspectives in current poststructural and postmodernist geographies, while Stuart Elden, in his 2001 *Mapping the Present,* argues that Heidegger's philosophy played a major role in the historical theories of critical theorist Michel Foucault, particularly his understanding of what Elden calls "spatial history."

In spite of the wide range of ways in which existentialism has been interpreted—both by its original founders and by geographers later drawing on the tradition—one can identify several conceptual claims that mark out a certain amount of common ground. These claims have been central for many (but not all) geographers seeking to make use of existential principles.

1. To study human beings existentially is to study human experiences, meanings, actions, situations, and events as they happen spontaneously in the course of daily life. On one hand, the world in which we find ourselves is inexhaustible and much more than each of us as unique individuals can ever experience or know. On the other hand, existentially, the world is only what each of us uniquely experiences and understands it to be.
2. There is no world "beneath" or "beyond" the world of our primordial lived experience, which is always and already before us as the world for which we have no choice but to have. Through knowledge, effort, and will, a person or group may over time have some possibility to change the constitution and tenor of their world, but in any particular moment of experience, our world is as it is; it cannot be otherwise.
3. Human awareness and consciousness are always intentional—i.e., necessarily oriented toward and finding their significance in a world of emergent meaning. We are never just aware but always aware of something, whether an object, living thing, idea, or the like. This always-present quality of intentionality is an invariant feature of human existence and demonstrates that human experience, action, and meaning always unfold in relation to the world in which we find ourselves.
4. This intentional relationship with the world means that person and world are not separate and two but indivisible and one. Human beings are inescapably immersed and enmeshed in their world—what Merleau-Ponty called "body-subject" and Heidegger called "*Dasein*," or "being-in-the-world." Because of this lived reciprocity between self and world, one cannot assign specific phenomena to either self or world alone. Everything experienced is "given" but also "interpreted," is "of the world" but also "of the person."
5. This lived reciprocity means that each person's existence gives meaning to his or her world, which in turn gives meaning to that person's existence as it emerges both for himself or herself and for others. This lived reciprocity also means that traditional philosophical dualities—

e.g., self-world, subject-object, body-mind, perception-cognition, thinking-feeling, personal-transpersonal, people-environment, individual-society, nature-culture, and so forth—must be called into question, revisioned, and rephrased through existential-phenomenological explication. One of the most difficult challenges is to describe the lived reciprocity of person and world in language and conception that do not fall prey to traditional philosophical dichotomies.

6. The everyday structure through which this lived reciprocity unfolds is the lifeworld—a person or group's day-to-day world of taken-for-grantedness that is normally unnoticed and therefore concealed as a phenomenon. One aim of existential study is to disclose and describe the various lived structures and dynamics of the lifeworld, a focus that has become central to existential-geographical research.
7. There are three dimensions of lifeworld that all must be considered in a thorough existential-phenomenological understanding of human existence, experience, and meaning: (a) a person or group's unique personal situation—e.g., one's gender, sexuality, physical and intellectual endowments, degree of ableness, personal likes and dislikes; (b) a person or group's unique social, cultural, and historical situation—e.g., the time and place in which one lives, economic and political circumstances, religious and societal background, technological infrastructure; (c), a person or group's situation as it involves their being typical human beings sustaining and sustained by a typical human world—e.g., the lived fact that we are bodily beings who are always and already "emplaced" physically in our world.

EXISTENTIAL PERSPECTIVES IN GEOGRAPHY

Foreshadowed by the humanist work of earlier geographers such as Johannes Granö, J. K. Wright, Clarence Glacken, and David Lowenthal, the existential tradition was initiated in the early 1970s largely by three geographers: Edward Relph, Yi-Fu Tuan, and Anne Buttimer. The first explicit discussion of the value that an existential approach might have for geography was in a 1970 *Canadian Geographer* article by Relph, who drew on the insights of existential phenomenology and emphasized that all knowledge arises from the world of experience, including peoples' everyday understanding of their geographical world. In his popular 1974 *Topophilia*, Tuan examined the positive, affective bond between people and place, while Buttimer, in a 1976 article in the *Annals of the Association of American Geographers*, considered how the phenomenological notion of lifeworld might offer insights into sense of place, social space, and time-space rhythms.

The most influential study in this early work was Relph's 1976 *Place and Placelessness,* an existential phenomenology of place, which he defined as a fusion of human and natural order and any significance spatial centre of a person or group's lived experience. The existential crux of place experience, Relph claimed, was insideness—the degree to which a person or group belong to and identify themselves with a place. Relph argued that the existential relationship between insideness and its experiential opposite outsideness is a fundamental dialectic in human experience. Through different degrees of insidenss and outsideness, different places take on different meanings and identities for different individuals and groups. For Relph, "existential insideness" is the foundation of the place concept because, in this mode of experience, place is experienced without any directed or self-conscious attention yet is laden with significances that are tacit and unnoticed unless the place is changed in some way—for example, one's home and community are destroyed by natural disaster.

The first comprehensive work to demonstrate the considerable topical range that existential approaches could offer geography was David Ley and Marwyn Samuels' 1978 *Humanistic Geography: Problems and Prospects,* an edited collection that included Samuels' chapter, "Existentialism and Human Geography." In this and later work, Samuels drew on Martin Buber's ideas regarding the significance of spatiality in human life to call for geographical research on what he called a "biography of landscape"—the lived foundations of geographical and spatial patterns, interconnections, and attachments. In practice, conceptual and applied efforts to identify and explore such "existential origins" continued to be conducted by geographers and other environmental researchers drawing on the perspective of existential phenomenology.

Major Themes in Existential Geography

Since the 1970s, partly through the conceptual foundations established by Buttimer, Ley, Relph, Samuels, and Tuan, existential work examining human beings' lived relationship with the geographical world has steadily continued, though overshadowed in the last two decades by the more vocal efforts of postmodernist, poststructural, and critical geographies. Most broadly, the aim of current existential-phenomenological work is to understand how qualities of the geographical world like place, home, journey, mobility, habitual embodiment, natural landscape, and so forth found and contribute to human existence, both broadly, in relation to human nature generally; and, specifically, for persons and groups living in particular places, cultural contexts, and historical moments. Three themes are highlighted here to exemplify this work: (1) lived body; (2) place; and (3) a lived environmental ethic.

1. Research on the lived body examines ways in which our existence as bodily beings contributes to our lived geographies. The fact that we are solid, upright bodies gives a sense of immediate centeredness to space and—in conjunction with upright posture and binocular vision—orients us within a sixfold directional axis of up-down, front-back, and left-right. We experience the world largely through the five senses, and existential-phenomenological research has studied how each sense offers a different but complementary way of knowing the world. Existential-phenomenological studies of the lived body have also examined specific environmental experiences of particular individuals or groups, thus Jonathan Cole and Kay Toombs explored how less-abled persons' loss of mobility leads to a changed interaction with the surrounding physical and human world, while sociologist Chris Allen examined the bodily encounters and resulting social geography of visually-impaired children.

   Beyond bodily structure and process, there is research on the pre-reflective but learned intentionality of the body, which Merleau-Ponty termed body-subject—the pre-conscious intelligence of body manifested through action. For geography, one of the most significant aspects of body-subject is its automatic, taken-for-granted ability to work in extended ways over time and space. One can ask how routine behaviors of individuals coming together regularly in space can transform that space into a place with a regular dynamic and character. David Seamon has explored how such "place ballets" can be established and sustained through environmental design and policy.

2. The theme of place has been a central focus in existential-phenomenological work since the seminal studies of Buttimer, Tuan, and Relph highlighted above. In philosophy, Edward Casey, Jeff Malpas, and Robert Mugerauer have written book-length accounts arguing for place as a central ontological structure founding human experience. As Casey wrote in his 1993 *Getting Back into Place*), "place, by virtue of its unencompassability by anything other than itself, is at once the limit and the condition of all that exists... To be is to be in place" (pp. 15-16).

   Much of this place research has focused on particular groups' lived relationships with particular places; one early example was David Ley's study of African-American neighborhoods in inner-city Philadelphia presented in his 1974 *The Black Inner City as Frontier Outpost*. More recent efforts include Ray Oldenberg's 1989 *The Great Good Place*, which highlights "third places"—public or semi-public establishments where people informally gather and socialize; Mindy Fullilove's 2004 *Root Shock*, a study of the traumatic impact that urban renewal had on African-American neighborhoods in several American cities; and Douglas Rae's 2003 *City*, an examination of traditional American urbanism grounded in lively streets and place-based community, using the city of New Haven, Connecticut, as a study focus.

3. Research involving a lived environmental ethic considers ways whereby people might become more sensitive to and involved with the natural world so that their wish

and will to care for the environment becomes stronger and more durable. Mugerauer, Relph, and philosopher Ingrid Stefanovic have all drawn on Heideggerian thinking to suggest possible ways whereby people might better care for the natural world. In his 1981 *Rational Landscapes and Humanistic Geography*, for example, Relph developed the concept of environmental humility—a way of seeing and understanding that is responsive to the best qualities of the Other and that might foster a compassion and gentle caretaking for places, people, and the things of nature. In a related way, Stefanovic drew on Heidegger's understanding of place and emplacement as means to reconsider the nature of environmental and economic sustainability.

CRITICISMS OF EXISTENTIAL GEOGRAPHY

With the development in the 1980s and 1990s of postmodernist, poststructural, and critical geographies, existential and humanistic geography has faced numerous conceptual and ideological criticisms that can most broadly be described by charges of: (1) essentialism; (2) authoritativeness; (3) voluntarism; and (4) an ideological bias toward bounded, static, exclusionary places.

As indicated by the writings of Buttimer, Relph, Samuels, and Tuan, early existential work in geography focused largely on human typicality with the result that critical and social-constructionist critics label existential studies as essentialist—i.e., presupposing and claiming an invariant and universal human condition only revealed when all "non-essentials" like culture, economics, or history are stripped away, leaving some inescapable core of human experience and existence. A second, related criticism, leveled especially by feminist geographers, is that the existential approach is authoritative in that it privileges the interpretive sensibilities of academic experts who arbitrarily claimed to provide an accurate depiction of the geographical situations and experiences of more ordinary human beings. This depiction, the feminist critique argues, is in fact grounded in an implicit masculinist point of view assuming that the experience of (mostly) academically trained men could represent all human situations—for example, the experiences of women, gays and lesbians, the less advantaged, particular racial and ethnic groups, and so forth.

As already pointed out, however, any thorough existential presentation of the geographical lifeworld requires that, in addition to human typicality, researchers must also recognize and examine the personal and cultural dimensions of particular environmental and place experiences; the already-cited work of Allen, Cole, Fullilove, Oldenburg, Rae, and Toombs are convincing examples of the conceptual and lived effectiveness of existential work dealing with specific individuals, groups, and places. Existential researchers claim that their people and place portrayals, grounded in the openness of phenomenological method, are more accurate and fair than social-constructivist or critical accounts that too often force fit their subjects through some pre-defined set of cultural, political, gender, or socioeconomic filters and thus end in lifeworld misrepresentation and distortion.

A third criticism of the existential approach is that it is voluntarist—i.e., that it tacitly views society and the world as a product of intentional, willed actions of individuals. This criticism arises from critical geographers, especially neo-Marxists and feminists, who give attention instead to the broader societal structures and power relations that underlie particular lifeworlds and places. As a way of philosophy that highlights self-awareness as a vehicle of personal and societal change, the existential perspective places greatest emphasis on individual freedom, understanding, and agency. On one hand, there is an underlying ideological assumption that individual will and personal growth provide the major means for making a difference in the larger world. On the other hand, an existential approach can examine power, exclusion, resistance, justice, political process and other central emphases of critical geographers, though little work has been done in this direction, perhaps because most existential thinkers instinctively favour an interest in experience, selfhood, and personal and group autonomy; one exception is political theorist Daniel Kemmis's 1990 *Community and the Politics of Place* and his 1995 *The Good City, the Good Life*, two books that explore how citizens' sense of responsibility for the place in which they live might facilitate a civilized politics.

A fourth criticism of the existential approach is that it portrays lifeworlds and places as bounded, static, exclusionary, and reactionary; that place, insideness, dwelling, and rootedness are ethically favored over non-place, outsideness, journey, and mobile, shifting modes of life and styles of identity. This criticism has been brought forward by poststructuralists, who emphasize relativist, shifting meanings and distrust any kind of permanent conceptual or lived structures. Existential thinkers respond that these poststructuralists misread existential conclusions and that, throughout existential-geographical work, there is a flexibility of conceptual expression—a recognition that an excess of place can lead to a provincialism and callousness just as an excess of journey can lead to a loss of identity or an impartial relativity that allows for commitment to nothing. One central question that thinkers like Kemmis, Oldenburg, and Seamon address is whether, through design and policy, progressive, connected places can be made that draw together human diversity through everyday environmental co-presence and co-awareness—e.g., the potential that a small-grained, permeable pathway system has for bringing people of difference together in city districts through informal, serendipitous sidewalk and street encounters.

Poststructuralist critics are also concerned that existential work too often seems a nostalgic paean to pre-modern times and places. How can authentic places, at-homeness, and dwelling exist in a postmodern era of human diversity, rapid technological change, globalization, and geographical and social mobility? This criticism, however, ignores a central conclusion of existential thinkers like Relph, Casey, Malpas, Mugerauer, and Stefanovic: that regardless of the particular cultural, technological, or historical situation, people will always need place because having and identifying with place are integral to what and who we are as human beings.

From this perspective, the postmodernist and poststructuralist devaluation of place as it supports individual and group identity and solidarity is questionable existentially and potentially devastating practically. Instead, the crucial theoretical and real-world question is how a conceptual and applied understanding of place might lead to the making of actual places that draw together diverse individuals and groups through a shared sense of environmental involvement and attachment. In our mobile, ever-changing, globally-dominated world, one of the few real-world ways to accommodate a pluralistic society may be the power of place to gather human differences together spatially and thereby sustain the autonomy of individuals and groups as, at the same time, they feel a sense of belonging and commitment to the larger place of which they are a part.

EXISTENTIAL GEOGRAPHIC THEORIES

Existential Phenomenology

It is possible to decribe a human being in terms of anatomy. However, it is highly improbable that anyone asked to describe oneself would give such an account. This is analogical to the description of a place. Instead of a merely physical account one has to try to understand the place in question. This has traditionally been the task of humanistic geography. In geography, humanism can be seen as sensibility to human feelings in geographical settings. The theoretical base for this is often said to be 'existential phenomenology', understood as a combination of the theories of phenomenology and existentialism.

Neither phenomenology nor existentialism is a simple set of axioms nor are they easy to describe. The paradigmatic thinker of phenomenology is Edmund Husserl (1859-1938), and that of existentialism Jean-Paul Sartre (1905-1980). Classification of some other thinkers like Martin Heidegger (1889-1976), or Maurice Merleau-Ponty (1908-1961) under these two labels is not easy. They all used the concept of 'phenomenology' in their writings—and so did Sartre—but they changed the emphasis of their study from the strictly epistemological stance of Husserl towards understanding the human life-world. This makes them existentialist, too, at least in some respects.

The original slogan of phenomenology is 'Back to things themselves!' It was a critique of academic philosophy, especially neo-Kantianism, and a chance to finish mere analyzing of concepts but to make a fresh philosophy of things. The major question dividing the stances of Husserl and Heidegger, according to Jean-Luc Marion (1998: 2), is whether the 'return to things' means returning to their objectivity, or to their Being. The first leads to epistemological cogitations, while the latter leads to more existential settings. Geographers have usually found the latter one more fruitful for their studies.

Entrikin (1976: 623) defines 'existential phenomenology' as a 'combination of the phenomenological method with the importance of understanding man in his existential world'. In philosophy the same concept is used to refer to the modes of existentialism that have phenomenological foundations—e.g. philosophies of Sartre, Heidegger, and Merleau-Ponty—and to separate them from the modes of phenomenology that do not have the same foundations, namely the philosophies of Søren Kierkegaard and Friedrich Nietzsche.

Pauli Tapani Karjalainen (1986: 55) compares the 'positivistic' and 'existential' spheres of geography saying that while the first one is practical—or ontic—the latter one is ontological. The existential is therefore the foundational level on which the practical level is based. He says that 'existential understanding is ontologically directed', and means that human beings are the foundation of environmental relations in the empirical world. On the other hand, ontology is not necessary existential. Any ontological system without a viewpoint, however, is irrelevant in geography—as pointed out by Barry Smith and David M. Mark (1998). They insist that topological and mereological means, while adequate in the 'table-top world', are not sufficient in describing the ontology of geographic kinds. What they propose instead is, however, a set of 'special mereotopological theories that depart in crucial ways from standard topology'.

Yi-Fu Tuan (1975: 152) proposes that experientally place is a continuum between locations in abstract spatial systems and centers of strong visceral meanings. As both extremes are rare or nearly non-existent, most of our place experiences lie somewhere in the middle range. The difference between ontologies proposed by Karjalainen (1986) and Smith and Mark (1998) is that they pick up different things of the world. Their fundamentality is an open question but for practical needs it seems to be sufficient to choose one that picks up the kinds needed in the study under consideration. The purpose of Smith and Mark is, for instance, to develop ontological tools for geographic information systems (GIS), a goal that differs in great extent from understanding human being in a lived world.

Augustin Berque (1998: 442), on the other hand, compares the subjective and thc objective in human milieu. He says that there is a difference between them in the system of logic. Physically, all things are as they are and follow the logic of subject. But they exist only through symbolic systems and techniques of humanity that follow the logic of predicat. The first is the classical Western system of logic where P cannot be not-P, and the latter is more a metaphoric logical system dealing with the process of P coming not-P. These two systems of logic are not contradictory, however. They just look at the world from different points of view.

INSIDENESS AND OUTSIDENESS

First part of the visit to a place is the arrival. No one, however, comes to a place without some expectations about it. Christian Norberg-Schulz (1997: 41) writes that arriving to a foreign city has sense only if the place has its own identity. Before arriving one travels through a landscape, and the city has to fit to the expectations which this landscape raises. According to him, city as a work of art should be consistent with its natural surroundings to 'take its place' and meet the expectations of a traveller.

It is not only the environing landscape that raises the expectations of a visitor. People do not just end up in a place but they usually have an intention to go there. In the case of tourists this intention is constructed by magazines, television, travel brochures, photos and stories of friends and relatives. As John Urry notes, this creates anticipation towards the place. Urry has developed the concept 'tourist gaze' to describe the manner how tourists do experience places. He points out that this gaze is socially organised and systematised as is the gaze of a medic, an example of Michel Foucault.

Urry says that tourists are in a way semioticians. They are looking for particular signs in the landscape, like typical English villages, typical American skyscrapers, or typical French castles. The professionals that operate in the tourist business develop different elements in places towards these anticipations. This way a standard experience of a place is produced. Tourism is a kind of game, and all the participants know its rules. The game stays in order because—according to Urry—tourists are not even seeking for authentic experiences but ones that are different from those which they encounter in their everyday life (Urry 1990: 3, 11-12).

Tourist has a home somewhere else, and in that way does not belong to the place where visiting. Tourist is an outsider. On the other hand, being *in* place tourist is also an insider. In Edward Relph's terminology tourist could be a behavioural insider. *Behavioural insideness* means that one knows when being in the place where one is. Behavioural insider makes observations about the place and the activities occuring there.

Besides tourists there exist also travellers. 'Travelling' is derived from French term *travail* which means work. Distinction to leisure-seeking tourism is evident: travelling takes an effort. The more individual character of travelling is marked also by Urry (1990: 3). The distinction between a tourist and a traveller, however, is not that sharp. One can be one day in one place a tourist, and another day, or in another place, a traveller. What is different is the mode of insideness. A traveller can perhaps achieve what Relph calls *empathetic insideness*. There is no sharp distinction between behavioural and empathetic insideness but the latter needs more effort to be achieved. It demands willingness to be open to the significancies of the place and to feel it.

One can also be an outsider in a place. If one experiences place just as a background for events one is an incidental outsider. *Incidental outsideness* is in essence an unselfconscious attitude which according to Relph is typical to people who identify themselves rather to some international or otherwise not place-bound community. Also a businessman who perhaps is an insider in some place may find cities where conferences or business meetings are held irrelevant.

Existential outsideness involves uninvolvement. It is alienation from people and places—according to Relph from all places: existential outsider is not at home anywhere. Relph does not explain why a sense of existential outsideness could not be local, i.e. exist only towards some places. It is anyhow different from *objective outsideness* which is the viewpoint of a naturalistic scientist. Objective outsider is a detached observer that comprehends places as 'things having certain attributes'. These attributes are then explained with the help of some locational theory.

Relph insists, however, that it is possible to become an insider without even visiting the place. *Vicarious insideness* is mode that can be achieved with means of art. It is one purpose of an artist or a poet 'to convey something of what it is to live there, to give a sense of that place'. On the contrary, *existential insideness* is possible only for people who live in that place since it involves deep and complete identity with the place. Existential insider feels belonging to place.

Hence, the conceptual division to an insider and an outsider is not the same as the division to a visitor and an inhabitant. Yet the fact that there are some modes of insideness that are unachievable to either one of them shows that the question of insideness and outsideness is not irrelevant in this context. In general, it could be said that visitor's place experiences tend to be more detached and more visual compared to the ones of an inhabitant. But to say that a visitor is an outsider, and an inhabitant an insider would be an oversimplification of the subject.

TO BE IN PLACE

'To be a human being means to be on the earth as a mortal. It means to dwell'. Therefore, dwelling is the way how one is on the earth. Heidegger (1971: 145) says that dwelling is attained only by means of building. It does not mean only the building of dwelling houses but all building. Everything that one builds is built to sustain one's dwelling.

Heidegger's way to approach place underwent a notable change during his philosophical career. In his early philosophy he referred to place only in other contexts like 'work world', or 'politics'. In the middle period of his career he took a less instrumental interpretation of place but gave to it and to other related terms like 'region' a more central position only in his later period. Even then, however, he did not give it such a fundamental role in his ontology like the one given for instance by Archytas. He reaches it indirectly.

One of the central themes in Heidegger's philosophy is 'to-be-in'. To-be-in is to belong to one's environment; or in other words, to be interested in the beings of one's surroundings. In his later work he uses a more concrete word—'dwelling' (*Wohnen*)—for the same subject. Dwelling for Heidegger is a kind of poetry. It is due to the worldliness of humans that we are able to encounter things, and the poetry of encountering them is a concrete and non-theoretical way of understanding reached by subordinating oneself to the Being.

Heidegger exemplifies the relationship of human and one's environment by studying the way one deals with surrounding entities in one's everyday life. The kind of dealing that is closest to humans has its own kind of knowledge about the entities concerned. It is not theoretical knowledge but phenomenological. Knowing about entities that get used or produced is knowing about their Being. The ontological mode of Being of these close entities—or equipments—is *readiness-to-hand*. There is another mode of Being, too, i.e. *present-at-hand*. However, as David E. Cooper (1999: 59) notes, Heidegger does not mean that world contains two kinds of entity. Everything is proximally encountered as ready-to-hand.

Jean-Paul Sartre speaks about 'situation'. According to him, situation is an ambiguous phenomenon. It is a necessary condition of human liberty since one is never free but in a situation. On the other hand, however, situation never exists without human liberty. Therefore, human beings are always necessarily free and necessarily in a situation. Sartre mentions various manners in which situation becomes manifest. These are *my place, my body, my past, my position*, and *my relation to other human beings*.

John O'Neill brings out an analogy between Sartre's 'situation' and an act of a theatre play. This means that it is not only placial but also a temporal phenomenon. Events in a situation have an intentional history, and this is what makes them meaningful. This is opposed to what O'Neill calls 'Humean history' being just a causal chain of events. On the other hand, as situation manifests itself in 'place' (*place*), Sartre (1943: 538) insists that one never simply *is* in place. Place either helps or prevents one to achieve one's aims. To be in place is thus to be far from, or near to.

What Sartre adds to the equipmental readiness-to-hand of Heidegger is the negativity as a property of situations. For instance, if one goes to a café in order to meet a friend there but the friend is not there, his absence is a real property of that café. Like equipmental and sign-like characters that Heidegger attributes to things, negativity is a profoundly human aspect of the world. Since they are also all essential aspects of the world, it means that the world is fundamentally human.

Edmunds V. Bunkse (1990: 103) criticizes Heidegger's stance as abstract and disembodied. Therefore he does not find it suitable for any practical purposes. According to him, this kind of detachedness does not serve as a theoretical foundation for humanistic geography. What he argues instead is that geographical thinking should be part of broader speculations about the world around us. This was, he says, the situation in the 19th century—especially in the work of Alexander von Humboldt.

Louise Sundararajan (1997) has a similar argument against Heidegger's concept of 'dwelling'. She says that in the framework of Heidegger, 'poetry has superseded the body as our vital connection to the earth'. Sundararajan argues that marginalisation of nature in this way leads to disembodied view of dwelling. What she proposes instead is a habitat theory that expands the Heideggerian concept and makes it part of a continuum that connects human world with nature.

Bunkse's plea for a mode of humanism that was associated with geographical thinking before it was institutionalised into a distinct discipline ressembles, however, Heidegger's seeking of the original character of Being in the ancient writings of the Greek philosophers. What Bunkse calls 'particularity' is a serious challenge for humanistically oriented geography.

MAPPING LIVED ENVIRONMENT

People make places. By modifying ones environment one creates a place—a significant part of space. According to Heidegger (1971: 152-155), spaces receive their being from places. Heidegger's example is a bridge. A bridge constructed over a stream gathers the earth and landscape around it. Therefore, it constitutes a place. On the other hand, place is connected to other places through space, and it is through these places that space becomes into existence. This is what Anne

Stenros calls the topological character of places and spaces. Place is topological since like a bridge it always connects the elements around it. Space is topological, too, since it is a system of places. Space connects places.

Ingrid Leman Stefanovic (1998) tries to illuminate some essential aspects of the evolution of sense of place by beginning with Heidegger's concept of 'being-at-home'. She conducts a study of two distinct places which are Cavtat, an old town in Croatia, and Mississauga, a suburban development in Ontario. Stefanovic identifies six themes of both her places that she finds essential to the sense of place.

In both communities, themes of 'clear centre', 'privacy and enclosure' and 'reflection of time' arouse in one way or another. Having clear centre is certainly one of the most important aspects of placeness. Heidegger's example is a bridge but it can be a central square, a tower with with nodal location, or a combination of them that makes place.

The most significant place in one's world is one's home. It is 'our corner of the world'. This dialectic between home and the world is the elementary structure of human territoriality. Hence home is the place, and world is the limitless space around it.

Guy Di Méo (1991; 1998) introduces a method of sociospatial metastructure in order to study human territoriality. It is based on the hierarchy of different spatial concepts. The most basic ones of them are practiced and perceived spaces that together constitute 'life-space' (*espace de vie*). This combined with social space and the space of imagination and conceptualisation constitutes 'lived space'. The first one is the concrete everyday world while the latter one, according to Armand Frémont (1974/1999: 249) who has introduced the concept to geography, is the opposite of the space of alienation. It is a space where one belongs to: a region.

Sociospatial metastructure, on the hand, is the structural form of represented space (*espace représenté*). To form it one has to add the structural relations of places to lived space. These are, according to Di Méo (1991: 124, 127), economical, ideological, and politico-administrative relations. In addition, one has to take into account different spatial levels of sociospatial formation which are local, regional, and national.

The setting of Di Méo is close to that of Henri Lefebvre, and his theory on the 'production of space'. There are some categorical difficulties in this kind of theorising. For instance, as pointed out by Tim Unwin (2000: 22), there is a categorical difference between 'the production of space' and, for instance, 'the production of human misery'.

While concentrating on the first one draws attention to an intellectual conceptualisation, and therefore looses touch of the lived experience of humanity. Therefore this so-called critical theory lies outside the interests of this study.

If looking for 'an epistemological tool that would successfully mediate between art and science, lived and conceptual realities'—as Bunkse (1990: 98) does—Di Méo's sociospatial metastructure is not really an answer. It fails because it stays in those areas of the humanities that are close to social sciences, a failure of most humanistically oriented geography as pointed out by D.W. Meinig. What is needed instead is to go inside the humanities and do research on its own terms.

Di Méo approaches Bunkse's proposal by introducing the sociospatial metastructure of Marius Champailler, a wine farmer from central France. He presents a map where the lived space and the outlying objectified space of Champailler are shown. It begins with the individual experience of a wine farmer but is, however, interpreted with superimposed structural categories. This makes the initially existential approach to understand one's lived world to transform into a detached presentation of spatial attributes.

Detachedness is problem also in the *cognitive mapping* of in behaviourally oriented studies. In psychology, for instance, the phenomenon of 'place attachment' is often approached by studying different kind of 'actors' contributing to it. Setha M. Low and Irwin Altman (1992: 4) argue (but do not argumentate) that it is compatible with, for instance, phenomenological approaches. Taken the fundamental differences of phenomenological and psychological theories this seems highly implausible.

Mapping places is mapping things that have significance. Richard Dey (1995) says that 'a map's main attraction is what it leaves to the imagination, for the explorer to fill in'. But, on the contrary, how does one map imagination? Should that not be a concern of a geographer? John K. Wright writes about his summer place in Maine:

You geographers know nothing about it except what you could reasonably infer from your general familiarity with the region where it lies.

You might infer something about it's climate, and you could draw some conclusions as to what it is *not* [—]. If, therefore, *terra incognita* be conceived as an area within which no observed facts are on record in scientific litterature or on maps, the interior of my place in Maine, no less than the interior of Antarctica, is a *terra incognita* [—]. [H]ence, if there is no *terra incognita* today in an absolute sense, so also no *terra* is absolutely *cognita* (Wright 1947: 3-4, his italics).

Wright (1947: 15) concludes his paper with often-cited words: '[F]or, perhaps, the most fascinating *terrae incognitae* of all are those that lie within the minds and hearts of men.' To map these terrae incognitae one has to combine Di Méo's (1991; 1998) mapping of lived space to Saint-Exupéry's geography lesson: mapping of individual sensory as well as pragmatic and poetic encounters with one's environment.

TRADITION OF REGIONAL GEOGRAPHY

'[A]nyone who inspects the world around him is in some measure a geographer' (Lowenthal 1961: 242). Some modes of geographical thinking have been a necessary condition of human life since the beginning. The term 'geography' has been used since about 300 BC when scholars in Alexandria began to use it. Even earlier, descriptions of different places in the known world were given by various writers like Herodotus who lived in the Fifth Century BC.

Methodological guidelines for performing a geographical description were initially presented by Strabo in the First Century BC. He writes that 'since different places exhibit different good and bad attributes, [—] some that are due to nature; for they are permanent, whereas the adventitious attributes undergo changes.' He reminds one that the latter ones are also significant to the nature of place—sometimes even after they have persisted since they 'somehow possess a certain distinction and fame'.

The dualistic character of geography seeking balance between human and nature is thus apparent already in the work of Strabo. However, there was not much progress in the methodology of regional geography over the next two thousand years. In the Middle Ages, the progress of methodological work did not disappear but it flourished more in the Islamic world than in the Christian parts of Europe.

In the Renaissance mode of thought the particularity of 'place' was substituted by universal 'space', and the supremacy of space was even enforced in the 16th and 17th centuries. In the vein of such thinkers as Galilei, Newton, and Leibniz, places were seen merely as momentary subdivisions of neutral and homogenic space. There was no interest to develop tools for describing particular places, or regions. On the other hand, the discovery and exploration of new continents aroused practical need for undergoing those kinds of studies, anyhow.

Bernhard Varenius was the first one to divide geography into general and specific parts, i.e. into systematic and regional geography. His *Geographia Generalis* which was published in 1650 included three sections. These were absolute (terrestrial), relative (cosmic), and comparative sections. The last one is the specific section of his study. Varenius himself did not really appreciate the last section and explained that it was included only as a concession of earlier approaches to the subject. This is quite understandable, taken the scientific atmosphere of the period.

The foundations of modern institutionalised geography were laid in the 19th century. Two Prussian geographers—or cosmographers—have a central role in this development. Alexander von Humboldt (1769-1859) made large expeditions especially to South America. He wrote his main work *Cosmos* as a physical description of the world but insisted that all phenomena are to be studied in relation to other physical and human phenomena. His contemporain Carl Ritter (1779-1859) specified the scientific base of geography more carefully saying that all phenomena should be studied in the light of other analogical phenomena in the other regions. Both of them were professors of geography in the University of Berlin but, nevertheless, in their time, geography was not yet institutionalised as a sharp-edged discipline but was part of broader speculations about the world around us. Notable steps towards the humanistic tradition in geography were taken by Paul Vidal de la Blache (1845-1918) and his students in the late 19th and early 20th centuries. They introduced a *point de vue* to geography. This is what Vidal himself calls 'terrestrial unity'. It is described by the concept of 'milieu' which is the ensemble of co-existing heterogenical beings that interact reciprocically with each other. The epistemological stance of Vidal was later called 'possibilism' as contrasted to deterministic stance of environmentalists. Vidal himself, however, never used that term.

In Germany, Ewald Banse (1883-1953) declared that geography should be redefined as art. Real geography, according to him, is 'a spiritual presentation of experienced impressions'. His plea got no response, however. German geography of the first four decades of the 20th century was dominated on the other hand by neo-Kantian thinkers such as Alfred Hettner (1859-1941), who based his epistemology on Immanuel Kant's idea of nomothetic and idiographic sciences, and on the other hand by landscape (*Landschaft*) geographers such as Siegfried Passarge (1867-1958) who saw 'landscape' as a regional concept that unites physical and human geography. Banse had some connections with the latter school of thought. Some traces of enviromental determinism of the late 19th century were also remaining in the form of 'regional-geographical model' (*Länderkundliche Schema*) where 'region' was approached as a sequence of geological structure, surface morphology, climate, drainage, plant and animal geography, settlement, economy, and population.

German geographical thinking—especially that of Hettner—influenced greatly to the development of North American geography. Hettnerian influence is particulary strong in the works of Richard Hartshorne. His main work *The nature of geography*, published in 1939, is still one of the foundational texts in geographical epistemology. Hartshorne's emphasis on the objectivity of chorological study, however, made him introduce some positivistic elements to his epistemology. The manner how Hartshorne delineates chorological sciences—eg. geography, astronomy and geophysics—and chronological sciences—e.g. history and paleontology—apart from the systematic sciences is derived via Hettner from Kant.

By the 1950s geography was dominated by positivistic epistemology with its abstract spatialisations. A notable exception was Eric Dardel (1899-1967). He derived from the etymology of the word 'geography' that the world is a kind of text that has to be interpreted in terms of human condition. Dardel's thoughts received more attention in the 1970s when phenomenological philosophy was introduced to Anglo-American geography. The concept of 'region', however, was widely substituted by that of 'place'. This was largely due to the more fundamental ontological status of the latter. On the other hand, the basic idea of describing the particularity of the world was the same.

In the 1980s 'regional' came back to geography when the so-called 'new regional geography' was introduced. As one of its proponents Mary Beth Pudup (1988: 369) says, the aim of this new mode of regional studies was to utilise the conceptual framework of social sciences in geography. Regional variances are thus seen as local responses to general conditions, namely the capitalist mode of production. This is criticized for instance by Hans Holmén (1995: 51) by noting that it is basically the same kind of abstracting theory as those positivistic spatial models that it tries to challenge. According to Holmén, regional aspect is therefore lost.

Anne Gilbert (1988: 210, 222) notes that the French mode of new regional geography stresses more the importance of cultural aspects and the specificity of regions. R. Brunet *et alii* (1982: 27) say that Anglo-Saxon geography is more psychological, and approaches the lived space through the concept of 'perception'. Anyway, there is an underlying normative aspect in new regional geography: it is not just a scientific understanding of the spatio-temporal world but an instrument for action. What Gilbert (1988: 222) insists is that this normative argument has been always implicitly involved in regional geography but, nevertheless, she presents no argument to support this allegation.

If 'new regional geography' is the new paradigm of regional geography or just a side track in a long tradition is not yet possible to declare. However, if the fundamental idea of geography as earth-writing is taken seriously the main emphasis should be given to region, or place, itself. Whether new regional geography can do this is highly dubious. J.H. Paterson (1974: 4) says that 'regional geography' is 'work in which the purpose of the study is to clarify a specific situation in a particular locality'. This is a more traditional but not in any way outmoded stance to the subject. It is also the stance taken in this study.

9

Cultural and Historical Behavioural of Geography

It took a while before the proposed humanistic approach was adopted. Only in the beginning of the 1970s some geographers took the initiative; however in 1947 John K. Wright already introduced *geosophy*, defined as the study of geographical knowledge, based on all people (and not only geographers). Every person has a geographical knowledge at his disposal which in some way determines their actions and way of living. His paper could have started the behavioural geography early, but looking at how much it was referenced in later papers it had not much influence.

David Lowenthal published a more widely cited paper in 1961 with a similar idea as John K. Wright: people have their own limited personal world but the view of the whole world is similarly among many. As Lowenthal states 'we elect to see certain aspects of the world and to avoid others', this is the way how we personally see the world. One quote emphasizes his study to personal worlds and how an individual connects to local and global worlds: "The surface of the earth is shaped for each person by refraction through cultural and personal lenses of custom and fancy. We are all artists and landscape architects, creating order and organizing space, time and causality in accordance with our apperceptions and predilections".

- note: apperception = the view of something related to past experience
- note: predilection = preference to something.

A second paper by Kirk (original ideas in 1951, reiterated in 1963) mentions that the environment is not simply a thing but given meaning by humans. When the meaning is given, this is passed through generations. Therefore the environment can be seen as two separate but not independent parts: phenomenal (the earth's surface) and behavioural (human perception and interpretation of the phenomenal). Due to geography often being used as a decision making tool, this behavioural environment has to be taken into effect all the time. For example when said that 'Kaohsiung is an industrial city', it only reflects the view of people from outside.

These views of Wright and Kirk, including the paper by Lowenthal, were hardly referred by other researchers, as the three were not members of a major college in the early 1960s. Brookfield (1964) evaluated work by cultural geographers on other societies and found there is the concept of behavioural environments. Prince (1971) suggested that historical geographers should study 3 worlds: the real (recorded documents and landscape), the abstract (models related to the past) and the perceived (seen through people's eyes). "We must understand man and his cultures before we can understand landscapes".

ANTI-POSITIVISM, IDEALISM AND HISTORICAL GEOGRAPHY

From the early 1970s some cultural and historical geographers proposed to look wider at geography, not only taking measured values as scientific values and proof. Several humanistic approaches were proposed, focused on decision-makers and their perceived worlds. Harris (1971) considers geography being related to particular parts of phenomena and not with spatial relations. He links geography to history and states 'To understand an event is to appreciate why it took place (humanistic) vs. to explain an event is to predict it (positivist)'. Four points were created for the nature of history: 1) it concerns a specific event; 2) explanation may take the thoughts of individuals into account; 3) explanation may use general laws and 4) explanation relies heavily on the judgment of the researcher. This also accounts for geography, as temporal and spatial features are important parts of life and therefore the views on each should be similar.

Guelke (1971) extended Harris' view by mentioning that when geography is a lawapplying science, it can hardly find any results except a very strong generalization, as humans don't follow any laws (ie. humans are unpredictable). To use models and theories, a way of testing these to be valid should be found (which has not happened) and whenever a model or theory is developed, extra hypotheses are added to account for the differences. His offered alternative is an idealist method: 'the explanation of an action is complete when the goal and its understanding of the situation are discovered', 'one must discover what he believed, not why he believed it'. This is because the reasons for an action were already know to the being researched. Chappell (1976) argued that this view would omit any reference to environmental constraints and influences on that person's actions. These constraints were accepted by Guelke (1976) but this would deviate from the geographer's domain.

Hay (1979) also argued Guelke's view by mentioning his idealist method is based on the ideas 1) that all theory must be based on norms ('ideas thought to be correct') and optimal decision-making, 2) that to be scientific means following laws and 3) that prediction is the same as knowledge of the future. In simple words, Guelke should not ask 'does this theory explain Y' but 'does this theory contribute to an understanding of Y?'. Also, when considering groups as study projects instead of individuals, the idealist alternative doesn't see that group behaviour is different from the behavioural sum of the individuals, objective facts must influence behavioural outcomes (example: Columbus discovers America because it was there, not that Columbus thought that was Asia) and it ignores the possibility of unconscious or subconscious behaviour.

Guelke was prepared for the question how an idealist interpretation can be verified, as was argued that two researches towards the same thing might have different outcomes. He mentions that where data suggests that a previous theory is incorrect, a new hypothesis has to be formed. However, due to the complexity of human nature, mistakes will always be there. The idealist philosophy of Guelke (1981) states that mental activity can't be controlled and that all knowledge is ultimately based on the individual's experience of the world: their mental views. A 'real' world independently of the mind does not exist and this therefore criticizes the positivist spatial science because it believes in a 'real' world explained by general laws. It also criticizes behavioural geography due to the statement in behavioural geography that images exist that can be measured accurately which then have strong relationships with actual behaviour.

Curry (1982) stated that reasons humans find are not necessarily based on logic. The behaviour must be studied in its context and the idealist geographer should take this into account. Guelke (1982) agreed with this and found that historical reconstruction of thought is necessary in the understanding of why humans act like they do.

PHENOMENOLOGY AND RELATED APPROACHES

Human geographers were more attracted to phenomenology though. It is based on the idea that there's no objective world independent of human existence: 'all knowledge relates to experience'. Entrikin (1976) defines 'phenomenologists describe rather than explain'. The environment is unique to every individual and phenomenology is the study of how the individual gives meaning to the environment. A further approach might be finding the elements which determine the individual giving meaning. The phenomenology approach was introduced by Relph (1970) and followed by Yi-Fu Tuan (1971). Tuan looks at geography as a mirror: 'to know the world is to know oneself, just as careful analysis of a house reveals much about both the designer and occupant'. Another quote states that 'humanistic geography achieves an understanding of the human world by studying people's relations with nature, their geographical behaviour as well as their feelings and ideas in regard to space and place'. In many of Tuan's following publications (until 1979) he explains this view more through many examples. His autobiography (1999) states the reason why he was interested in this field; he wanted to figure out 'the meaning of existence, what are we doing here and what do we want out of life?'. He mentions 'inscapes', landscapes which have different meaning to different people.

In 2002 Tuan states that for surviving daily life geography is much more important than history. Although history teaches us what (not) to do, common tasks are mostly based on geography. It's easier to call animals geographers than historians. Mercer and Powell (1972) argued that land-use patterns can never be understood by just looking at them. Research methods should be developed which view a problem through the eyes of the people being researched. Buttimer (1974) states that an existentially aware geographer is more interested in encountering people and situations open-minded than using analytic methods to understand them. Prediction, except for the most routinized, is impossible.

Buttimer (1976) also introduced the 'lifeworld', a combination of the world of facts and human experiences. It rejects positivism as that separates the observer from the studied object (it doesn't take human experience into account), but idealism should also be rejected as it accepts the existence of a 'real world' outside human's consciousness. Phenomenology does include all of these and therefore is a better way in understanding geographical factors by stimulating human development but not forcing it. Walmsley (1974) accepted the cases mentioned by Buttimer but mentioned that the factual concepts shouldn't disappear completely. Gregory (1978) criticized both positivism and phenomenology. Social science has to be performed in the society and not on it, but for phenomenology it fails to recognize constraints laid on society. Therefore the idealism and phenomenology needs to incorporate these constraints ('Radical Geographies').

Both idealism and phenomenology however was more a talk about ideas of change than actually performing it in practice. Billinge (1977) wondered when it was performed in practice, if it would actually be considered science: 'we can justify our partially formulated hypothesis ... [and] cease worrying about the validity of our reconstruction and ... label the whole exercise phenomenological'. Pickles (1985) criticized that geographers who attempted to adopt the phenomenological approach actually misunderstood it in how to apply it. He mentions that the next step to be taken is to figure out how to apply it.

Phenomenology is closely associated with existentialism and some geographers have difficulty in separating the two. Phenomenology says that a person's consciousness associates meaning to objects while existentialism says that a person makes himself (aka in phenomenology the surroundings have influence). Samuel (1978) therefore saw that for every landscape there's someone who can be held responsible.

All of above suggest that humanistic geography is concerned with the study of individuals and their construction of plus behaviour in the environment or landscape analysis with respect to the meaning attached to it. It is therefore different from human geography which investigates behaviour and the everyday activities in an environment. It is based on the critiques of positivism, which makes large assumptions about nature and decision-making and seeks scientifically verifiable laws of human behaviour. It sees the humans as 'living, acting, thinking' individuals. Entrikin (1976) argues that humanistic geography doesn't offer any alternatives for scientific geography and therefore is only just a criticism.

Critics state that humanistic geography only focuses on the less important parts of applied geography and not with improving the world. Buttimer (1979) thinks this could be done by manipulating and managing individuals and their environments instead of improving the 'human becoming'. Relph (1981) this implies that geography should be used to plan everything in the most efficient way. This also decreases the specific characteristics and individuality of communities and places: a location should be uniform. Humanistic geography is compared to this statement a reaction to preserve communities' and places' individuality. The treatment of a landscape should be seen by individuals as encouragements of what they are and how they can control themselves and their environment.

The Practice of Humanistic Geography

Much of the practice has been concerned with exploring and explaining the reasons and meanings of human actions. Many of the works have been stimulated by the view that life is seen as a process of experience, experiment and evaluation. To understand social life through this view field work with close connection to the people studied is required. Pocock (1983) describes that this can also be reached through strategies 'from library search to observation to experiencing'. The landscape as a creation of those living/lived in it is an important source; Lowenthal (1985) sees the landscape not as a mirror of the past but as an insight to the present. Even though it's based on historic shaping, living with it happens in the present, as does the decisions we make what (not) to preserve from the past. It tells us more about what people want to preserve from the past than how the past was experienced.

Novels work in the same way, but Porteous (1985) mentions that one has to be careful to select the literature, as it can be written by insiders or outsiders and places are described as home or away. The home-insider provides the sense of the place, the away-outsider experiences alienation, the home-outsiders don't develop relationships with the environment and away-insiders are travellers reporting experiences. Also science fiction provides insight in the future thinking of the society.

The problem however of using written information as source in research is the base of the language: text enables the distribution of information but also limits it through the meaning of the used words. Describing a phenomenon in words assigns the phenomenon to a category and therefore actually simplifies its meaning (Olsson (1982), more explored in 'Postmodernism'). The added problem to this will be that geographers themselves create texts as well, leading to a double interpretation (double hermeneutic, Dilthey (1980)). First the geographers interpret the texts they read and then write about it in their words, which will be read by others and maybe differently understood. The geographer writing about it also makes a selection of what he thinks is important. In the same sense each person's own history and upbringing might cause them to think differently about any source he encounters.

HUMANISTIC AND CULTURAL GEOGRAPHY

Even though successful applications of each philosophy in geography can be found, only few geographers got interested in it. Boal and Livingstone (1989) don't mention any specific philosophy but make a general statement about the forming of these philosophies: 'the purpose of geography is not to tell us what the world really is but it is the search for the right words to describe it'. Each created philosophy tries to approach it in their own way. The above mentioned humanistic approach without taking people's beliefs into account is called cultural geography. Foote and Domosh (1989) argued that the 'old' cultural geography is more based on the research into historic information while the 'new' cultural geography is more interested in also emphasizing everyday life and landscapes. The humanistic approach was seen as an attempt to define a 'new' cultural geography. Another debate going on was the difference between the American cultural geography and British social geography. Duncan (1994) sees this debate as the younger generation attacking the older generation on their theories, while the older generation didn't even know these theories existed in the first place.

Alternative methods of studying cultural geography were offered but these of course got criticized as well. Jackson (1987) links it to the concept of ideology and future work suggests further links with radical geography ('Radical Geographies').

The definition of culture itself is also discussed, and many adopted Duncan's (1994) definition: 'created and maintained by the society and flexible with the use in life and activities'. Culture is the medium through which people experience, discuss and establish change (Cosgrove and Jackson 1987). For Mitchell (1995) culture is the medium which is used to differentiate the world. To understand human differentiation, behaviour, experience and discussion culture has to be theorized. However, laws for culture can't be made but a powerful idea of culture is present. He mentions that cultural geography still hasn't been able to exactly explain what culture is. It however does exist and allows classifying people into distinct groups with each group having their differences. Culture is also crucial in geopolitics and economics. Mitchell (1995): 'culture is an idea that integrates by dividing; it is a strategy for control' and it has to be studied how it affects both positive and negative views of societies (more in 'Postmodernism').

Cook and Crang (1995) describe cultural geography with humanistic geography as mostly describing the human social phenomena, opposed to the positivist approach. Although other research identified 43 different ways to do this, main focus on four of these is enough: observation of the participant (the researcher lives and works among the study group), interviewing (conversations between researcher and study group), focus groups (treating people as members of an interacting community instead of individuals) and filmed approaches (visual media expresses more than words could describe). Finally, when this research is conducted, the composing of information is a major task. While doing this, ethical codes and the relationship between the researcher and study group is very important to take into account ('Applied Geography and the Relevance Debate').

THE GEOGRAPHY

Geography is the science that deals with the study of the Earth and its lands, features, inhabitants, and phenomena. A literal translation would be "to describe or write about the Earth". The first person to use the word "geography" was Eratosthenes (276-194 B.C.).

Four historical traditions in geographical research are the spatial analysis of natural and human phenomena (geography as a study of distribution), area studies (places and regions), study of man-land relationship, and research in earth sciences. Nonetheless, modern geography is an all-encompassing discipline that foremost seeks to understand the Earth and all of its human and natural complexities—not merely where objects are, but how they have changed and come to be. Geography has been called 'the world discipline'. As "the bridge between the human and physical sciences," geography is divided into two main branches—human geography and physical geography.

Traditionally, geographers have been viewed the same way as cartographers and people who study place names and numbers. Although many geographers are trained in toponymy and cartology, this is not their main preoccupation. Geographers study the spatial and temporal distribution of phenomena, processes and features as well as the interaction of humans and their environment.

As space and place affect a variety of topics such as economics, health, climate, plants and animals, geography is highly interdisciplinary. "...mere names of places...are not geography...know by heart a whole gazetteer full of them would not, in itself, constitute anyone a geographer. Geography has higher aims than this: it seeks to classify phenomena (alike of the natural and of the political world, in so far as it treats of the latter), to compare, to generalize, to ascend from effects to causes, and, in doing so, to trace out the great laws of nature and to mark their influences upon man. This is 'a description of the world'—that is Geography. In a word Geography is a Science—a thing not of mere names but of argument and reason, of cause and effect. " — *William Hughes, 1863*

Geography as a discipline can be split broadly into two main subsidiary fields: human geography and physical geography. The former focuses largely on the built environment and how space is created, viewed and managed by humans as well as the influence humans have on the space they occupy. The latter examines the natural environment and how the climate, vegetation & life, soil, water, and landforms are produced and interact. As a result of the two subfields using different approaches a third field has emerged, which is environmental geography. Environmental geography combines physical and human geography and looks at the interactions between the environment and humans.

BRANCHES

Physical Geography

Physical geography (or physiography) focuses on geography as an Earth science. It aims to understand the physical lithosphere, hydrosphere, atmosphere, pedosphere, and global flora and fauna patterns (biosphere).

Human Geography

Human geography is a branch of geography that focuses on the study of patterns and processes that shape human interaction with various environments. It encompasses human, political, cultural, social, and economic aspects. While the major focus of human geography is not the physical landscape of the Earth, it is hardly possible to discuss human geography without referring to the physical landscape on which human activities are being played out, and environmental geography is emerging as a link between the two. Various approaches to the study of human geography have also arisen through time and include:

- Behavioural geography
- Feminist geography

- Culture theory
- Geosophy.

Environmental Geography

Environmental geography is the branch of geography that describes the spatial aspects of interactions between humans and the natural world. It requires an understanding of the traditional aspects of physical and human geography, as well as the ways in which human societies conceptualize the environment. Environmental geography has emerged as a bridge between human and physical geography as a result of the increasing specialisation of the two sub-fields. Furthermore, as human relationship with the environment has changed as a result of globalization and technological change a new approach was needed to understand the changing and dynamic relationship. Examples of areas of research in environmental geography include emergency management, environmental management, sustainability, and political ecology.

Geomatics

Geomatics is a branch of geography that has emerged since the quantitative revolution in geography in the mid 1950s. Geomatics involves the use of traditional spatial techniques used in cartography and topography and their application to computers. Geomatics has become a widespread field with many other disciplines using techniques such as GIS and remote sensing. Geomatics has also led to a revitalization of some geography departments especially in Northern America where the subject had a declining status during the 1950s. Geomatics encompasses a large area of fields involved with spatial analysis, such as Cartography, Geographic information systems (GIS), Remote sensing, and Global positioning systems (GPS).

Regional Geography

Regional geography is a branch of geography that studies the regions of all sizes across the Earth. It has a prevailing descriptive character. The main aim is to understand or define the uniqueness or character of a particular region which consists of natural as well as human elements. Attention is paid also to regionalization which covers the proper techniques of space delimitation into regions.

Related Fields

- Urban planning, regional planning and spatial planning: use the science of geography to assist in determining how to develop (or not develop) the land to meet particular criteria, such as safety, beauty, economic opportunities, the preservation of the built or natural heritage, and so on. The planning of towns, cities, and rural areas may be seen as applied geography.
- Regional science: In the 1950s the regional science movement led by Walter Isard arose, to provide a more quantitative and analytical base to geographical questions, in contrast to the descriptive tendencies of traditional geography programs. Regional science comprises the body of knowledge in which the spatial dimension plays a fundamental role, such as regional economics, resource management, location theory, urban and regional planning, transport and communication, human geography, population distribution, landscape ecology, and environmental quality.
- Interplanetary Sciences: While the discipline of geography is normally concerned with the Earth, the term can also be informally used to describe the study of other worlds, such as the planets of the Solar System and even beyond. The study of systems larger than the earth itself usually forms part of Astronomy or Cosmology. The study of other planets is usually called planetary science. Alternative terms such as Areology (the study of Mars) have been proposed, but are not widely used.

Techniques

As spatial interrelationships are key to this synoptic science, maps are a key tool. Classical cartography has been joined by a more modern approach to geographical analysis, computer-based geographic information systems (GIS). In their study, geographers use four interrelated approaches:

- Systematic-Groups geographical knowledge into categories that can be explored globally.
- Regional-Examines systematic relationships between categories for a specific region or location on the planet.

- Descriptive-Simply specifies the locations of features and populations.
- Analytical-Asks *why* we find features and populations in a specific geographic area.

Cartography

Cartography studies the representation of the Earth's surface with abstract symbols (map making). Although other subdisciplines of geography rely on maps for presenting their analyses, the actual making of maps is abstract enough to be regarded separately. Cartography has grown from a collection of drafting techniques into an actual science. Cartographers must learn cognitive psychology and ergonomics to understand which symbols convey information about the Earth most effectively, and behavioural psychology to induce the readers of their maps to act on the information. They must learn geodesy and fairly advanced mathematics to understand how the shape of the Earth affects the distortion of map symbols projected onto a flat surface for viewing. It can be said, without much controversy, that cartography is the seed from which the larger field of geography grew. Most geographers will cite a childhood fascination with maps as an early sign they would end up in the field.

Geographic Information Systems

Geographic information systems (GIS) deal with the storage of information about the Earth for automatic retrieval by a computer, in an accurate manner appropriate to the information's purpose. In addition to all of the other subdisciplines of geography, GIS specialists must understand computer science and database systems. GIS has revolutionized the field of cartography; nearly all mapmaking is now done with the assistance of some form of GIS software. GIS also refers to the science of using GIS software and GIS techniques to represent, analyze and predict spatial relationships. In this context, GIS stands for Geographic Information Science.

Remote Sensing

Remote sensing is the science of obtaining information about Earth features from measurements made at a distance. Remotely sensed data comes in many forms such as satellite imagery, aerial photography and data obtained from hand-held sensors. Geographers increasingly use remotely sensed data to obtain information about the Earth's land surface, ocean and atmosphere because it: a) supplies objective information at a variety of spatial scales (local to global), b) provides a synoptic view of the area of interest, c) allows access to distant and/or inaccessible sites, d) provides spectral information outside the visible portion of the electromagnetic spectrum, and e) facilitates studies of how features/areas change over time. Remotely sensed data may be analyzed either independently of, or in conjunction with, other digital data layers (e.g., in a Geographic Information System).

Quantitative Methods

Geostatistics deal with quantitative data analysis, specifically the application of statistical methodology to the exploration of geographic phenomena. Geostatistics is used extensively in a variety of fields including: hydrology, geology, petroleum exploration, weather analysis, urban planning, logistics, and epidemiology. The mathematical basis for geostatistics derives from cluster analysis, linear discriminant analysis and non-parametric statistical tests, and a variety of other subjects. Applications of geostatistics rely heavily on geographic information systems, particularly for the interpolation (estimate) of unmeasured points. Geographers are making notable contributions to the method of quantitative techniques.

Qualitative Methods

Geographic qualitative methods, or ethnographical; research techniques, are used by human geographers. In cultural geography there is a tradition of employing qualitative research techniques also used in anthropology and sociology. Participant observation and in-depth interviews provide human geographers with qualitative data.

History

The oldest known world maps date back to ancient Babylon from the 9th century BC. The best known Babylonian world map, however, is the *Imago Mundi* of 600 BC. The map as reconstructed by Eckhard Unger shows Babylon on the

Euphrates, surrounded by a circular landmass showing Assyria, Urartu and several cities, in turn surrounded by a "bitter river" (Oceanus), with seven islands arranged around it so as to form a seven-pointed star. The accompanying text mentions seven outer regions beyond the encircling ocean. The descriptions of five of them have survived. In contrast to the *Imago Mundi*, an earlier Babylonian world map dating back to the 9th century BC depicted Babylon as being further north from the centre of the world, though it is not certain what that centre was supposed to represent.

The ideas of Anaximander (c. 610 B.C.-c. 545 B.C.), considered by later Greek writers to be the true founder of geography, come to us through fragments quoted by his successors. Anaximander is credited with the invention of the gnomon,the simple yet efficient Greek instrument that allowed the early measurement of latitude. Thales, Anaximander is also credited with the prediction of eclipses. The foundations of geography can be traced to the ancient cultures, such as the ancient, medieval, and early modern Chinese. The Greeks, who were the first to explore geography as both art and science, achieved this through Cartography, Philosophy, and Literature, or through Mathematics. There is some debate about who was the first person to assert that the Earth is spherical in shape, with the credit going either to Parmenides or Pythagoras. Anaxagoras was able to demonstrate that the profile of the Earth was circular by explaining eclipses. However, he still believed that the Earth was a flat disk, as did many of his contemporaries. One of the first estimates of the radius of the Earth was made by Eratosthenes.

The first rigorous system of latitude and longitude lines is credited to Hipparchus. He employed a sexagesimal system that was derived from Babylonian mathematics. The parallels and meridians were sub-divided into 360°, with each degree further subdivided 602 (minutes). To measure the longitude at different location on Earth, he suggested using eclipses to determine the relative difference in time. The extensive mapping by the Romans as they explored new lands would later provide a high level of information for Ptolemy to construct detailed atlases. He extended the work of Hipparchus, using a grid system on his maps and adopting a length of 56.5 miles for a degree. From the 3rd century onwards, Chinese methods of geographical study and writing of geographical literature became much more complex than what was found in Europe at the time (until the 13th century). Chinese geographers such as Liu An, Pei Xiu, Jia Dan, Shen Kuo, Fan Chengda, Zhou Daguan, and Xu Xiake wrote important treatises, yet by the 17th century, advanced ideas and methods of Western-style geography were adopted in China.

During the Middle Ages, the fall of the Roman empire led to a shift in the evolution of geography from Europe to the Islamic world. Muslim geographers such as Muhammad al-Idrisi produced detailed world maps (such as Tabula Rogeriana), while other geographers such as Yaqut al-Hamawi, Abu Rayhan Biruni, Ibn Battuta and Ibn Khaldun provided detailed accounts of their journeys and the geography of the regions they visited. Turkish geographer, Mahmud al-Kashgari drew a world map on a linguistic basis, and later so did Piri Reis (Piri Reis map). Further, Islamic scholars translated and interpreted the earlier works of the Romans and Greeks and established the House of Wisdom in Baghdad for this purpose. Abû Zayd al-Balkhî, originally from Balkh, founded the "Balkhî school" of terrestrial mapping in Baghdad. Suhrâb, a late tenth century Muslim geographer, accompanied a book of geographical coordinates with instructions for making a rectangular world map, with equirectangular projection or cylindrical equidistant projection. In the early 11th century, Avicenna hypothesized on the geological causes of mountains in *The Book of Healing* (1027).

Abu Rayhan Biruni (976-1048) first described a polar equi-azimuthal equidistant projection of the celestial sphere. He was regarded as the most skilled when it came to mapping cities and measuring the distances between them, which he did for many cities in the Middle East and Indian subcontinent. He often combined astronomical readings and mathematical equations, in order to develop methods of pin-pointing locations by recording degrees of latitude and longitude. He also developed similar techniques when it came to measuring the heights of mountains, depths of valleys, and expanse of the horizon. He also discussed human geography and the planetary habitability of the Earth. He hypothesized that roughly a quarter of the Earth's surface is habitable by humans. He also calculated the latitude of Kath, Khwarezm, using the maximum altitude of the Sun, and solved a complex geodesic equation in order to accurately compute the Earth's circumference, which were close to modern values of the Earth's circumference. His estimate of 6,339.9 km for the Earth radius was only 16.8 km less than the modern value of 6,356.7 km. In contrast to his predecessors who measured the Earth's circumference by sighting the Sun simultaneously from two different locations, al-Biruni developed a new method of using trigonometric calculations based on the angle between a plain and mountain top which yielded more accurate measurements of the Earth's circumference and made it possible for it to be measured by a single person from a single location. He also published a study of map projections, *Cartography*, which included a method for projecting a hemisphere on a plane.

The European Age of Discovery during the 16th and 17th centuries, where many new lands were discovered and accounts by European explorers such as Christopher Columbus, Marco Polo and James Cook, revived a desire for both accurate geographic detail, and more solid theoretical foundations in Europe. The problem facing both explorers and geographers was finding the latitude and longitude of a geographic location. The problem of latitude was solved long ago but that of longitude remained; agreeing on what zero meridian should be was only part of the problem. It was left to John Harrison to solve it by inventing the chronometer H-4, in 1760, and later in 1884 for the International Meridian Conference to adopt by convention the Greenwich meridian as zero meridian.

The 18th and 19th centuries were the times when geography became recognized as a discrete academic discipline and became part of a typical university curriculum in Europe (especially Paris and Berlin). The development of many geographic societies also occurred during the 19th century with the foundations of the Société de Géographie in 1821, the Royal Geographical Society in 1830, Russian Geographical Society in 1845, American Geographical Society in 1851, and the National Geographic Society in 1888. The influence of Immanuel Kant, Alexander von Humboldt, Carl Ritter and Paul Vidal de la Blache can be seen as a major turning point in geography from a philosophy to an academic subject.

Over the past two centuries the advancements in technology such as computers, have led to the development of geomatics and new practices such as participant observation and geostatistics being incorporated into geography's portfolio of tools. In the West during the 20th century, the discipline of geography went through four major phases: environmental determinism, regional geography, the quantitative revolution, and critical geography. The strong interdisciplinary links between geography and the sciences of geology and botany, as well as economics, sociology and demographics have also grown greatly especially as a result of Earth System Science that seeks to understand the world in a holistic view.

IMPORTANCE OF GEOGRAPHY IN WORLD POLITICS

The West has been chastened by the war in Iraq, argues Robert D. Kaplan in The Revenge of Geography, an article published in Foreign Policy Magazine in 2009. He says that, like the war in Vietnam, the Iraq war was provoked mainly by fear. Today, we are more realists in contrast with the 1990s when the western world was very idealistic, says Kaplan. But idealism and fear were among the main causes for the break out of the war in Iraq. Idealism, a feature of the last years of the 20th century, was a direct result of the fall of communism; and the fear that replaced idealism as a major "psyho-political" mood for the beginning of 21st century, was a direct result of the 9/11 terrorist attacks. America was flushed with success in the end of the Cold War and it wanted to preserve this precious world of the 1990s. The surprise and disappointment that the terrorist attacks caused had turned into a rage and fear, and the world's most powerful nation reacted to the new threat in a way that can be described as a "panic." The reason and political prudence in American politics have returned uncertainly, but only after the sobering effect of the Iraq war.

Today's realism, says Kaplan, is more than mere opposing of the wars in Middle East. "Realism means recognizing that international relations are ruled by a sadder, more limited reality than the one governing domestic affairs. It means valuing order above freedom, for the latter becomes important only after the former has been established. It means focusing on what divides humanity rather than on what unites it. In short, realism is about recognizing and embracing those forces beyond our control that constrain human action-culture, tradition, history, the bleaker tides of passion that lie just beneath the veneer of civilization."

Kaplan says that realism in international politics demands a better understanding of geography. The geography is one of the basic factors that determine the events on the international scene. The importance of geography has been forgotten by the politicians, who believed that globalization dilutes the differences caused by geography. Indeed, says Kaplan, globalization reinforced the significance of geography. Mass communications and economic integration has been weakening many states, exposing a Hobbesian world of small, fractious regions. Kaplan's advice is that Western politicians and strategists need to "return to the map," and particularly to what he calls the political geography of the "shattered zones" of Eurasia.

In The Revenge of Geography Robert Kaplan makes a synopsis of the most influential geopolitical theorists-the French historian Fernand Braudel (*The Mediterranean and the Mediterranean World in the Age of Philip II*), the U.S. naval captain and author of *The Influence of Sea Power Upon History, 1660-1783* Alfred Thayer Mahan, Dutch-American strategist Nicholas Spykman, and the father of modern geopolitics Sir Halford J. Mackinder ("*The Geographical Pivot of History*").

Writing his world history Fernand Braudel did not underestimate the importance of geography. Behind the historical trends and events he saw environmental forces. To Braudel, for example, the poor, precarious soils along the Mediterranean, combined with an uncertain, drought-afflicted climate, spurred ancient Greek and Roman conquest. This means that people and states often do not control their own destinies. There is something more than desires and rational plans, something that pushes their will in one or another direction... and it is geography-climate, terrain, soil, and neighbors.

Alfred Thayer Mahan thought that the naval power had always been the decisive factor in global political struggles. Nicholas Spykman saw the seaboards of the Indian and Pacific oceans as the keys to dominance in Eurasia and the natural means to check the land power of Russia. Mackinder's work, says Kaplan, is the archetype of the geographical discipline. His understanding of geopolitics was summarized in one sentence: "Man and not nature initiates, but nature in large measure controls." Mackinder looked at European history as "subordinate" to that of Asia, for he saw European civilization as merely the outcome of the struggle against Asiatic invasion. Key discoveries of the Columbian epoch, Mackinder writes, only reinforced the cruel facts of geography. In the Middle Ages, the peoples of Europe were largely confined to the land. But when the sea route to India was found around the Cape of Good Hope, Europeans suddenly had access to the entire rimland of southern Asia, to say nothing of strategic discoveries in the New World.

The wisdom of geographical determinism, says Kaplan, endures across the chasm of a century because it recognizes that the most profound struggles of humanity are not about ideas but about control over territory, specifically the heartland and rimlands of Eurasia. Of course, says Kaplan, ideas matter, and they span geography. And yet there is a certain geographic logic to where certain ideas take hold. Communist Eastern Europe, Mongolia, China, and North Korea were all contiguous to the great land power of the Soviet Union. Classic fascism was a predominantly European affair. And liberalism nurtured its deepest roots in the United States and Great Britain, essentially island nations and sea powers both. Such determinism is easy to hate but hard to dismiss.

In his article Kaplan depicts a kind of catastrophic future in which geography serves as a common base for numerous changes, conflicts and possible cooperation between states. He quotes Yale University professor Paul Bracken who in 1999 warned that there is no room anymore in the world and especially in Eurasia (*Fire in the East*). The lack of empty geographical space for expansion, combined with the population growth explosion, crowd psychology of impoverished masses, and technological development, the possession of weapons of mass destruction by countries such as North Korea, Pakistan and probably soon Iran, makes our world extremely dangerous place.

Kaplan supports his view of importance of geography with concrete examples of present and smolder conflicts in Middle East, Arabian Peninsula, China, Pakistan, Afghanistan and India. He compares these zones of conflict with the earthquake faults that need attention and understanding in order to avert the devastation from future shocks.

Kaplan finishes with following: "In this century's fight for Eurasia, like that of the last century, Mackinder's axiom holds true: Man will initiate, but nature will control. Liberal universalism and the individualism of Isaiah Berlin aren't going away, but it is becoming clear that the success of these ideas is in large measure bound and determined by geography. Geographical determinists must be seated at the same honored table as liberal humanists. Embracing the dictates and limitations of geography will be especially hard for Americans, who like to think that no constraint, natural or otherwise, applies to them. But denying the facts of geography only invites disasters that, in turn, make us victims of geography."

10

Idealism and Critical Realism in Geography

IDEALISM

Idealism is the philosophical theory which maintains that experience is ultimately based on mental activity. In the philosophy of perception, idealism is contrasted with realism, in which the external world is said to have an apparent absolute existence.

Epistemological idealists (such as Kant) claim that the only things which can be directly *known for certain* are just ideas (abstraction). In literature, idealism means the thoughts or the ideas of the writer.

In the philosophy of mind, idealism is the opposite of materialism, in which the ultimate nature of reality is based on physical substances.

Idealism and materialism are both theories of monism as opposed to dualism and pluralism. Idealism sometimes refers to a tradition in thought that represents things of a perfect form, as in the fields of ethics, morality, aesthetics, and value.

In this way, it represents a human perfect being or circumstance. Idealism is a philosophical movement in Western thought, and names a number of philosophical positions with sometimes quite different tendencies and implications in politics and ethics; for instance, at least in popular culture, philosophical idealism is associated with Plato and the school of platonism.

IDEALISM AND ANCIENT PHILOSOPHY

Antiphon

In his chief work *Truth*, Antiphon wrote: "*Time* is a thought or a measure, not a substance." This presents time as an ideational, internal, mental operation, rather than a real, external object.

PLATO

Plato is called an idealist because of his theory of Forms or doctrine of Ideas, which are "ideal" in the dictionary sense. Most interpreters, ancient and modern, hold that Plato does not describe the Forms as being in any mind. Instead, he describes them as having their own independent existence—for which the textual evidence is adduced from various translations of the dialogues. Indeed, some anti-idealist commentators say that in the dialogues Socrates often denies the reality of the material world. However, it is clear that the Platonic Socrates merely denies the ideal reality of the non-ideal realm, which he sometimes compares to shadows. An exact interpretation of the dialogues, which are notoriously misrepresented, involves knowledge of linguistics, hermeneutics, philology, semantics, and the philosophy of language, as well as good grounding in classical studies. Athenian Greek philosophical terms, like most English abstract nouns, have more than one meaning. It seems clear that Plato is not, at any rate, a subjective idealist, unlike Berkeley.

Plato's Allegory of the Cave is sometimes interpreted by anti-platonists as drawing attention to the modern European philosophical problem of knowing external objects—the question that is often attributed to Descartes, Locke, Berkeley, and other early modern philosophers. According to certain materialistic interpretations of Plato, which construe matter as an entirely external reality, the Forms of which the Cave-dwellers are ignorant are not external to them in the way that so-called material objects are for modern thinkers. Again, some anti-idealistic readers hold that for Plato the Forms are true realities, but they are not outside of us in a spatial sense like material objects, which some natural scientists call physical bodies. For these interpreters, one might say, the issue that Plato's allegory addresses is the problem of how one can know what is truly real and good—a theme which apparently is opposed to the so-called modern question of our knowledge of the external world.

Plotinus

Nathaniel Alfred Boll wrote of this Neoplatonist philosopher: "With Plotinus there even appears, probably for the first time in Western philosophy, *idealism* that had long been current in the East even at that time, for it taught that the soul has made the world by stepping from eternity into time, with the explanation: 'For there is for this universe no other place than the soul or mind' (neque est alter hujus universi locus quam anima), indeed the ideality of time is expressed in the words: 'We should not accept time outside the soul or mind' (oportet autem nequaquam extra animam tempus accipere)."

Similarly, professor Ludwig Noiré wrote: "For the first time in Western philosophy we find idealism proper in Plotinus, where he says, "The only space or place of the world is the soul," and "Time must not be assumed to exist outside the soul." It is worth noting, however, that like Plato but unlike Schopenhauer and other modern philosophers, Plotinus does not worry about whether or how we can get beyond our ideas in order to know external objects.

Anaxagoras

Pre-Socratic philosopher Anaxagoras, who arrived in Athens some time after 480 BC taught a form of idealism. He was known as Nous or Mind, because he taught that "all things" were created by Mind and that Mind held the cosmos together and gave to human beings a connection to the cosmos, or a pathway to the divine.

TYPES OF IDEALISM

Subjective Idealism (or phenomenalism) is a theory which describes a relationship between human experience of the external world, and that world itself, in which objects are nothing more than collections (or bundles) of sense data in those who perceive them. Proponents include George Berkeley, Arthur Collier, A. A. Luce and John Foster. Objective idealism is the view asserting that the act of experiencing has a reality combining and transcending the natures of the object experienced and of the mind of the observer. Proponents include Thomas Hill Green, Josiah Royce, Benedetto Croce and Charles Sanders Peirce.

Actual Idealism is a form of idealism developed by Giovanni Gentile that grew into a 'grounded' idealism contrasting the Transcendental Idealism of Immanuel Kant and the Absolute idealism of G. W. F. Hegel. Transcendental idealism is a doctrine founded by German philosopher Immanuel Kant in the eighteenth century. Kant's doctrine maintains that human experience of things is similar to the way they appear to us — implying a fundamentally subject-based component, rather than being an activity that directly (and therefore without any obvious causal link) comprehends the things as they are in and of themselves.

Monistic idealism is a metaphysical theory which states that consciousness, not matter, is the ground of all being. It is a monistic theory because it holds that there is only one type of thing in the universe, and a form of idealism because it holds that one thing to be consciousness. In India this concept is central to Vedanta philosophy. Proponents include Amit Goswami and the Hindu philosophy Kashmir Shaivism.

Absolute idealism is an ontologically monistic philosophy attributed to G. W. F. Hegel. It is Hegel's account of how being is ultimately comprehensible as an all-inclusive whole. Hegel asserted that in order for the thinking subject (human reason or consciousness) to be able to know its object (the world) at all, there must be in some sense an identity of thought and being.

Other Proponents include Bernard Bosanquet and F. H. Bradley. Pluralistic Idealism is the view that there are many individual minds which together underlie the existence of the observed world. Unlike absolute idealism, pluralistic idealism does not assume the existence of a single ultimate mental reality or Absolute. According to pluralistic idealism, it is individual minds which make possible the existence of the physical universe. Proponents include Gottfried Leibniz.

Personal Idealism also known as Personalism is the view that the minds which underlie reality are the minds of persons. Proponents include George Holmes Howison, Borden Parker

Bowne and J. M. E. McTaggart. Epistemological idealism is a subjectivist position in epistemology that holds that what one knows about an object exists only in one's mind. It is opposed to epistemological realism. Proponents include Brand Blanshard.

Theistic Idealism was founded by the 19th-century philosopher Hermann Lotze. It is a theory of the world ground, in which all things find their unity, it has been widely accepted by theistic philosophers and Protestant theologians. Hindu idealism is essentially monotheist, espousing the view that consciousness, which at its root emanates from God (Brahman, Purusha or Svayam bhagavan), is the essence or meaning of the phenomenal reality.

The presence of idealist concepts in Indian thought has been emphasized by Rupert Sheldrake and Fritjof Capra. These ideas have also been developed by P.R. Sarkar and advanced by his disciple Sohail Inayatullah, notably in the theory of Microvitum.

MODERN PHILOSOPHY

Yangming

Wang Yangming was a Ming Chinese idealist Neo-Confucian philosopher, official, educationist, calligraphist and general. He held that objects do not exist entirely apart from the mind because the mind shapes them. He believed that it is not the world that shapes the mind, but the mind that gives reason to the world. Therefore, the mind alone is the source of all reason. He understood this to be an inner light, an innate moral goodness and understanding of what is good.

Malebranche

Nicolas Malebranche, a student of the Cartesian School of Rationalism, disagreed that if the only things that we know for certain are the ideas within our mind, then the existence of the external world would be dubious and known only indirectly. He declared instead that the real external world is actually God. All activity only appears to occur in the external world. In actuality, it is the activity of God. For Malebranche, we directly know internally the ideas in our mind. Externally, we directly know God's operations. This kind of idealism led to the pantheism of Spinoza.

Renouvier

Charles Bernard Renouvier was the first Frenchman after Nicolas Malebranche to formulate a complete idealistic system, and had a vast influence on the development of French thought. His system is based on Immanuel Kant's, as his chosen term "néo-criticisme" indicates; but it is a transformation rather than a continuation of Kantianism.

Leibniz

Leibniz expressed a form of Idealism known as Panpsychism in his theory of monads, as exposited in his Monadologie. He held Monads are the true atoms of the universe, and are also entities having perception. The monads are "substantial forms of being." They are indecomposable, individual, subject to their own laws, un-interacting, and each reflecting the entire universe. Monads are centers of force; substance is force, while space, matter, and motion are phenomenal. For Leibniz, there is an exact pre-established harmony or parallel between the world in the minds of the alert monads and the external world of objects. God, who is the central monad, established this harmony and the resulting world is an idea of the monads' perception. In this way, the external world is ideal in that it is a spiritual phenomenon whose motion is the result of a dynamic force. Space and time are ideal or phenomenal and their form and existence is dependent on the simple and immaterial monads. Leibniz's cosmology, with its central monad, embraced a traditional Christian Theism and was more of a Personalism than the naturalistic Pantheism of Spinoza.

Berkeley

Gecrge Berkeley, also known as Bishop Berkeley (Bishop of Cloyne), was an Irish philosopher whose primary achievement was the advancement of a theory he called immaterialism (later referred to as "subjective idealism" by others). This theory contends that individuals can only know directly sensations and ideas of objects, not abstractions such as "matter". The theory also contends that ideas are dependent upon being perceived by minds for their very existence, a belief that became immortalized in the dictum, "esse est percipi" ("to be is to be perceived").

Collier

Arthur Collier published the same assertions that were made by Berkeley. However, there seemed to have been no influence between the two contemporary writers. Collier claimed that the represented image of an external object is the only knowable reality. Matter, as a cause of the representative image, is unthinkable and therefore nothing to us. An external world, as absolute matter, unrelated to an observer, does not exist for human perceivers. As an appearance in a mind, the universe cannot exist as it appears if there is no perceiving mind. Collier was influenced by John Norris's (1701) *An Essay Towards the Theory of the Ideal or Intelligible World.* The idealist statements by Collier were generally dismissed by readers who were not able to reflect on the distinction between a mental idea or image and the object that it represents.

Kant

Immanuel Kant held that the mind shapes the world as we perceive it to take the form of space-and-time. It is said that Kant focused on the idea drawn from British empiricism (and its philosophers such as Locke, Berkeley, and Hume) that all we can know is the mental impressions, or *phenomena*, that an outside world, which may or may not exist independently, creates in our minds; our minds can never perceive that outside world directly. Kant made the distinction between things as they appear to an observer and things in themselves, "... that is, things considered without regard to whether and how they may be given to us....".... if I remove the thinking subject, the whole material world must at once vanish because it is nothing but a phenomenal appearance in the sensibility of ourselves as a subject, and a manner or species of representation. – *Critique of Pure Reason A383*

Kant's postscript to this added that the mind is not a blank slate, *tabula rasa* (contrasting with the philosophy of John Locke), but rather comes equipped with categories for organising our sense impressions. Perhaps this Kantian sort of idealism opens up a world of abstractions (i.e., the universal categories minds use to understand phenomena) to be explored by reason, but perhaps, in sharp contrast to Plato's, confirms uncertainties about a (un)knowable world outside our own minds. We cannot approach the *noumenon*, the "Thing in Itself" (German: *Ding an sich*) outside our own mental world. (Kant's idealism is called *transcendental idealism.*)

Apparently Kant distinguished his transcendental or critical idealism from previous varieties: The dictum of all genuine idealists, from the Eleatic school to Bishop Berkeley, is contained in this formula: "All knowledge through the senses and experience is nothing but sheer illusion, and only in the ideas of the pure understanding and reason is there truth." The principle that throughout dominates and determines my idealism is, on the contrary: "All knowledge of things merely from pure understanding or pure reason is nothing but sheer illusion, and only in experience is there truth." – *Prolegomena, 374*

Fichte

Johann Fichte denied Kant's noumenon, and held that consciousness constitutes its own foundation, that the mental life of the Ego, of pure selfhood, relies upon nothing wholly external to itself, and that the hypothesis of an outer world of any kind is the same thing as admitting a Kantian realm. We may say that Fichte was the first German philosopher to make an attempt at a presuppositionless theory of knowledge, wherein nothing outside of thought is assumed to exist apart from the primordial analysis of the Ego. So that his philosophy could be solely grounded in itself, he assumed nothing without his Fichtean deductions from first principles, and elaborated what he called a Wissenschaftslehre. (Apparently Fichte's theory is very similar to Giovanni Gentile's Actual Idealism, except that Gentile's theory appears to go even further by denying any grounds, derived from pure thought, for the Ego or personality.)

Schelling

Friedrich Wilhelm Joseph Schelling (1775–1854) claimed that the Fichte's "I" needs the Not-I, because there is no subject without object, and vice versa. So there is no difference between the subjective and the objective, that is, the ideal and the real. This is the Schelling's "absolute identity": the ideas or mental images in the mind are identical to the extended objects which are external to the mind.

Hegel

Hegel is another German philosopher whose dialectical system has been called *idealistic*. In his *Science of Logic* (1812–1814) Hegel argued that finite qualities are not fully "real," because they depend on other finite qualities to determine them. Qualitative *infinity*, on the other hand, would be more self-determining, and hence would have a better claim to be called fully real. Similarly, finite natural things are less "real"—because they are less self-determining—than spiritual things like morally responsible people, ethical communities, and God. So any doctrine, such as materialism, that asserts that finite qualities or merely natural objects are fully real, is mistaken. Hegel called his philosophy *absolute idealism*, in contrast to the "subjective idealism" of Berkeley and the "transcendental idealism" of Kant and Fichte, philosophies which were not based (like Hegel's idealism) on a critique of the finite, and a dialectical philosophy of history. Some commentators have maintained that Hegel's dialectical system most closely resembles that of Plato and Plotinus, however, there is an exact historical difference between ancient and modern thought, at least in the history of philosophy. One might say that none of these three thinkers associate their idealism with the so-called epistemological thesis that what we know are ideas in our minds.

It is perhaps a noteworthy fact that some commentators of Hegel fail to distinguish Hegelian idealism from either the philosophy of Berkeley or Kant. Hegel certainly intends to preserve what he takes to be true of German idealism, in particular Kant's insistence that ethical reason can and does go beyond finite inclinations. However, some commentators hold that Hegel does not endorse Kant's conception of the thing-in-itself, or the type of epistemological perplexities that led Kant to that view. Still less does Hegel endorse Berkeley's doctrine that to be is to perceive or to be perceived—in the purely Berkeleyian sense. The guiding ideal behind Hegel's absolute idealism is the scientific thought, which he shares with Plato and other great idealist thinkers, that the exercise of reason and intellect enables the philosopher to know ultimate historical reality, which in the Hegelian system is the phenomenological constitution of self-determination,—the dialectical development of self-awareness and personality in the realm of History. By giving this Ideal a central role in his philosophy, Hegel made a lasting contribution to that part of the Western mindset, beginning in earnest with Plato and his Pre-Socratic predecessors, which makes Idealism the basis of civilization and progress in the world.

Schopenhauer

In the first volume of his *Parerga and Paralipomena*, Schopenhauer wrote his "Sketch of a History of the Doctrine of the Ideal and the Real". He defined the ideal as being mental pictures that constitute subjective knowledge. The ideal, for him, is what can be attributed to our own minds. The images in our head are what comprise the ideal. Schopenhauer emphasized that we are restricted to our own consciousness. The world that appears is only a representation or mental picture of objects. We directly and immediately know only representations. All objects that are external to the mind are known indirectly through the mediation of our mind. Schopenhauer's history is an account of the concept of the "ideal" in its meaning as "ideas in a subject's mind." In this sense, "ideal" means "ideational" or "existing in the mind as an image." He does not refer to the other meaning of "ideal" as being qualities of the highest perfection and excellence. In his *On the Freedom of the Will*, Schopenhauer noted the ambiguity of the word "idealism" by calling it a "term with multiple meanings."

[T]rue philosophy must at all costs be *idealistic*; indeed, it must be so merely to be honest. For nothing is more certain than that no one ever came out of himself in order to identify himself immediately with things different from him; but everything of which he has certain, sure, and therefore immediate knowledge, lies within his consciousness. Beyond this consciousness, therefore, there can be no *immediate* certainty.... There can never be an existence that is objective absolutely and in itself; such an existence, indeed, is positively inconceivable. For the objective, as such, always and essentially has its existence in the consciousness of a subject; it is therefore the subject's representation, and consequently is conditioned by the subject, and moreover by the subject's forms of representation, which belong to the subject and not to the object. – *The World as Will and Representation, Vol. II, Ch. 1*

It is evident that Schopenhauer's "idealism" is based primarily on considerations having to do with the relation between our ideas and external reality, rather than being based (like Plato's, Plotinus's, or Hegel's "idealism") on considerations having to do with the nature of reality as such.

British Idealism

British idealism enjoyed ascendancy in English-speaking philosophy in the later part of the 19th century. F. H. Bradley of Merton College, Oxford, saw reality as a monistic whole, which is apprehended through "feeling", a state in which there is no distinction between the perception and the thing perceived. Like Berkeley, Bradley thought that nothing can be known to exist unless it is known by a mind.

We perceive, on reflection, that to be real, or even barely to exist, must be to fall within sentience.... Find any piece of existence, take up anything that any one could possibly call a fact, or could in any sense assert to have being, and then judge if it does not consist in sentient experience. Try to discover any sense in which you can still continue to speak of it, when all perception and feeling have been removed; or point out any fragment of its matter, any aspect of its being, which is not derived from and is not still relative to this source. When the experiment is made strictly, I can myself conceive of nothing else than the experienced. – *F.H. Bradley, 'Appearance and Reality', Chapter 14*

Bradley was the apparent target of G. E. Moore's radical rejection of idealism. Moore claimed that Bradley did not understand the statement that something is real. We know for certain, through common sense and prephilosophical beliefs, that some things are real, whether they are objects of thought or not, according to Moore. In this way, he disagreed with Bradley's assertion that we cannot think of anything that really exists unless we have a thought of it in our mind.

J. M. E. McTaggart of Cambridge University, argued that minds alone exist, and that they only relate to each other through love. Space, time and material objects are for McTaggart unreal. He argued, for instance, in *The Unreality of Time* that it was not possible to produce a coherent account of a sequence of events in time, and that therefore time is an illusion. His book *The Nature of Existence* (1927) contained his arguments that space, time, and matter cannot possibly be real. In his *Studies in Hegelian Cosmology*, Cambridge, 1901, p. 196, he declared that metaphysics are not relevant to social and political action. McTaggart "... thought that Hegel was wrong in supposing that metaphysics could show that the state is more than a means to the good of the individuals who compose it." For McTaggart, "...philosophy can give us very little, if any guidance in action.... Why should a Hegelian citizen be surprised that his belief as to the organic nature of the Absolute does not help him in deciding how to vote? Would a Hegelian engineer be reasonable in expecting that his belief that all matter is spirit should help him in planning a bridge?

American philosopher Josiah Royce described himself as an objective idealist. Thomas Hill Green and Bernard Bosanquet are also prominent members of the British idealism movement. John Foster is a British philosopher. He is the author of The case for Idealism, which defends a form of subjective idealism. He argues that the physical world is the logical creation of the natural (non-logical) constraints on human sense-experience. Foster's latest defence of his views is in his book A World for Us: The Case for Phenomenalistic Idealism.

Karl Pearson

In *The Grammar of Science*, Preface to the 2nd Edition, 1900, Karl Pearson wrote, "There are many signs that a sound idealism is surely replacing, as a basis for natural philosophy, the crude materialism of the older physicists." This book influenced Einstein's regard for the importance of the observer in scientific measurements. In § 5 of that book, Pearson asserted that "...science is in reality a classification and analysis of the contents of the mind...." Also, "...the field of science is much more consciousness than an external world."

CRITICISM

Immanuel Kant

In the 1st edition (1781) of his Critique of Pure Reason, Kant described idealism thus: We are perfectly justified in maintaining that only what is within ourselves can be immediately and directly perceived, and that only my own existence can be the object of a mere perception. Thus the existence of a real object outside me can never be given immediately and directly in perception, but can only be added in thought to the perception, which is a modification of the internal sense, and thus inferred as its external cause.... In the true sense of the word, therefore, I can never perceive external things, but I can only infer their existence from my own internal perception, regarding the perception as an effect of something external that must be the proximate cause.... It must not be supposed, therefore, that an idealist is someone who denies the existence of external objects of the senses; all he does is to deny that they are known by immediate and direct perception.... – *Critique of Pure Reason, A367 f.*

In the 2nd edition (1787) of his Critique of Pure Reason, he wrote a section called Refutation of Idealism to distinguish his transcendental idealism from Descartes's Sceptical Idealism and Berkeley's Dogmatic Idealism. In addition to this refutation in both the 1781 & 1787 editions the section "Paralogisms of Pure Reason" is an implicit critique of Descartes' Problematic Idealism, namely the Cogito. He says that just from "the spontaneity of thought" (cf. Descartes' Cogito) it is not possible to infer the 'I' as an object. Kant also defined idealism in the following manner: "The assertion that we can never be certain whether all of our putative outer experience is not mere imagining is idealism."

Soren Kierkegaard

Kierkegaard's primary criticism against Hegel is based on Hegel's claim to have developed a fully comprehensive system that could explain the whole of reality. The quote commonly used to express this idea, whether fair to Hegel or not, is, "What is rational is actual; and what is actual is rational," in the *Elements of the Philosophy of Right* (1821). Kierkegaard asserts that reality can be a system for God, but it cannot be so for any human individual, because both reality and humans are incomplete, and all philosophical systems imply completeness. Kierkegaard attacked Hegel's idealist philosophy in several of his works, but most succinctly in *Concluding*

Unscientific Postscript (1846). In the *Postscript*, Kierkegaard, as the pseudonymous philosopher Johannes Climacus, argues that a logical system is possible but an existential system is impossible. Hegel argues that once one has reached an ultimate understanding of the logical structure of the world, one has also reached an understanding of the logical structure of God's mind. Climacus claims Hegel's absolute idealism mistakenly blurs the distinction between existence and thought. Climacus also argues that our mortal nature places limits on our understanding of reality. As Climacus argues:

> So-called systems have often been characterized and challenged in the assertion that they abrogate the distinction between good and evil, and destroy freedom. Perhaps one would express oneself quite as definitely, if one said that every such system fantastically dissipates the concept existence.... Being an individual man is a thing that has been abolished, and every speculative philosopher confuses himself with humanity at large; whereby he becomes something infinitely great, and at the same time nothing at all.

A major concern of Hegel's *Phenomenology of Spirit* (1807) and of the philosophy of Spirit that he lays out in his *Encyclopedia of the Philosophical Sciences* (1817–1830) is the interrelation between individual humans, which he conceives in terms of "mutual recognition." However, what Climacus means by the aforementioned statement, is that Hegel, in the *Philosophy of Right*, believed the best solution was to surrender one's individuality to the customs of the State, identifying right and wrong in view of the prevailing bourgeois morality. Individual human will ought, at the State's highest level of development, to properly coincide with the will of the State. Climacus rejects Hegel's suppression of individuality by pointing out it is impossible to create a valid set of rules or system in any society which can adequately describe existence for any one individual. Submitting one's will to the State denies personal freedom, choice, and responsibility.

In addition, Hegel does believe we can know the structure of God's mind, or ultimate reality. Hegel agrees with Kierkegaard that both reality and humans are incomplete, inasmuch as we are in time, and reality develops through time. But the relation between time and eternity is outside time and this is the "logical structure" that Hegel thinks we can know. Kierkegaard disputes this assertion, because it eliminates the clear distinction between ontology and epistemology. Existence and thought are not identical and one cannot possibly think existence. Thought is always a form of abstraction, and thus not only is pure existence impossible to think, but all forms in existence are unthinkable; thought depends on language, which merely abstracts from experience, thus separating us from lived experience and the living essence of all beings. In addition, because we are finite beings, we cannot possibly know or understand anything that is universal or infinite such as God, so we cannot know God exists, since that which transcends time simultaneously transcends human understanding.

Friedrich Nietzsche

Friedrich Nietzsche was the first to mount a logically serious criticism of Idealism. He argued that Kant's argument for his transcendental idealism rests on a confusion between a tautology and/or petitio principii, and is therefore an invalid argument. In his book *Beyond Good and Evil*, Part 1 On the Prejudice of Philosophers Section 11, he ridicules Kant for admiring himself because he had undertaken and (thought he) succeeded in tackling "the most difficult thing that could ever be undertaken on behalf of metaphysics."

"But let us reflect; it is high time to do so. 'How are synthetic judgements a priori possible?' Kant asked himself-and what really is his answer? 'By virtue of a faculty'-but unfortunately not in five words,...The honeymoon of German philosophy arrived. All the young theologians of the Tübingen seminary went into the bushes all looking for 'faculties.'...'By virtue of a faculty'-he had said, or at least meant. But is that an answer? An explanation? Or is it not rather merely a repetition of the question? How does opium induce sleep? 'By virtue of a faculty,' namely the virtus dormitiva, replies the doctor in Moliére." This argument Nietzsche advances can also be constructed to read that Kant was making a tautological argument (i.e. necessarily true). An argument that has a necessarily true premise cannot make any synthetic a priori statements, because (qua Kant) the synthetic cannot be necessarily true. In addition to the Kant's idealism, Nietzsche in the same book attacks the idealism of Schopenhauer and Descartes via a similar argument to Kant's original critique of Descartes. Quoting Nietzsche: "There are still harmless self-observers who believe that there are "immediate certainties"; for example, "I think," or as the superstition of Schopenhauer put it, "I will"; as though knowledge here got hold of its objects purely and nakedly as "the thing in itself," without any falsification on the part of either the subject or the object. But that "immediate certainty," as well as "absolute knowledge" and the "thing in itself," involved a *contradictio in adjecto*, I shall repeat a hundred times; we really ought to free ourselves from the seduction of words!"

G. E. Moore

The first criticism of Idealism that falls within the analytic philosophical framework is by one of its co-founders G. E. Moore. This 1903 seminal article, *The Refutation of Idealism*. This is one of the first demonstrations of Moore's commitment to analysis as the proper philosophical method.

Moore proceeds by examining the Berkeleian aphorism *esse est percipi*: "to be is to be perceived". He examines in detail each of the three terms in the aphorism, finding that it must mean that the object and the subject are *necessarily* connected. So, he argues, for the idealist, "yellow" and "the sensation of yellow" are necessarily identical-to be yellow is necessarily to be experienced as yellow. But, in a move similar to the open question argument, it also seems clear that there is a difference between "yellow" and "the sensation of yellow". For Moore, the idealist is in error because "that *esse* is held to be *percipi*, solely because what is experienced is held to be identical with the experience of it". Though far from a complete refutation, this was the first strong statement by analytic philosophy against its idealist predecessors, or at any rate against the type of idealism represented by Berkeley. This argument did not show that the GEM is logically invalid.

Bertrand Russell

Despite Bertrand Russell's hugely popular book *The Problems of Philosophy* (this book was in its 17th printing by 1943) which was written for a general audience rather than academia, few ever mention his critique even though he completely anticipates David Stove's GEM both in form and content. In chapter 4 (Idealism) he highlights Berkeley's tautological premise for advancing idealism.

Quoting Russell's prose (1912:42-43): "If we say that the things known must be in the mind, we are either un-duly limiting the mind's power of knowing, or we are uttering a mere tautology. We are uttering a mere tautology if we mean by 'in the mind' the same as by 'before the mind', i.e. if we mean merely being apprehended by the mind.

But if we mean this, we shall have to admit that what, in this sense, is in the mind, may nevertheless be not mental. Thus when we realize the nature of knowledge, Berkeley's argument is seen to be wrong in substance as well as in form, and his grounds for supposing that 'idea'-i.e. the objects apprehended-must be mental, are found to have no validity whatever. Hence his grounds in favour of the idealism may be dismissed."

A.C. Ewing

Published in 1933, A. C. Ewing, according to David Stove, mounted the first full length book critique of Idealism, entitled *Idealism; a critical survey*. Stove does not mention that Ewing anticipated his GEM.

David Stove

The Australian philosopher David Stove argued in typical acerbic style that idealism rested on what he called "the worst argument in the world". From a logical point of view his critique is no different from Russell or Nietzsche's—but Stove has been more widely cited and most clearly highlighted the mistake of proponents (like Berkeley) of subjective idealism.

He named the form of this argument-invented by Berkeley—"the GEM". Berkeley claimed that "[the mind] is deluded to think it can and does conceive of bodies existing unthought of, or without the mind, though at the same time they are apprehended by, or exist in, itself". Stove argued that this claim proceeds from the tautology that nothing can be thought of without its being thought of, to the conclusion that nothing can exist without its being thought of. Alan Musgrave recently extended this argument to attack Conceptual Idealism.

John Searle

In *The Construction of Social Reality*, John Searle offers an attack on some versions of idealism. Searle conveniently summarises two important arguments for (subjective) idealism. The first is based on our perception of reality:

1. All we have access to in perception are the contents of our own experiences

2. The only epistemic basis we can have for claims about the external world are our perceptual experiences therefore,

*3. the only reality we can meaningfully speak of is the reality of perceptual experiences (*The Construction of Social Reality *p. 172)*

Whilst agreeing with (2), Searle argues that (1) is false, and points out that (3) does not follow from (1) and (2).

The second argument for (subjective) idealism runs as follows:

Premise: Any cognitive state occurs as part of a set of cognitive states and within a cognitive system

Conclusion 1: It is impossible to get outside of all cognitive states and systems to survey the relationships between them and the reality they are used to cognize

*Conclusion 2: No cognition is ever of a reality that exists independently of cognition (*The Construction of Social Reality *p. 174)*

Searle goes on to point out that conclusion 2 simply does not follow from its precedents.

Philip J. Neujahr

"Although it would be hard to legislate about such matters, it would perhaps be well to restrict the idealist label to theories which hold that the world, or its material aspects, are dependent upon the specifically cognitive activities of the mind or Mind in perceiving or thinking about (or 'experiencing') the object of its awareness." (*Kant's Idealism*, Ch. 1)

Idealism in Religious Thought

A broad enough definition of idealism could include most religious viewpoints. The belief that personal beings (e.g., God/

s, angels & spirits) preceded the existence of insentient matter seems to suggest that an experiencing subject is a necessary reality. Also, the existence of an omniscient God suggests, regardless of the actual nature of matter, that all of nature is the object of at least one consciousness. Materialism sees no incoherence in a scenario of there being a cosmos where no sentient subject ever develops; a wholly unknown universe where neither any subject, nor any object of a subject's experience ever exists. Historically, Mechanistic Materialism has been the favorite viewpoint of Atheist philosophers. Still, idealistic viewpoints that have not included God, supernatural beings, or a post-mortem existence have sometimes been advanced.

While many religious philosophies are indeed specifically idealist, for example, some Hindu denominations view regarding the nature of Brahman, souls, and the world are idealistic, some have favored a form of substance dualism. Early Buddhism was not subjective idealistic. Some have misinterpreted the Yogâcâra school of Mahayana Buddhism that developed the consciousness-only approach as a form of metaphysical idealism, but this is incorrect. Yogâcâra thinkers did not focus on consciousness to assert it as ultimately real, but rather because it is the cause of the karmic problem they are seeking to eliminate.

Some Christian theologians have held idealist views, substance dualism has been the more common view of Christian authors, especially with the strong influence of the philosophy of Aristotle among the Scholastics. Several modern religious movements, for example the organizations within the New Thought Movement and the Unity Church, may be said to have a particularly idealist orientation.

The theology of Christian Science includes a form of subjective idealism: it teaches that all that exists is God and God's ideas; that the world as it appears to the senses is a distortion of the underlying spiritual reality, a distortion that may be corrected by a reorientation (spiritualization) of thought. Such a reorientation, Christian Science teaches, results in healing, as the world of appearance adjusts to approximate more nearly to the underlying divine reality. Christian Science is consequently a form of monistic (theistic) idealism, since it teaches that there is in reality no matter: all is Spirit (God) and its manifestation. In Christian Science teaching, there is no ultimate division or dualism between Spirit and its expression (the spiritual universe including the true identity of each one of us) any more than there is between the sun and the light which shines forth from it.

A Course in Miracles, a spiritual self-study course published in 1976, represents an explicitly idealist, pure nondualistic thought system. In the Course, only God and His Creation, which is Spirit and has nothing to do with the world, are real. The physical universe is an illusion and does not exist. The Course compares the world of perception with a dream. It arises from the projection of the dreamer, i.e. the mind ("projection makes perception," T-21.in.1:5), according to its wishes (perception "is the outward picture of a wish; an image that you wanted to be true," T-24.VII.8:10). The purpose of the perceptual world is to ensure our separate, individual existence apart from God but avoid the responsibility and project the guilt onto others. As we learn to give the world *another purpose* and recognize our perceptual errors, we also learn to look past them or "forgive," as a way to awaken gradually from the dream and finally remember our true Identity in God. The Course's nondualistic metaphysics is similar to Advaita Vedanta. However, *A Course in Miracles* differs in that it adds a "motivation" for the illusory existence of the perceptual world.

Other uses

In general parlance, "idealism" or "idealist" is also used to describe a person having high ideals, sometimes with the connotation that those ideals are unrealisable or at odds with "practical" life, or naively at variance with empirical observations of the real world. The word "ideal" is commonly used as an adjective to designate qualities of perfection, desirability, and excellence. This is foreign to the epistemological use of the word "idealism" which pertains to internal mental representations. These internal ideas represent objects that are assumed to exist outside of the mind.

IMPORTANT PHILOSOPHERS OF IDEALISM

The nature and identity of the "mind" upon which reality is dependent is one issue that has divided idealists of various sorts. Some argue that there is some objective mind outside of nature, some argue that it is simply the common power of reason or rationality, some argue that it is the collective mental faculties of society, and some focus simply on the minds of individual human beings.

Platonic Idealism

According to Platonic Idealism, there exists a perfect realm of Form and Ideas and our world merely contains shadows of that realm.

Subjective Idealism

According to Subjective Idealism, only ideas can be known or have any reality (it is also known as solipsism).

Transcendental Idealism

According to Transcendental Idealism, develped by Kant, this theory argues that all knowledge orginates in perceived phenomena which have been organized by categories.

Absolute Idealism

According to Absolute Idealism, all objects are identical with some idea and the ideal knowledge is itself the system of ideas. It is also known as Objective Idealism and is the sort of idealism promoted by Hegel. Unlike the other forms of idealism, this is monistic — there is only one mind in which reality is created.

CRITICAL REALISM IN GEOGRAPHY

Critical realism is a philosophy of and for the social sciences that has had an impact on methodology in geography since the 1980s, although there have always been realist elements in geographical thought. With the rise of critical realism, these and further elements were developed and promoted self consciously, while non or anti realist elements were attacked.

A DEFINITION

Critical realism argues that the natural and social worlds we study exist largely independently of the researcher, and that there is necessity in the world which enables and constrains what can happen. Causation is to be understood in terms of the powers that objects possess rather than in terms of empirical regularities among events; if and when these causal powers are activated, the results depend on contexts, and are unlikely to be regular. Since social phenomena such as actions and ideas are intrinsically meaningful, unlike the subject matter of the physical sciences, their meaning also has to be interpreted. The world can only be understood in terms of available discourses. While there are no privileged routes for discovering the truth about the world, and empirical tests are themselves fallible, it is often possible to distinguish better from worse accounts in terms of their adequacy for informing material practice.

INTELLECTUAL CONTEXT

Critical realist philosophy was developed by Roy Bhaskar out of his earlier work on the philosophy of natural science ('transcendental realism'). The latter sought an alternative to both those positions which treat knowledge as straightforwardly based on observation and experience (empiricism) and for which truth is a simple matter of correspondence between statements and the objects to which they refer, and various relativist positions which treat the truth of theories as purely relative to discourses. Critical realism also steers a course between positions which regard social science as the same as natural science and those which treat it as entirely different.

REALISM AND FALLIBILISM

The most fundamental realist assumption is that much of the world can exist independently of our knowledge of it. The plausibility of this assumption rests upon the fallibility of knowledge; the fact that knowledge claims sometimes prove to be mistaken and generate false expectations implies that the world is not a product of our thought but is whatever it is regardless of what we think about it. Realists reject the empiricist view that reality is whatever we can experience since this implies an improbable coincidence between the world and the limits of our sensory powers, and implies that either knowledge is already complete, or that new knowledge creates new objects. Critical realists accept that our observations and knowledge are always formed through available discourses or are theory laden', so that we can never escape from our conceptual frameworks to see how they compare with the world they seek to represent. However, that observation is theory laden does not necessarily mean that it is entirely determined by theories and so it can still be possible to compare the adequacy of different theories from within discourses and find observations which contradict expectations. This offers a way of avoiding the relativist view that truth is merely relative to theoretical systems. It also implies that science can make progress in explaining the world even though absolute truth is not an intelligible goal.

Critical realism therefore does not involve claims to have a privileged access to the truth about the world, a uniquely realistic view, for the very independence of the world from our knowledge of it renders such claims problematic. It must necessarily view all knowledge as in principle fallible, although this does not mean, of course, that it is all false or all equally true or untrue.

KEY ARGUMENTS AND THEIR INFLUENCE ON GEOGRAPHY

Critical realism became influential in geography partly for the above reasons, for geographers, like other scientists, were seeking a way of understanding science that avoided the unappealing alternatives of empiricism and relativism. However, a further important factor was probably its view of causation and systems. Some of the first discussions of critical realism in geography emphasized this issue and its implications for the nature of theorizing in geography.

The scientific revolution in geography, exemplified by location theory and spatial analysis, had largely assumed that causation was a matter of empirical regularities or constant conjunctions among causes and effects. It was expected that understanding of the regularities in spatial organization of phenomena would grow to the point where it would be possible to formulate laws about them. This regularity based view of causation had dominated the philosophy of science despite the fact that, particularly in social sciences like human geography, there appear to be few enduring precise empirical regularities, so that the search for laws of social and spatial behaviour has been singularly unsuccessful. For realists this is unsurprising. For them, causation is a matter of what produces change, not a matter of empirical regularities in sequences of events. Objects have causal powers, that is, the power to act in certain ways. A seed has the power to germinate, a person the power to work. These objects have these powers in virtue of their structures, such as the biochemical constitution of the seed, or the anatomical and mental structures of a person.

Whether these powers are ever activated depends on conditions whose presence is contingent, that is, neither necessary nor impossible, such as moisture and solar energy in the case of the seed or a need for food in the case of the person. Furthermore, the particular effects which follow when these causal powers are activated depends on conditions which again are contingent. The germination of the seed may be encouraged by fertilizer or halted by herbicides, the attempt of the person to work may be hampered by lack of tools or encouraged by their availability.

This alternative conception of causation has far reaching implications.

First, since it dissociates causation from empirical regularities, it enables understanding of how unique events, as much as repeated ones, can be caused.

Second, it focuses on necessity rather than regularity or the search for empirical order.

Third, in view of this, explanation does not require repeated observations: what makes something happen has nothing to do with the number of times it has or has not been observed to happen. It follows from this that the old debate in geography between idiographic and nomothetic approaches the former a supposedly nonscientific study of the unique, the latter a supposedly scientific search for laws was falsely based. Regardless of whether phenomena were unique or widely replicated, they could be explained in the same way.The uniqueness of many geographical phenomena no longer posed a threat to geography's scientific status.

Fourth, it became possible to see that the search for generalizations is distinct from explaining how causes work; generalizations, as the term suggests, attempt to tell us how common or extensive certain phenomena are, and this is different from explaining how they are produced. The greater part of standard literature on the philosophy and methodology of science had confused these two things, and many geographers had done so too.

Fifth, the realist account offers a way of understanding how it is possible for the same cause to produce different effects and for different causes to produce the same effects, since the relationship between causal powers and empirical outcomes is not one of automatic regularity but is dependent on the conditions within which they are located.

An example of this can be given from a kind of economic geography which was popular at the same time critical realism became influential. The geography of industrial restructuring looked at changes in economic geography in terms of how competitive pressures upon firms to restructure produced responses.

In realist terms, competitive pressures on profit margins were considered as the main causal power of interest here, with their effects being mediated by a wide range of contextual circumstances, such as the particular cost structures of the firms under pressure, the scope for technological change, and the availability of various kinds of labour. Thus, in an industry such as clothing, which had little scope for further automation or speeding up work, and in which wages were a major element of costs, a common response was to seek out cheaper sources of labour, sometimes by relocating.

By contrast, in industries which were more technology intensive and had scope for further automation, a more common response was technological innovation. By such means, it was possible to explain how the same or similar causes could produce radically different results according to context, whereas approaches which rested upon the discovery of empirical regularities foundered. Similar research also illustrated how a single kind of outcome job losses could have completely different causes, e.g., a drop in demand for the firm's products, or the introduction of automation during steady or rising demand, or reorganization of work routines to eliminate idle time and intensify work.

One of the most important and lasting influences of critical realism on geography has been on its empirical research designs.

Hitherto, the dominance of conceptions of explanation as tied to generalizations about empirical regularities had been used to privilege extensive research designs which sought to uncover such regularities or patterns of covariation. Although these are, as the term indicates, useful for establishing how extensive certain phenomena are, they do not necessarily identify causes, as opposed to spurious correlations.

The latter are likely to be thrown up by extensive research because it preselects groups of objects taxonomically, that is, on the basis of similarities (e.g., industries of a certain kind), rather than functional connection.

By contrast, intensive research designs, including ethnographic case studies, focus on causal rather than taxonomic groups and follow up causal connections wherever they lead often between heterogeneous objects, such as firms of different kinds. Intensive research is typically more exploratory, since the purpose is to discover the relevant causal groups. It is often time consuming to do this for large numbers of cases, and therefore it is not always a good basis for generalization. However, as we have seen, this lack of generalizability does not undermine the status of causal explanations of the particular cases which are studied intensively. Conse quently, having formerly been regarded as unscientific, intensive studies have now become more accepted in geographical research.

Critical realism acknowledges that the methodology of social science must diverge from that of the natural sciences because human, social phenomena are intrinsically meaningful. While the objects that, say, geologists study, are what they are regardless of any meaning people may give to them, objects such as socially segregated urban areas depend on the meanings actors give to them.

To understand what these are, one has to know what their meaning is in society, whereas the nature of a rock does not depend on how its constituents understand one another, as they do not. Consequently, an important part of the methodology of human geography, no less than other social sciences, is interpretive understanding. For example, to understand the geography of the Middle East, we would have to understand what significance its land had for Jews and Arabs in terms of their identities.

Although this interpretive understanding has also been the focus of humanistic geography, critical realists make certain qualifications which the latter might not. The three most important are as follows. First, critical realists argue that although we have to interpret the understandings that actors have of their situations in order to make sense of how they act, their understanding is not necessarily a good one, indeed it may be systematically flawed. Moreover, these misunderstandings may have important effects which actors cannot explain. Thus a mysogynist may believe that the proper spatial location for women is in the home, on the false grounds that they are incapable of coping with life in the public sphere; the falsity of this understanding makes a difference to what happens and therefore has to be acknowledged in scientific accounts. Further, different actors may give contradictory accounts of the same situation: where this is the case the researcher cannot sit on the fence and say both are correct. Actors accounts of situations therefore face social scientists accounts both as objects of study and rivals. It is therefore likely that researchers accounts will be at least implicitly critical of actors accounts a conclusion which humanistic geographers are generally unwilling to accept. It is primarily for this reason that Bhaskar's philosophy of social science is called critical realism.

Second, among the intrinsically meaningful aspects of social phenomena are actors reasons. Critical realists argue that reasons can be causes, since they can be responsible for producing change, by prompting actions. This, of course, implies that realists do not limit causation to physical processes. To deny that reasons are causes is to imply that the giving of reasons by actors is ineffectual and redundant, which of course makes it unclear why they are given. Third, an insistence on the necessity of interpretive understanding should not allow us to forget that social life is also material, embodied, and spatially situated, and that things happen to people, so that, for example, they can be dominated, sometimes regardless of their understanding of the situation.

The realist facility for explaining irregular processes was particularly attractive to a discipline such as geography, concerned as it is with spatial differentiation and uneven development, and hence unable to ignore as, say, economics tries to do the problems of applying equilibrium models or making generalizations which are supposed to hold across time and space. The systems which geography and other social sciences study are open, that is, their elements can themselves be undergoing internal qualitative change actors aging and learning, for example and the relations among the elements are not constant, with the result that any empirically regular behaviors are unlikely to be durable or widespread. Evolutionary change and disequilibrium rather than equilibrium are the norm.

Where previous attempts at scientific explanation in geography had tried to evade the prevalence of differentiation and irregularity, on the mistaken grounds that explanation required the discovery of regularity, human geography began to re embrace differentiation, nowhere more strikingly than in Doreen Massey's influential Spatial Divisions of Labour. This was closely followed by a burgeoning literature on locality studies, which typically focussed on how economic restructuring worked out in different localities, and how those differences impacted back on the restructuring process.

CRITICAL RECEPTION

Some geographers feared that such concerns heralded an abandonment of theory and generalization and a slide towards the empiricist documentation of facts, indicating a resistance to the critical realist de emphasis of generalization. These fears were not merely methodological but partly about a weakening attachment in economic geography to a particular kind of theory Marxism and also a tendency to treat critical realism as a source of substantive theory rather than as a philosophy, when it had no such pretensions. At the same time, some of the attempts to use critical realism in localities studies invited justified criticism by arbitrarily translating it into the study of general, supralocal causal processes interacting with local contingent conditions. However, critical realism did not license such an extraordinary alignment of scale and necessity: the supralocal is no more or less the realm of necessity than the local, nor is the local any more the realm of contingency than the supralocal.

Towards the end of the 1980s a newer generation of geographers became influenced by postmodernism. In some ways this continued the emphasis on differentiation only phrased as difference which had connotations of social differences of identity. Societies were seen as inherently messy, and skepticism towards grand universalizing accounts of the world grew. One of the positive features of this literature was that it gave greater concern to the textual nature of accounts of the world. At the same time, some postmodernist writers rekindled relativist, anti realist tendencies, although sometimes by mischaracterizing realism as claiming privileged access to the truth rather than as having a fallibilist view of knowledge. The debate continues.

11

The Rediscovery of Environmental Causation

The fundamental questions of human experience continue to vex us academically and as a society. Of the major questions that we challenge ourselves with, geography and geographers historically focus most intensively on pondering those related to how we construct our relationships with the non-human world and how that non-human world in turn affects us. These concerns address, according to Kates (1987, 532), 'the central question of the human-environment tradition: what is and what ought to be our relationship to the natural world?'

The impact of people on the environment occupies a central concern of society; an array of researchers and policymakers have begun to recognise the need to address environmental problems and crises through a consideration of humans together with their environment. Societal and scientific determination to solve current and future environmental problems highlights the need to develop better understandings of the human-environment condition. While new lines of inquiry and investigation breathe life into science, they can also represent problems.

One such problem arises when new lines of research resuscitate theoretical dead ends such as environmental determinism. Although vanquished by the works of cultural and political ecologists throughout the last 100 or so years, we are now surprised that environmental determinism reappears. Perhaps our collective surprise belies naivete, as Kates (1987, 527) reminds us, 'such is the power of good theory that practice seldom discourages it even when findings are to the contrary... each subsequent scholarly generation would redefine and expand the equation'.

We contend that the Pulitzer Prize winning book Guns, germs and steel (GGS) (Diamond 1997) is emblematic of the dangers posed by uncritically melding determinist scientific thinking with questions of human relationships to the environment. To justify this claim, this paper outlines the intellectual history of human-environment thought in geography, highlighting how apparent progress away from environmental determinism is ignored by some contemporary writers. GGS is not the only example of the rebirth of determinism, although certainly the most commercially and publicly popular. Diamond's engaging literary style and grasp of recent accomplishments in both archaeology and biology has made GGS a remarkably popular work of nonfiction, winning the Pulitzer Prize and continuing to post strong sales, television specials and public-speaking engagements. Other parties that share Diamond's favouring of environmental influence have benefited from the popularity of his work and found a more receptive audience to their own environmentally deterministic take on human-environment relations.

Neo-environmental determinist arguments mirror early conceptions of human-environment relations that attributed causal determinacy to the 'natural' environment. The widespread readership of GGS has thrust the question of environmental determinism (sometimes called geographic determinism or environmental causation) once again into the mainstream of popular thought and catalyzed the arguments of environmental determinists. In response, academics have either challenged its central thesis (Blaut 2000), or relented to reconsidering the role of the environment in shaping human history (Sachs 2005). We contend that the recent success of GGS and its less influential sequel, Collapse (Diamond 2004a), represents the persistence of an environmental determinist logic, hereafter referred to as neo-environmental determinism, and that this resurgence threatens negative consequence if uncritically adopted by policymakers. The popularity of GGS and other associated works suggests that the human-environment field has failed to communicate adequately its research advances, allowing the seeming intuitiveness of environmentally deterministic logic to resurge.

Popular acclaim for GGS alone would not necessitate the reconsideration of environmental determinism; however, its assimilation within the international development literature has significant implications for development policy, as it is emblematic of a recent shift toward a renewed interest in the determinative qualities of the natural environment. Concurrently, we argue that GGS itself serves as a catalyst for neo-environmental deterministic arguments forwarded by key development policy advisors. GGS's neo-environmental determinism originates in a particular perspective defined by its lack of appreciation for previous human-environment research and the inherent complexity of human-environment relations.

To demonstrate problems associated with the re-embrace of environmental determinism, this paper achieves three, linked goals. It develops an appreciation for the direction of human-environment research, highlighting advances since early environmental determinism that are in direct conflict with the arguments of neo-environmental determinism. We critique neo-environmental determinist arguments, exemplified by the work GGS, and test the degree of similarity shared with early theories of environmental causation. Finally, we identify the potential impacts of neo-environmental determinism by examining its influence on those who create and influence international development policy.

HISTORY OF HUMAN-ENVIRONMENT RESEARCH

Human-environment research within geography is a vast and sometimes divergent field of study, encompassing a diversity of research topics and embracing a wide range of emphases. The major subdivisions of this type of work include risks and hazards, resource and conservation, water geographies and cultural and political ecology (CAPE). This paper focuses its attention particularly on CAPE research and its juncture with neo-environmental determinism epitomised by the work GGS. An examination of the lineage of CAPE provides ample evidence to its own diverse theoretical pedigree. At the core of CAPE work, however, is Kates' unifying meta-question that binds the various threads of human-environment research and provides the inspiration for the diverse research questions pursued by its investigators.

Scientific questions, when well formulated, produce a series of other questions that probe issues of identity, ethics, change, impacts and the very definitions of the words 'humanity' and 'environment'. Complicating the most basic task of defining the vocabulary at the centre of this question has been the changing use of terms as well as evolving perceptions of the environment. The specific terminology employed has varied over time, but some notable usages include the man-land tradition, man-environment relationships (Grossman 1977), nature and society, people and nature (Sayer 1979), and human-environment relationships (Kates 1987).

The conceptual division between people and the environment has also been closely intertwined with changing assertions as to what determines the human-environment condition. Determinism, as used in this paper, refers to the attribution of significant influence to general attributes of the human-environment relationship and should not be construed as an assertion of absolute or complete influence. The separation of humankind from nature, and the search for determinism within this relationship, are mutually constitutive and appear to varying degrees during all moments of human-environment research. In essence, the development of this field of study can therefore be characterised by shifts in thought along a continuum of determinacy between humans and their environment. We complicate this continuum, however, by subdividing the human into two scales of interest, recognising the three axes of household, society and environment.

Household

Household specifically refers to the smallest human variable considered within a particular study. This could include an individual, an entire extended family or some minimum management unit of an environmental resource. Different moments in research have assigned varying importance to this unit, and several approaches have been adopted to explain household behaviour, ranging from cultural explanations to agricultural economics and beyond.

Society

Society refers to groupings of households that vary depending on the concept of society employed. Some examples would include cultural groups, populations subjected to the same government, informal unifying institutions, societies and divisions based on the political economy. Generally, society has been viewed as determining human-environment relationships, in that they set the decision context for the household, often in reference to perceptions of how the environment functions or is shaped.

Environment

The environment refers to the elements that compose the physical or conceived aspects of nature, along with their groupings in landscapes and ecosystems, with special reference to that which is considered the 'non-human'. During different times, the environment has been attributed varying degrees of determinism. Employing these compound axes, we trace the historic continuum of human-environment research by demonstrating that at different moments, greater causation has been attributed to factors associated with one or the other of these three axes. This activity uses just a few keystone works published at different times to develop generalisations about the theoretical frameworks shared during each period. The characterisation of strong determinism versus weak determinism is a conceptual device that compares the theoretical weight given to each of the three aspects of human-environment research at any given moment. Any such approach necessarily simplifies complexity and should therefore be understood as informative of the characteristics of each moment rather than of any given researcher. For a more in-depth review of the development of CAPE within the field of human-environment research, one can refer to Robbins (2004) and Zimmerer and Bassett's (2003a 2003b) recent works on political ecology.

Moment of environmental determinism (1890-1920) Early work in human-environment relations had deterministic roots that stretched deep into classical history, linking with the traditional thinking that the environment held fundamental sway over humanity (Glacken 1967). Plato, Aristotle, Hippocrates and Montesquieu all wrote on the influence of climate on the development of governments and on stimulating the progress of societies. An acceptance of this direction of influence, strictly from the environment to humans, persisted throughout a number of centuries and found renewed scientific merit following Darwin (1859) and Wallace's (1855) theory of evolution—albeit that neither were environmental determinists. It was believed by some that their theory of evolution was the bridge linking all organisms (including humans) to the natural laws governing the environment. Fredrich Ratzel is often identified as one of this moment's central figures as a result of his oft-quoted student Ellen Churchill Semple (1911, 1) who wrote:

> *Man is a product of the earth's surface. This means not merely that he is a child of the earth, dust of her dust; but that the earth has mothered him, fed him, set his tasks, directed his thoughts, confronted him with difficulties that has strengthened his body and sharpened his wits... She has entered his bone and tissue, into his mind and soul.*

Environmental factors were asserted as the determinative cause of racial differences, cultural practices, moral values, ingenuity and the ultimate capabilities of any given population.

This moment is characterised as being highly deterministic with relation to the environment and nearly completely lacking in any determinism with regard to the household and society. The failure of environmental determinists to prove that similar environments yielded the same response in human populations, and their inability to account for the ways humans intentionally modified their environment, greatly weakened the arguments of this approach and remains the fatal flaw of renewed interest in environmentally deterministic theories (Ellen 1982).

II. Moment of cultural possibilism (1920-1960/present) The free will of individuals, as constrained or enabled by the environment, became the focus of a new theoretical framework forwarded by academics with training outside the natural sciences (Ellen 1982). As one of the exemplars of this period, Sauer (1925) distanced himself from the problems of environmental determinism, but approached what some have instead termed a cultural determinism (Leighly 1987). Writing about the response of people to the environment, Sauer (1941, 7) states that: 'Such behaviour does not depend upon physical stimuli nor on logical necessity, but on acquired habits, which are the culture of the group'. The inductive, diachronic research techniques advocated by Sauer (1941) and his contemporaries in anthropology sought to illustrate how culture could be unified and contextualised within the medium of the physical environment (Steward 1955). This approach, termed cultural ecology, viewed culture as the sum total of individuals in a society, and it was anticipated that correlations could be made between cultural practices and specific environmental attributes (Steward 1955).

We characterise the 'moment of cultural possibilism' as reducing the determinism of the environment to a force of constraint or to act as an enabler—preserving only a muted sense of influence. The household was often defined as an individual who was seen as inventive and in direct exchange with the natural environment, meaning that there were few other mediating factors considered to intrude upon individual interactions with the environment. Lastly, society was conceived as the sum total influence of individual households, which, when combined, yielded a culture group with a distinct material connection to the environment termed the cultural landscape. While still actively supported, this moment was eclipsed by studies that questioned the concept of culture and promised the formation of generalised theories that transcended the ideographic tendencies of the case study.

Moment of systems (1960-present) Scholars reconceived culture during the 'moment of systems' as the product of human interaction with the environment, defined as the mode of life associated with a specific material and symbolic practice. It was thus viewed as functional and adaptive, in that cultural differences represented an enhancement of the human-environment interaction. Cultural adaptation was studied through the examination of regional ecology and environmental perception of peoples, as mediated by culture (Butzer 1990). These adaptationists examined how cultural groups responded to changing environmental conditions through studies of land use and resource procurement. Referring to the modified use of ecology, systems theory and cybernetics, Butzer (1990, 685) states: 'societies can be regarded as interlocking, human ecosystems. They operate on the basis of individual initiatives and actions, embodied in aggregate community behaviour and institutional structures'. The modified application of these theories was employed to examine system-wide characteristics that could either lead to adaptation or maladaptation by the cultural group (Butzer 1990).

This moment in human-environment research was characterised with a middle-range determinism spread among the household, society and environment. As the driving force of adaptation, the environment was again infused with more determinative force, while determinism within the household was more subdued. Society, while retaining some determinism, held only minor sway in the relationship, as it was viewed as the product of ecological interactions with the household.

Moment of behaviouralism (1965-present) Dissatisfied with the limits of the input/output approaches of systems theory, researchers later refocused attention on what was termed active participants. Vayda and McCay (1975) suggested that an individual-oriented approach promised to explain group characteristics, such as environmental interaction. Brookfield (1964, 300) presaged this perspective, advocating micro-geography as an acceptable approach, stating that 'the study of process with its concomitant need to inquire into human organisation and motivation can only be pursued effectively by selecting very small groups of people, usually occupying only very limited territories'. Subgroups, smallholders and individuals were no longer cast as passive agents, as in environmental determinism, but as active participants in land use and decision-making. This perspective led to endogenous conclusions that linked specific human-environment interactions with individuals, situated within the context of culture and regional ecology. Attention was also turned to developing mid-range theories to explain smallholder decisions that could provide insights into regional and global concerns (Brookfield 1964).

This moment was characterised by a strengthening in the determinism of both the household and society. Households represented active participants who were considered inventive in their responses, while the constraints and opportunities provided by society were attributed a moderate degree of determinism. The determinism ascribed directly to the environment weakened during this period, as it was viewed more passively as providing constraints and opportunities. It was realised during this moment that households confronted with the same ecological and social problems have a range of potential responses at their disposal, complicating explanations that rely on simplistic causal relations.

Moment of structuralism (1980-1990/present) Political ecology, a dominant theoretical approach of this moment, was founded on the concept that ecological arguments are never socially neutral but are influenced by structural forces that condition the choices available (Peet and Watts 2004). Developed partly as a critique of the dominant paradigms of risk-hazards research and cultural ecology, political ecology identified several theoretical weaknesses in the previous human-environment research (Blaikie and Brookfield 1987). A list of these critiques include the prevalence of a positivist and Western perspective, an uncritical assumption of the role of politics and the larger economy in subsistence cultures, and the failure of cultural ecology to progress toward an overarching meta-theory (Robbins 2004). Early political ecology took exception to the concept of voluntaristic agent smallholders as the primary force in shaping nature-society relationships (Peet and Watts 2004). Political ecologists focused:

> *not [on] isolated or subsistence communities in harmony with their physical environment, but rather peasant societies marked by the presence of the markets, social inequalities, conflict and forms of social and cultural disintegration associated with their integration into a modern world system. Here maladaptation, rather than adaptation, was the order of the day.*

The 'moment of structuralism' is characterised by the elevation of society to the position of greatest determinacy as institutions, governments, class, race and economic structures are viewed as the dominant influence mediating human relations with the environment. The household was viewed as dominated by the collective, with any agency being minor and accorded to it by the collective. Likewise, the environment was viewed as a passive influence on human-environment relations, serving as a stage for political economic actions and receiving the brunt of impacts originating from collective human systems. This moment recognised the ability of society, in all its organisational forms, to influence the balance of the human-environment relationship, potentially outweighing household adaptations and even the most favourable or restrictive environmental situations.

Moment of integrative human ecologies (1987-present) Researchers have begun to assert that the combination of CAPE approaches, generally referred to as hybrid or integrative ecologies (Zimmerer and Bassett 2003a), may offer explanations that range across both temporal and spatial scales. Integrative methods distinguish themselves from recent developments in political ecology alone by rejecting the a priori theoretical grounding of political economy.

This has led to the rejection of the tendency to 'understand "the local" in the context of political economic and other forces at "higher" levels that ultimately home in on the local'. An 'actor-oriented' approach, developed by CAPE, has been espoused as necessary to understanding how individuals might manipulate their own situations within the ecological, structural and cultural framework in which they are located. Power and other structural influences such as profit and political constraints thus persist as research foci within this integrative framework. However, their earlier determinative roles are discounted with the consideration of other influences. This has allowed integrative human ecologies to overcome some criticism of political ecology by making room for the consideration of the environment as an actor influence in human-environment relations.

This moment is characterised by the convergence of influence between the household and society. While maintaining a strong degree of causation, society is no longer viewed as immutable, particularly as the household is attributed greater ingenuity in manipulating their situation and possessing the ability to influence the society through group action (protest, elections, unions). The environment also receives an increased allotment of determinism, as it functions both as a factor of constraint as well as a market source. This moment recognises that simple, causal explanations of human-environment phenomena err when they attribute causal determinacy to one of the three axes, while ignoring additional significant mediating or contributing factors from the other axes.

GUNS, GERMS AND STEEL: ENVIRONMENTAL DETERMINISM REVISITED

Jared Diamond's (1997) work, Guns, germs and steel: the fates of human societies, ambitiously chronicles the development of the human race to the present state of the world. The stated goal of the book is to explain why differences exist between human societies and more specifically why wealth and power has been concentrated in the hands of a few societies. In answering this question, Diamond (2005, 81) guides the reader through a synthesis of archaeological and biological knowledge that he uses to identify the source of 'ultimate causation' as being the natural environment.

His knowledge of the major accomplishments within these fields is impressive, as is his weaving of their various conclusions together into a concise and forceful argument. We contend, however, that his work is flawed fundamentally, from his conclusions back to the manner in which he structured his research question at the beginning of the book. The flaws are not due to ill-conceived arguments or erratic writing, rather they stem from imposing a modernist, scientific determinism to the question of human history, society formation, political action and conquest. Diamond sees the environment as the determinative factor in human-environment relations, as methods, subject matter and evidence are restricted to the natural environment. Now a decade since publication, GGS maintains a significant influence on the future direction of human-environment research, as its popularity, both among the general public and professional community, cements the book's position to force renewed consideration of nature's determinative influence. A critical examination of the argument presented in GGS does not rehash past critiques, such as appeared in the journal Antipode, but is necessary to lay out the arguments that form the basis for modern neo-environmental determinism.

The determinism attributed to the environment in GGS is forwarded as the basis of both the success and the failure of societies to place themselves in positions of economic and technological strength. Environmental constraints are postulated specifically as fundamental weaknesses that can doom any society to future failure. In this manner, Diamond echoes the mistakes of earlier environmental determinists. His arguments concerning the advantages of geographical environments fail to prove that similar environments yield the same response in human actions and society formation, particularly as one considers the immense generalisations Diamond makes concerning the topography of Europe and Asia (Blaut 2000 2005). Likewise, GGS fails to acknowledge the ingenuity and capabilities of individuals and societies to surmount sizeable physiographic barriers and environmental limitations through adaptive social organisations and technological innovations.

The arguments of GGS quickly factor out human consciousness, desire, political power and the formation of culture as determinative in the distribution of wealth and power. Diamond instead appears to espouse the subtle logic that if a society can, it will. His approach for answering the question of why disparities exist in the world relies on first identifying the immediate causes (guns, germs and steel), and then explaining their occurrence by identifying the ultimate causes for their uneven global distribution. Referring to explanations that stop at the factors that allowed Europeans to invade and subjugate other peoples, Diamond (2005, 23) states:

> *However, this hypothesis is incomplete, because it still offers only a proximate (first-stage) explanation identifying immediate causes. It invites a search for ultimate causes: why were Europeans, rather than Africans or Native Americans, the ones to end up with guns, the nastiest germs, and steel?*

The assumption is that, given the same technological and biological endowments, all societies would behave in a manner similar to colonial Europe. Thus, to explain the history of colonisation and subjugation, all one needs to do is figure out what it is that most determines what societies can and cannot accomplish—representing an elevation of limiting factors to the level of causation.

Diamond characterises culture as an irrational byproduct of humans that stymies their development through taboos, restrictive customs, and the obstruction of innovation. Regarding the acceptance of innovations in agriculture, particularly the domestication of plants, Diamond (2005, 154) writes:

Our broad conclusion is that people can recognize useful plants, would therefore have probably recognized better local ones suitable for domestication if any had existed, and aren't barred from doing so by cultural conservatism or taboos. The fact is that... some societies will be more open to innovation, and some will be more resistant. The ones that do adopt new crops, livestock, or technology may thereby be enabled to nourish themselves better and to outbreed, displace, conquer, or kill off societies resisting innovation.

References to culture are similarly characterised throughout the book in the negative sense of inhibitory conservatism, juxtaposed to the innovation that Diamond suggests are the natural results of evolutionary biological competition, a throwback to the evolutionary arguments made by earlier environmental determinists.

GGS begins with an experience recalled by the author that initially directed his thoughts in writing this book. Diamond (2005, 14) describes an inquisitive native of New Guinea, named Yali, who poses the apparently unsolicited question:

Why is it that you white people developed so much cargo [technological innovations and weapons] and brought it to New Guinea, but we black people had little cargo of our own?

The fact that Yali, a charismatic and intelligent native, first raises the question reduces the appearance that Diamond is alone in marvelling at the seemingly obvious power and economic superiority of the West. The author nevertheless feels the need to absolve himself from the earlier works that compared the development of different societies based on the environment, namely environmental determinism.

Diamond distinguishes his work from that of earlier environmental determinists by constructing a historical strawman, depicting the approach as consumed with climatic variation:

A genetic explanation isn't the only possible answer to Yali's question. Another one, popular with inhabitants of northern Europe, invokes the supposed stimulatory effects of their homeland's cold climate and the inhibitory effects of hot, humid, tropical climates on human creativity and energy.

Diamond precedes this description of environmental determinism by alluding to the historic racist arguments of European superiority, as early environmental determinists were faulted for being at least implicitly compliant in bolstering racist colonial endeavours (Robbins 2004). The characterisation of early environmental determinism as forcibly racist allows Diamond to distance himself from this work by claiming a secondary objective, namely putting to rest any lingering racist explanations for societal differences. The neo-environmental determinism of GGS, however, explicitly echoes the arguments of early determinism, particularly with regard to environmental influence on selecting intelligence. In contrast to the standard racist application of this argument, Diamond reverses the tables and suggests that natives lacking in modern amenities and health care are probably smarter than Westerners. He states:

> *In mental ability New Guineans are probably genetically superior to Westerners, and they surely are superior in escaping the devastating developmental disadvantages under which most children in industrialized societies grow up.*

Such an argument represents a foray into the theoretical terrain captured in the already cited quote from Semple, where she claims that the environment works to direct the thoughts and permeates the minds of people (Semple 1911).

Diamond's principal argument revolves around what natural factors have given which societies a 'head start' in the race of existence. The metaphor of a race, introduced at the beginning of GGS, is more than a literary device. Entailed in the race metaphor is the concept of a linear progression to human history, implying a starting point and the necessary passing of successive developmental stages (Peet and Watts 2004). Diamond believes that the development path of all societies progresses through the successive stages of hunter/gather, pastoralism, sedentary agriculture and lastly the development of complex, socially stratified societies. This assertion has been heavily criticised, as it ignores that all these purported stages of development exist concurrently and persist even within societies that maintain extensive contact with outsiders (Robbins 2003). The supposition that all societies progress through the same stages of development is highly suspect and more a reflection of Western popular thought than an accepted theory on societal development.

Perhaps an even more pernicious result of the race metaphor is the premise that all societies are in direct competition with one another. Much of the world prior to the period of European colonialism would have been surprised to learn that they were in a race for world domination. On the contrary, the concept of a race was more than a metaphor for Europeans as France, Britain, Spain, Portugal, the Netherlands and Germany all competed to acquire resource rich colonies. Diamond advances this colonial logic in his book by characterising the world's people as athletes, all competing for the top spot of dominant society (Diamond 2005, 50). Not only is this argument Eurocentric, it is also completely defensible if the human race is treated as any other plant or animal population subject to evolutionary competition. The evolutionary competition perspective is central to Diamond's argument that environmental factors are the ultimate cause of difference between human societies, as it establishes the societal competition necessary for the natural selection of the 'fittest' societies. As Diamond rejects any complex notion of the influence of socio-cultural variations, he asserts that random arrangements of environmental factors must have determined which societies have become the most successful. Within such lines of reasoning there is no place for socio-cultural tendencies, such as pacifist societies, or for the consideration of morally reprehensible actions, such as slavery and genocide. Instead, those whose environments have provided them with the greatest advantages will necessarily come to dominate all others societies, by whatever means are at their disposal.

If mapped onto the history of the human-environment field, GGS would closely reproduce the distribution of determinism that characterised earlier theories of environmental determinism. The only variation would be that society, as depicted in GGS, is considered to hold some minor degree of determinism, as governments and cultures are mentioned as proximate causes of what Diamond identifies as a successful society—one that is able to amass power and wealth at the expense of other societies. Environmental factors, however, are viewed as the ultimate causes determining the manifestation of both government and culture at any given stage of development.

While, at first, many geographers embraced Diamond's work (accepting him into the academic community and attending his lectures in droves), many both in and outside the field have expressed serious reservations regarding the nature of his geographic focus. Andrew Sluyter (2003) identifies GGS as another in a series of recent works that have come to 'rely on the same faulty categorical thinking' (Sluyter 2003, 816). His concern is that the popularity of the work may suggest that GGS's 'neo-environmental determinism' might actually be indicative of a broader intellectual transformation to integrated research which is focused on addressing the human-environmental repercussions of modernisation (Sluyter 2003). Characterising such a convergence Sluyter (2003, 817) writes:

> *In the short run, as scientists from both sides of the nature/society dichotomy scramble to deal with modernization's boomerang effects by integrating research on nature and society, opportunists are able to achieve some renown by reviving environmental determinism as a quick and dirty integration of the natural and social sciences.*

If these predictions are true, the recent trend toward a levelling of determinative influence among the household, society and the environment could be rejected for a strong environmental determinism of a type similar to that forwarded by GGS. The chance that one work would result in such a sea change is unlikely; however, the broad acclaim GGS has received among the general public, and its attention within academia, indicate that Diamond's arguments have found some traction. The possibility that neo-environmental determinism is embraced among development professionals risks future programmatic failures and accompanying social consequences, as the influence of socio-cultural factors (ranging from the household to society) are discounted in the face of challenging environmental limitations.

NEO-ENVIRONMENTAL DETERMINISM IN PUBLIC POLICY

Schoenberger's (2001) 'Interdisciplinarity and social power' addresses the problem of renewed interest in environmental determinism among policy-oriented economists. She notes that several well-known economists at top research universities have recently begun to use 'geography', meaning the natural environment, as an explanatory mechanism in theories grappling with the causes and persistence of uneven development. These economic thinkers include David Landes,

Andrew Mellinger and John Gallup at Harvard University; and Jeffrey Sachs at Columbia University. Schoenberger (2001, 374) points out that the use of geography by these notable scholars, rather than being a boon, has been quite detrimental to the discipline of geography, as they seem to be engaging in 'disciplinary reductionism' rather than actual interdisciplinary work. These scholars limit geography to 'a spatial container for imperfect competition', ignoring or failing to take into consideration the larger body of research within the discipline of geography that refutes attributing causal determinacy to the environment (Schoenberger 2001, 378). Geography, as Schoenberger (2001, 378) points out, is regarded as simply a location in these economic theories which:

> *eliminates any possible analysis of how space is produced, how the production of a built environment (so important for those increasing returns) is connected with social and economic processes in the short and long run, how the characteristics of place are produced and how they enter productively into economic relationships, and so on.*

The theories deployed by these key economists are the refurbished version of early twentieth century environmental determinism espoused by Jared Diamond, scrubbed clean of its racist insinuations, but nonetheless still reliant on its faulty deterministic logic (Schoenberger 2001).

Schoenberger addresses the implications of this superficial engagement with geography by outside scholars as a failing of the geographic discipline to engage with the wider academic and social community. She argues that the discipline not only needs to communicate more internally across the human and physical divide, but that geographers also need to assert themselves in the academic arena and 'create the interdisciplinary projects and take them out into the world', rather than have famous economists act as our geographic spokespeople (Schoenberger 2001, 380). We contend that these words apply with equal importance to the interdisciplinary field of human-environment research.

While Schoenberger's concerns about interdisciplinary research are important, we would like to extend her arguments further and address the policy implications of neo-environmental determinist economists who hold significant social power. She addresses the social power relationships in interdisciplinary work, in terms of who has 'control over socially valued resources' and who gets to determine what is considered valuable. We contend that the influence of these well-known economic-minded thinkers over the direction and funding of international development is a critical, but overlooked, aspect of the social power wielded by those espousing a form of neo-environmental determinism. The question then emerges, beyond a cursory and lacklustre engagement with the field of geography, what effect have these well-known economists had on the actual development policy formation and international aid? Before investigating the policy implications, a more thorough review of the theoretical positions of these economists is in order.

In 1998, Gallup, Sachs and Mellinger presented a paper at the Annual World Bank Conference on Development Economics which was then published a year later in a special issue of International Regional Science Review focusing on geography and economic development (Gallup et al. 1999). The authors' treatise on the effects of geography on development argues that those countries which are landlocked, have few navigable rivers, and possess a tropical climate are doomed by their physical geography to high disease rates, low productivity and increased transportation costs. Reinforcing this argument, the authors review the work of Jared Diamond, citing GGS extensively. All of this leads the authors to the seemingly self-evident conclusion that geography matters and those landlocked countries in tropical areas are at a serious disadvantage for economic growth.

Taken out of the historic socio-cultural context, the simplicity of this environmentally focused conclusion has grave implications for development policy. The authors state:

> *the policy implications of these findings, if the findings are true, are staggering. Aid programs should be rethought, and the crucial issue of migration should be brought into much sharper focus. The research agenda needs to be reshaped in light of the importance of geographic variables.*

Implicit is the suggestion that the geographic advantages of a region should be increasingly considered in the determination of the aid given to human beings. Gallup et al. (1999) also recommend research into the connection between migration and geography, reasoning that those in geographically undesirable areas will have to migrate en masse, as the authors do not consider socio-cultural adaptations capable of overcoming environmental limitations of the type reviewed.

Sachs (2003, 38) likewise argues for greater determinative weight to be given the natural environment in his work 'Institutions matter, but not for everything: the role of geography and resource endowments in development shouldn't be underestimated'.

This particular article is a reply to an ongoing debate in the field of economics, between those who believe that institutions explain almost everything, and those who agree with Sachs in ascribing a strong determinacy to the natural environment (Sachs 2003). In this chapter, Sachs attempts to distance himself from traditional environmental determinism by stating: 'It is a common mistake to believe—and a weak argument to make—that geography equals determinism' (p. 40). Immediately following this statement, he compares the fates of a poor coastal country, whose chances are favourable of escaping the poverty trap, with that of a poor landlocked country stating:

> *An equally poor landlocked region, however, may be stuck in poverty in the absence of outside help. A major project to construct roads and a port would most likely exceed local financing possibilities and may well have a rate of return far below the world market cost of capital. The market may be right: it is unlikely to pay a market return to develop the hinterland without some kind of subsidy from the rest of the world. Nor will institutional reforms alone get the goods to market.*

Sachs is not arguing for ignoring geographically disadvantaged countries or regions for development projects/ investments; indeed, many of his suggestions for aid programmes are generous and would be beneficial for impoverished areas. It is his persistent neo-environmental deterministic stance and lack of recognition of the prior failings of economic policies that is troubling. Writing about the challenges facing structural adjustment programs (SAPs), he does not question the validity or efficacy of these policies or their implementation, but rather blames the failure of countries subjected to these frequently austere measures on their natural geography.

> *The structural adjustment era in sub-Saharan Africa, for example, was very disappointing in this dimension. Although the region focused on economic reforms for nearly two decades, it attracted very little foreign (or even domestic) investment, and what it did attract largely benefited the primary commodity sectors. Indeed these economies remained almost completely dependent on a few primary commodity exports. The reform efforts did not solve the underlying fundamental problems of disease, geographical isolation, and poor infrastructure.*

The lack of recognition that SAPs aimed at development can actually deepen poverty, through the elimination of social welfare programmes, the mandated servicing of debts, and economic restructuring, is an egregious omission. As Mike Davis points out in his recent book Planet of slums: 'In Harare the 1991 SAP raised the cost of living 45 percent in a single year and 100,000 people ended up in hospital wards suffering from effects of malnutrition' (Davis 2006, 160). The tendency of SAPs to exacerbate poverty and environmental degradation was uncovered earlier by researchers from a number of fields, including CAPE, studying the institutional influences on human-environment relationships. The flaw in development programmes is not to be found in the natural geography of a country, it is the neoliberal economic agenda that places complete faith in the market to remedy the social, political and economic problems of poverty. When the market fails, as has often been the case in international development programmes, policy advisors like Sachs find theoretical reassurance by blaming a country's natural environment.

Sachs' neo-environmental determinist stance closely echoes the popularised arguments of Diamond, but is all the more troubling given his influence on the world political stage. Among his acclaims is his membership in the Brookings Institution, a political think tank with many current and former members possessing considerable social power. He is also Director of the Earth Institute at Columbia University and serves as a special adviser to the United Nations (UN) Secretary General on the UN Millennium Development Goals. Although it is important to recognise that Sachs is an advocate for increasing aid and assistance to developing countries, his failure to acknowledge adequately the role of history, failed economic policies and the fallibility of the Western development model as the principal contributing factors to the economic problems of developing countries is troubling.

While the primary audiences of Sachs and Diamond represent the separation between global development professionals and the general public, respectively, their shared belief in ascribing significant determinism to the natural environment has brought them together in a number of publications with broad readership and access to development policymakers. In a recent chapter in the journal Nature, Diamond (2004b) rearticulates his neo-environmental determinist views and offers specific developmental policy suggestions based upon the arguments he first made in his book GGS. A quarter of the citations in this recent work have Sachs listed as first author, with striking conceptual and evidentiary similarities between the authors. Sachs et al. (2001) is but one example of the recent intellectual convergence that has occurred between some leading development thinkers and the rise of a neo-environmental determinism, typified and popularised by Diamond (1997). Comparing Diamond (2004b) with the writings of Sachs et al. (2001), one is left to ponder whether the authors truly believe that greater investments in human health, family planning and environmental protection would alleviate the geographic constraints that they contend have had such a significantly determinative impact throughout the length of human history.

It must be recognised that neo-environmental determinism, as captured in GGS and the theorising of some development economists, represents a departure from mainstream human-environment research that must be addressed by the discipline. Although Jared Diamond and Sachs advocate for increased aid as a way to overcome geographic barriers, it is not inconceivable that those inside and outside the academy might use the neo-environmental perspective to justify increasingly harsher approaches towards nations in tropical regions, a scenario not without historical precedent. Semple's work, which characterised the first moment of human-environment work, was used by academics to justify colonial endeavours as a necessary investment in foreign countries under the pretence of the 'white man's burden'. Referring to this particular historical moment in human-environment research, Peet states 'this synthesis could be employed in the service of power, specifically to legitimate as natural the expansion of Europe into world dominance' (Peet 1998, 14). It is not hard to imagine this contemporary thread of neo-environmental thought, a slightly altered recycling of the first moment's positions, being co-opted to demand extensive and wide-ranging domestic reforms, further reducing the efficacy of social welfare programs, under the threat of reduced international aid. Such is not inconceivable, given the contention by Sachs et al. (2001) and Diamond (2004b) that the geographic disadvantages experienced by much of the developing world represent an intractable challenge that can only be overcome through directed assistance by the developed world. If the history and lessons of environmental research are forgotten or simply ignored, we risk repeating the mistakes of the past, not only damaging the legitimacy of a field of inquiry, but more importantly putting at risk those people considered to be the world's most vulnerable.

12

Marxist Geography

Marxist geography is a critical geography which utilises the theories and philosophy of Marxism to examine the spatial relations of human geography. In Marxist geography the relations that geography has traditionally analyzed-natural environment and spatial relations-are reviewed as outcomes of the mode of material production. To understand geographical relations, the social structure must also be examined. Marxist geography attempts to change the basic structure of society.

PHILOSOPHY AND METHODOLOGY

Marxist geography is radical in nature and its primary criticism of the positivist spatial science centered upon its methodologies, which failed to account or demonstrate the underlying mechanisms of capitalism and exploitation that underlie human spatial arrangements. As such, early Marxist geographers were explicitly political in advocating for social change and activism; they sought, through application of geographical analysis of social problems, to alleviate poverty and exploitation in capitalist societies. Marxist geography makes exegetical claims regarding how the deep-seated structures of capitalism act as a determinant and a constraints to human agency. Most of these ideas were developed in the early 1970s by dissatisfied quantitative geographers; David Harvey is generally regarded as the primary trail-blazer of the Marxist movement in human geography.

In order to accomplish such philosophical aims, these geographers rely heavily upon Marxist social and economic theory; drawing on Marxian economics and the concept of historical materialism to tease out the manner in which the means of production control human spatial distribution in capitalist structures. Marx is also invoked to examine how spatial relationships are affected by class. The emphasis is upon structure and structural mechanisms; emphasis on this aspect of society has yielded results but also criticism.

Criticism

Marxist geography's emphasis on constraints of structure upon human agency has been criticized extensively as deterministic; not allowing for the human agency and autonomy, whose action appears determined by capitalism's structural mechanisms in Marxist analysis. By contrast, Humanistic geography is a differing critical geography, which concentrates upon human will and autonomy in explaining geography's patterns. Unsurprisingly, much of the criticism directed at Marxists has emerged from the humanistic fold (though humanistic geography is itself seen as lacking for failing to account for behavioural constraints imposed by social structures). Marxist geography is also subject to critiques of historical materialism and its applicability to modern day post-industrial and capitalist societies. The importance Marxists place on the notion of class is also subject to critique. Marxist geographers have responded in kind to these polemics.

DICTIONARY OF MARXIST THOUGHT

Geographical knowledge deals with the description and analysis of the spatial distribution of those conditions (either naturally-occurring or humanly-created) that form the material basis for the reproduction of social life. It also tries to understand the relations between such conditions and the qualities of social life achieved under a given mode of production.

The form and content of geographical knowledge depends upon the social context. All societies, classes, and social groups possess a distinctive 'geographical lore', a working knowledge of their territory and of the spatial distribution of use values relevant to them. This 'lore', acquired through experience, is codified and socially transmitted as part of a conceptual apparatus with which individuals and groups cope with the world. It may be transmitted as a loosely-defined spatial-environmental imagery or as a formal body of knowledge-geography-in which all members of society or a privileged elite receive instruction. This knowledge can be used in the quest to dominate nature as well as other classes and peoples. It can also be used in the struggle to liberate peoples from so-called 'natural' disasters and from internal and external oppression.

Bourgeois geography, as a formal body of knowledge, underwent successive transformations under the pressure of changing practical imperatives. Concern for accuracy of navigation in earlier centuries gave way later on to cartographic practices designed to establish private property and state territorial rights. At the same time the creation of the world market meant ' the exploration of the earth in all directions' in order to discover 'new, useful qualities of things' and so promote the 'universal exchange of products of all alien climates and lands' (Marx *Grundrisse*). Working in the tradition of natural philosophy, geographers such as Alexander von Humboldt (1769-1859) and Carl Ritter (1779-1859) set out to construct a systematic description of the earth's surface as the repository of exploitable use values (both natural and human) and as the locus of geographically differentiated forms of economy and social reproduction. By the late nineteenth century, geographical practices and thought were deeply affected by direct engagement in the exploration of commercial opportunities, the prospects for primitive accumulation and the mobilization of Empire and colonial administration. The division of the world into spheres of influence by the main imperialist powers also gave rise to geopolitical perspectives in which geographers such as Friedrich Ratzel (1844-1904) and Sir Halford Mackinder (1861-1947) dealt with the struggle for control over space, i.e. over access to raw materials, labour supplies and markets, in direct terms of geographical control. In recent years, geographers have concerned themselves with 'rational management' ('rational' usually from the standpoint of accumulation) of natural and human resources and spatial distributions.

Two strongly opposed currents of thought stand out in the history of bourgeois geography. The first, deeply materialist in its approach, nevertheless holds to some version of environmental or spatial determinism (the doctrine that forms of economy, social reproduction, political power, are determined by environmental conditions or location). The second, deeply idealist in spirit, sees society engaged in the active transformation of the face of the earth, either in response to God's will or according to the dictates of human consciousness and will. The tension between these two currents of thought has never been resolved in bourgeois geography. The latter has, in addition, always preserved a strong ideological content. Although it aspires to universal understanding of the diversity of social life, it often cultivates parochial, ethnocentric perspectives on that diversity. It has often been the vehicle for transmission of doctrines of racial, cultural, or national superiority. Ideas of 'geographical' or 'manifest' destiny, of the 'white man's burden' and of the 'civilizing mission' of the bourgeoisie, are liberally scattered in geographical thought. Geographical information (maps, for example) can be all too easily used to prey upon fears and promote hostility between peoples, and so justify imperialism, neo-colonial domination, and internal repression (particularly in urban areas).

Marx and Engels paid little attention to geography as a formal discipline, but they frequently drew upon the works of geographers (such as Humboldt) and their historical materialist texts are suffused with commentary on matters geographical. They implied that the fundamental opposition in bourgeois thought could be bridged. They argued that by acting upon the external world and changing it we thereby also changed out own natures, and that although human beings made their own histories they did not do so under social and geographical circumstances of their own choosing. But Marx, evidently concerned to distance himself from determinist current in bourgeois thought, usually downplayed the significance of environmental and spatial differentiations. The result is a somewhat ambivalent treatment of geographical questions.

For example, Marx often made it sound as though there was a simple, unilinear historical progression from one mode of production to another. But he also accepted that Asiatic society possessed a distinctive mode of production, in part shaped by the need to build and maintain large scale irrigation projects in semi-arid environments. He also later attacked those who transformed his 'historical sketch of the genesis of capitalism into an historico-philosophical theory of the general path of development prescribed by fate to all nations', and argued that he had merely sought to 'trace the path by which, in Western Europe, the capitalist economic system emerged from the womb of the feudal economic system' (letter to Otechestvenniye Zapiski, November 1877). Even in Western Europe, considerable variation existed because of the uneven penetration of capitalist social relations under local circumstances showing 'infinite variations and gradations in appearance'.

Marx also sought an analysis of capitalism's historical dynamic without reference to geographical perspectives on the grounds that the latter would merely complicate matters without adding anything new. But in practice he is forced to recognize that the physical productivity of labour is affected by environmental conditions which in turn form the physical basis for the social division of labour. The value of labour power (and wage rates) consequently vary from place to place, depending upon reproduction costs, natural and historical circumstances. Differential rent can also in part be appropriated because of differentials in fertility and location. To the degree that such differentials create geographical variation in wage and profit rates, Marx looks to the mobilities of capital (as money, commodities, production activity, etc.) and labour as means to reduce them. In so doing he is forced to consider the role of geographical expansion-colonization, foreign trade, the export of capital, bullion drains, etc.-on capitalism's historical dynamic. He accepts that geographical expansion can help counteract any tendency towards falling profit rates but denies that the crisis tendencies of capitalism can be permanently assuaged thereby. The contradictions of capitalism are merely projected onto the global stage. But Marx does not attempt any systematic analysis of such processes. A planned work on crises and the world market never materialized.

Marx's commentaries possess a unifying theme. Though nature may be the subject of labour, much of the geographical nature with which we work is a social product. The productive capacities of the soil, for example, are neither original nor indestructible (as Ricardo held) because fertility can be created or destroyed through the circulation of capital. Spatial relations are also actively shaped by a transport and communications industry dedicated, in the bourgeois era, to the reduction of turnover time in the circulation of capital (what Marx called 'the annihilation of space by time'). Distinctive spatial configurations of the productive forces and social relations of capitalism (investment in physical and social infrastructures, urbanization, the territorial division of labour, etc.) are produced through specific processes of historical development. Capitalism produces a geographical landscape in its own image, only to find that image is seriously flawed, riddled with contradictions. Environments are created that simultaneously facilitate but imprison the future paths of capitalist development.

Subsequent Marxist work often failed to appreciate the subtly nuanced 'geographical lore' omnipresent in Marx's and Engel's texts. Lenin's *Development of Capitalism in Russia* is an early exception. The dominant tendency was to view nature and hence geographical circumstance as unproblematically social. Karl Wittfogel's attempt (1896-) to reintroduce geographical determinism into Marxist thought, though itself seriously flawed, reopened the questions of the relations between mode of production and environmental conditions. The practical requirements of reconstruction, planning, industrial and regional development in the Soviet Union also led to the emergence of geography as a formal discipline within a Marxist framework. A deep and almost exclusive concern with the development of the productive forces on the land was associated with an analysis in which the concrete development of such productive forces was seen as the moving force in a geographically differentiated social history. This style of thinking flowed westward, mainly through the work of French geographers such as Pierre Georges (1909-).

The study of imperialism and the world market (a topic which Marx had left untouched) introduced a more explicitly spatial imagery into Marxist thought in the early years of the twentieth century. Hilferding, Lenin, Bukharin, and Luxemburg dramatically unified themes of exploitation, geographical expansion, territorial conflict and domination, with the theory of accumulation of capital. Later writers pursued the spatial imagery strongly. Centers exploit peripheries, metropolises exploit hinterlands, the first world subjugates and mercilessly exploits the third, underdevelopment is imposed from without, etc. Class struggle is resolved into the struggle of periphery against the centre, the countryside against the city, the third world against the first. So powerful is this spatial imagery that it freely flows back into the interpretation of structures even in the heart of capitalism. Regions are exploited by a dominant metropolis in which ghettos are characterized as 'internal neo-colonies'. The language of *Capital* (the exploitation of one class by another) tends to give way in some Marxist work to a compelling imagery in which people in one place exploit those in another. There was, however, very little in this Marxist tradition which grappled with the concrete processes whereby class antagonisms are translated into spatial configurations, or with the way in which spatial relations and organization are produced under the imperatives of capitalism.

New life was breathed into these questions during the 1960s, as the radical critique of bourgeois geography gathered strength. The attempt to reconstitute formal geographical understandings from a socialist perspective had some peculiar advantages. Traditional bourgeois geography, dominated by conservative thinkers attached to the ideology of empire, was nevertheless global, synthetic and materialist in its approach to ways of life and social reproduction in different natural and social environments. It was a relatively easy target for criticism and lent itself easily to historical materialist approaches. Yet there was little to appeal to in Marxist geographical thought and only a brief flurry of an indigenous radical tradition in the anarchism of Elisée Reclus (1830-1905) and Kropotkin (1842-1921).

The radical thrust initially concentrated on a critique of ideology and geographical practice. It called into question the racism, classism, ethnocentrism and sexism in geographical texts and teaching. It attacked the dominantly positivist stance of geographers as a manifestation of bourgeois managerial consciousness. It exposed the role of geographers in imperialist endeavors, in urban and regional planning procedures directed towards social control in the interests of capital accumulation. It sought to uncover the hidden assumptions and class biases within geography through a thorough critique of its philosophical basis. But it also sought to identify and preserve those facets of geography relevant to socialist reconstruction and to merge the positive aspects of bourgeois geography with a reconstituted understanding of the geography buried in Marx's and Engel's texts. The more mundane techniques-from mapping to resource inventory and analysis-appeared usable (as the Soviet experience had shown), but were too close to bourgeois practice for comfort, and the assumption of their social neutrality was troubling. Something more was needed. Bourgeois geographers had long sought to understand how different peoples fashion their physical and social landscapes as a reflection of their needs and aspirations and they had also shown that different social groups-children, the aged, social classes, whole cultures,-possess different and often incomparable forms of geographical knowledge. It was a short step to create a more dialectical view, based on Marx's thesis that by acting upon and changing the external world we change our own natures. From this a new agenda for geography could be constructed-the study of the active construction and transformation of material environments (both physical and social) through particular social processes, together with critical reflection on the geographical knowledge (itself contributory to those social processes) which resulted. It follows that contradictions within a social process (such as those founded on antagonism between capital and labour) are necessarily manifest in both the actual geographical landscape (the social organization of space) and our interpretations of that landscape.

Marxist geographical inquiry is in its infancy in the West. It seeks the reformulation of bourgeois questions, and new perspectives on Marxist theory and practice. It seeks deeper insights into how different social formations create material and social landscapes in their own image. It explores how capitalism transforms and creates nature as new productive forces embedded in the land and sets in train irreversible and often damaging processes of ecological change. It examines how spatial configurations of productive forces and social relations are created and with what effects-uneven geographical development, the spatial integration of world capitalism through the geographical mobility of capital and labour. It seeks to explain how the exploitation of people in one place by those in another (peripheries by centers, rural areas by cities) can arise in a social formation dominated by the antagonism between capital and labour. It investigates how spatial organization (e.g. segregation) relates to all reproduction of class relations. Above all, geographers seek understanding of how crises are manifest geographically, through processes of regional growth and decay, inter-regional competition and restructuring, the export of unemployment, inflation, surplus productive capacity, degenerating into inter-imperialist rivalries and war.

MARXIST GEOGRAPHY

The study of geographical questions using the analytical insights, concepts, and theoretical framework of Marxism. Although not inherently limited to one kind of society, Marxist geography has tended to focus on the various geographies of capitalism.

Before the 1960s, geography in North America and western Europe had experienced only a very limited radical critique, and postwar Soviet geography (where, at least outwardly, the influence of Marxism was much greater) was in practice more technocratic than radical. In the English-speaking world Marxist geography emerged in the early 1970s in response to two sets of events: the critique of 'establishment geography', and in particular its reformulation of geography as a narrowly conceived spatial science based on the supposedly 'objective' philosophy of positivism; and the political struggles and uprisings of the late 1960s in Europe, the Americas and Australia. These struggles took aim at poverty, racism and the imperialism of the Vietnam war, and prompted a new generation of activism: the civil rights, feminist, environmental and anti-war movements as well as a new left.

Marxists argued that positivist spatial science was flawed in three basic ways. First, insofar as existing geographical relations were treated as spatial patterns rather than the outcome of social processes, ruling social ideologies were reaffirmed; geographers might map urban segregation according to class and race, for example, but never interrogate the political and economic processes that produced such unequal geographies. Second, despite its avowed scientific objectivity, spatial analysis was devoted to providing 'socially useful' results that amounted to a 'spatial technology' for capital; locational analysis sought to identify the most efficient locations for factories, supermarkets and social services, for example, accepting traditional class-based economic definitions of'efficient location' (Massey, 1973). Third, universal spatial laws of the sort sought by positivist spatial analysis ignore the historical and geographical variability of spatial arrangements in different societies.

If the emergence of a radical alternative to establishment geography can be dated to 1969, when a group of graduate students and faculty at Clark University published the first volume of Antipode: A Radical Journal of Geography, its consummation came in 1973 with the publication of David Harvey's highly influential Social justice and the city. This book traced a personal and political journey from a constellation of unsatisfying liberal assumptions towards a systematic Marxist analysis and demonstrated the ways in which spatial form and urban geographies are integral to an exploitative social and economic system. ghetto formation, for example, is the result of a housing market that discriminates on the basis of class and race and yet is also a vital urban form through which the costs of social reproduction are minimized. In this light, supposed scientific objectivity seems both unrealistic and politically motivated to endorse rather than criticize the exploitation and oppression inherent to capitalism. A revolutionary geographical theory, Harvey argued, was necessary not just to comprehend current geographies but also to change them, and in the process to change the societies that produced them.

Marxist geography is a varied and internally differentiated theoretical and political tradition. It can be encapsulated under three (albeit overlapping) headings.

Political economic analyses. political economy explains the geography of capitalism as the outcome primarily of political and economic relationships and processes in the wider society. While therefore borrowing from Marxian economics, it also attempts to understand capitalist society as spatially and environmentally constituted. Early documentation of spatial inequality and community advocacy was superseded by critique and theory. The urban geographies of capitalism can thereby be understood as resulting from the inherent contradiction between class struggle and accumulation (Harvey, 1978). urbanization is both the most rational geographical means (for capital) of centralizing productive capital, and at the same time an encouragement to oppositional struggle insofar as it congregates large numbers of people with similar experiences of exploitation and oppression in a single place. Capitalist urbanization represents a further contradiction: on the one hand it brings about an extraordinary economic and geographical fixation of capital in the built environment as factories, offices and infrastructure as a condition of economic expansion. Yet at the same time, the changing conditions of production, circulation and realization of capital demand that capital investments be infinitely fluid. Given the long-term fixation of capital investment in the built environment, it is not surprising that economic crisis has a particularly sharp effect on urban landscapes.

Suburbanization can thereby be conceived less as a heroic fable of the middle-class consumerism, and more as a distinct geographical form of urban development that expresses the social geography of class inequality and the economic geography of class-based consumption. Suburbanization was actively planned and publicly subsidized, and represented a putative solution to the crisis of accumulation in the 1920s and 1930s. At the urban core, gentrification can be seen as an economic as well as a social question, resulting as much from geographical patterns of investment and disinvestment in the urban space economy as from consumer choice, and as part of a larger pattern of urban restructuring and uneven development at the urban scale. There is also an intricate connection between class and other social relationships such as gender and race. Socialist feminists have shown the importance of gender relations in the making of contemporary urban form. The requirements of social reproduction, the patterns of women's labour, and class-differentiated ideologies of gender have all shaped capitalist urbanization. Suburbanization was premised on the gender relations of postwar expansion, while gentrification results in part from the changing social and economic roles of women, the changing definitions of family, and the restructuring of the Fordist regime of accumulation.

Regional geographies have been transformed by a similar process, by deindustrialization, and by changes in the organization of labour and capital and technology. These shifts are integrally connected with economic and social crises and bring new geographies of industrial and non-industrial growth, new ensembles of production. At the global scale, greatest attention has been paid to the geography of underdevelopment. Blaut has consistently questioned western versions of the origins of capitalism and capitalist ideologies of nationalism. How has colonial and imperial expansion led to specific geographical patterns and structures in underdeveloped societies (cf. colonialism)? The answer comes in a number of forms. In environmental terms, underdevelopment has led to a highly destructive social ecology characterized by chronic famine and the systematic disruption of the means of social reproduction. In social and economic terms, underdevelopment leads to a decentred and imbalanced regional structure that emphasizes communications with the colonial capital and Europe rather than between neighbouring regions (Slater, 1975): thus the fastest way from Mali to neighbouring Niger may still be via Paris. Today the focus has shifted from understanding the ways in which imperial societies imposed specific geographies toward a more complicated inquiry into the ways that different imperial and local traditions came together to produce different political landscapes in different places.

The temporal rhythms of capital investment, accumulation and crisis are matched by a geographical logic of economic expansion and decline. Capital seeks a spatial fix for economic crises (Harvey, 1982), whether by disinvesting heavily in one place or investing heavily in another. In Marx's (1973) renowned phrase, the accumulation of capital relies upon a highly dynamic 'annihilation of space by time'. This implies the simultaneous development of the forces of communication and the cyclical creation of newly built environments for production, consumption and reproduction. But it also implies an equally fervid destruction of capital invested in the built environment, thereby creating new opportunities for expansion. This is the process that Schumpeter (1942), following Marx, later called 'creative destruction'. More broadly, the geography of capitalism is a perpetual maelstrom of construction and destruction that is captured in the general theory of uneven development.

There are of course many debates over all of these issues, and critiques of political economy approaches have resulted in a broadening and sharpening of Marxist concerns. With the maturation of a social theory tradition in geography, the broader structural analyses of 1970s and early 1980s political economy have been complemented by greater attention to questions of human agency and resistance, by cultural as well as political economic constructions of landscape (Mitchell, 1996), and by attempts to understand the connections between class, gender and race as interwoven sources of socio-spatial difference. In the wake of so-called globalization, a whole range of questions concerning the relationship between global and local have also emerged (Swyngedouw, 1992).

Theories of space. The critique of positivism and of abstract spatial science called into question the conceptions of space employed in geographical discourse. Geography has until recently been dominated by the familiar concept of absolute space space as a field or container, primordially empty until filled with objects and events. The Marxist critique objected that this was only one of various possible concepts of space, and that when twinned with dubious assumptions of scientific objectivity it encouraged geographers to see abstract spatial forms and processes separate from the concrete social processes that created them. Social processes were disguised within spatial forms and spatial processes, in an ideological move that Marxist geographers identified as spatial fetishism (Anderson, 1973). Obviously this conceptual critique intersects with the rationale for a political economic analysis. In concrete terms, it leads to a focus on the space-economy, but it also encouraged a more philosophical avenue of research.

For a reconstruction of space, Marxist geography looked to physics and beyond to relative and relational conceptions of space, to the connection of space and time (Thrift, 1983) and to the production of space (Lefebvre, 1991). Space is seen in relation to material events and processes (social as well as natural), no longer prior to nature: material objects do not so much fill up space; rather, their placement produces space. Absolute space is not entirely vanquished, but it is rendered relational; the absoluteness of private landed property, for example, represents socially constructed absolute space.

We do not know why capitalism has survived since Marx's time, Lefebvre says, but we do know how: by producing space. Lefebvre argues that a contemporary science of society is necessarily a science of space. In opposition to the homogeneity of abstract space continually imposed by capitalism, he identifies a differential space constructed through opposition to capitalism, class struggle and the actions of emerging social movements. The production of differential space is the object of revolutionary theory and practice for Lefebvre, and its agents are class struggle, emerging social movements and social activism.

Nature and society-nature relations. It is a common misconception that Marx had little to say about nature and the environment. His critique of capitalist society was built on an explicit vision of the relationship between society and nature. Rather than assuming that nature and society represent separate realms, Marxist theory posits their fundamental interconnectedness, achieved practically in the performance of social labour. Labour converts naturally occurring material into social commodities, and in transforming the form of nature, simultaneously changes its own (human) nature. Capitalist society produces wealth 'only by sapping' the original sources of all wealth the soil and the labourer.

This has led to the suggestion that geographers ought to develop a 'geographical materialism' comparable to Marx's historical materialism. Others have suggested a more socially centred vision of nature (Burgess, 1978). But it is also possible to derive from Marx the argument that human societies, and especially capitalism, are involved in the production of nature. It may sound quixotic to talk about the production of nature since, after all, nature is precisely that which we are used to thinking of as the antithesis of human society and social construction. Yet the strangeness of the idea may belie a persistent bifurcated ideology of nature: nature is deemed either external to human society or else as universal, including quite literally everything in the world (Whatmore, 1998). To the extent that the form of the Earth has been entirely altered by productive human activity, however, and no part of the world remains unaffected, the production of nature is a reality. This does not imply that somehow natural laws of gravity or chemical interaction cease to operate, nor that nature is thereby controlled. Control and production are two quite separate issues. It does suggest forcefully that the natural world can no longer be separated conceptually or ontologically from the social world, and that an environmental politics is a quintessentially social politics. This has two results. First, it disqualifies the romantic appeal from the deep ecologist to conservationist to a pre-existing, Edenic nature unaffected by social production and social change, to which we ought to return; or the appeal to biological essentialism that gives authority to much ecofeminism. Second, it disqualifies the technocratic appeal to 'society-nature interactions' insofar as this perspective also assumes the initial separation of society and nature. As Cosgrove (1984) has explained, it 'is not the relationship between human beings and the land that governs their social organization, but ultimately their relations with each other in the course of production'. 'The production of nature' suggests the political question: how do we as a society want to produce nature, and how will these decisions be made?

Marxist analyses of nature-society relations have also focused on more concrete questions. Considerable effort has been aimed at reinterpreting the conventional wisdom on environmental hazards. Where traditional hazard specialists draw a distinction between natural and technological hazards, Marxists have stressed that this distinction perpetuates an ideology of nature separate from society and encourages a belief in natural hazards as inevitable. 'Natural' hazard is in fact a misnomer, since all hazards (as opposed to natural events) are by definition social (O'Keefe et al., 1976). With a clear correlation between on the one side income and social class and on the other vulnerability to hazard, a disproportionate number of deaths due to so-called natural disasters are in the underdeveloped world. By the same token, any given environment has vastly different meanings for different people: a hazard for one population may be a recreational resource for another.

Supposedly natural events, such as the Sahel famine of 1968-74, the wider African famine of the 1980s and 1990s, and certainly global warming, are now understood as quintessentially social events traceable to the broad structure and specific operation of capitalist social relations (Watts, 1983). Likewise, the Irish starvation of the 1840s, traditionally blamed on potato blight, resulted from the dependence enforced by British imperialism of Irish peasants on the potato: as peasants starved, English landlords continued to export large quantities of Irish beef to the English market (Regan, 1980). The production of food in general involves an extraordinary appropriation of nature along class lines (Goodman and Redclift, 1991), and the class politics of rainforest destruction are now evident (Hecht and Cockburn, 1990). In the consumption sphere, too, access to nature is privatized (Heiman, 1988), and the disruption of local patterns of social ecology due to capitalist expansion fundamentally disrupts established processes and traditions of social reproduction.

A central ideological plank of traditional environmental geography holds that the population and resources of a place are intricately dependent on each other, and that 'overpopulation' should be defined in relation to available resources. There is an implicit retention here of Malthusian assumptions about the separateness and fixity of nature vis-Ã -vis population (Harvey, 1974). But given global economic trade and financial flows, and very unequal patterns of political power, it is doubtful that a place's resources have a determining effect on strictly local population growth or socio-economic development. Resource availability and resource scarcity are themselves socially constructed.

The first phase of Marxist research in geography, lasting until the early 1980s, was concerned, above all else, with demonstrating the ways in which capitalism, as a coherent social system, was responsible for the configuration of specific landscapes the urban geography of capitalism, its regional patterns, environmental depredation and underdevelopment at the global scale. The primary intent was to import Marxist ideas and a Marxist framework into geography as a means of analysing questions of traditional geographical concern. This involved a sustained rediscovery of Marx and Marxist ideas and their application to geography, but it was only half the battle; Marxists were no more convinced about geography than most geographers were about Marxism. And yet by the early 1980s, Marxism had come to hold an unprecedented influence within geography, compared to the other social sciences. In part this was a result of uneven intellectual development: in the 1960s, when social theory was dearly needed, geography embodied virtually no social theory beyond the assumptions of positivism. Geographers compensated for this lacuna with such an embrace of Marxism that within 15-20 years, a disproportionate number of the most influential geographers were Marxists (Bodman, 1992). A second phase of Marxist geography began in the early 1980s and was marked by several shifts. First, the focus was no longer so much on unearthing Marx and Marxism but rather on using them critically and in relation to other emerging social theory. This involved a significant broadening of Marxist geography (Gregory, 1994). But, second it involved an expansion and a corollary of the initial project. It was no longer simply a matter of convincing geographers that Marxism had something to offer that was already achieved but rather of taking the case to Marxism that a geographical, and especially a spatial, perspective was vital for Marxism and social theory more broadly. This ambitious 'spatialization of social theory' (Soja, 1989) gathered steam precisely as Marxism itself was subject to increasingly critical analysis by geographers. The second phase of Marxist research also heralded an attempt to rewrite cultural geography in a radical vein and the reconsideration of 'landscape' as a central geographical concept. Mitchell (1996) has taken the argument furthest with an attempt to install labour struggles at the centre of a new political-cultural explanation of landscape formation. This is part of a larger project aimed at developing a labour geography (Herod, 1997, 1998).

The broadening of Marxist geography in the 1980s and 1990s was the product of internal maturity as well as increasing challenges from outside, as geographers became more versed in social theory and the political climate lurched decisively to the right. These challenges came from several directions. The humanist critique (Duncan and Ley, 1982) tapped a widespread discomfiture with a Marxism portrayed as unnecessarily structuralist. It led variously toward a humanist socialism of the sort advanced by E.P. Thompson or toward the structuration theory of Anthony Giddens (1979, 1981) which dissected the Marxist dialectic into 'structure' and 'human agency' as a means of investigating their connection. A related argument came from realism, some proponents of which argued that Marxism overestimated the range of 'necessary' (i.e. structurally determined) relationships in contemporary capitalism, and that contingent relationships largely accounted for the production of specific geographies (Sayer, 1984).

The feminist engagement with Marxism has a varied history. feminist geography first emerged in the early 1970s in close connection with radical and socialist analyses, exploring issues of social reproduction, community and women's work, and connecting broader feminist debates with geographical questions, mostly at the urban scale. By the late 1980s, emerging feminist theory took a much more critical approach to Marxism, in part out of frustration that a newly influential Marxism only marginally considered questions of gender. Debate flared around Harvey's (1989) The condition of postmodernity, but a commitment to reintegrating class and gender is already evident. Linda McDowell (1991) especially warns that the baby of Marxist insights and class analysis should not be thrown out with the bathwater of a social theory blind to gender differences.

After the late 1980s, the social sciences and humanities underwent a sustained cultural turn and geography was no exception. If in some quarters the resort to culture became a means of denying the relevance of political economy or of providing an alternative to Marxism, it has quickly become clear that some of the most interesting and innovative work seeks to reintegrate economic and cultural insights depending on Marxist as well as other theoretical traditions.

The inspiration for this cultural turn had various interwoven threads. Attempts to construct feminist theory had already focused away from the logics of economic expansion and crisis toward the relations of social reproduction and daily experiences. postmodern theorists posited that Marxism and positivism, socialism and capitalism were all products of the eighteenth-century Enlightenment which valued rationality over irrationality, science over subjectivity, the global over the local, the universal over the partial and fragmented. Arguing that these definitive assumptions of modernism no longer pertain, postmodernists generally rejected attempts to read the meaning of contemporary societies from their social and economic structures, focusing instead on cultural systems of signs. Theorists of post-structuralism argue that power is expressed and cemented not simply in large-scale social structures but in the fine gauze of daily social interaction, and that social discourse plays a central role in the construction of power relations. The critique of discourse therefore marks a vital political intervention.

If Marxism both generated and provoked much of this new generation of political theory, it has also transformed in response to their challenge. Harvey's (1989) critique spearheaded a more critical attitude to postmodernist claims across a number of disciplines, and the sobering economic realities of the late 1990s have encouraged a broad modulation of cultural questions with a revived sense of the importance of economic relations. By the same token, Marxist economic geography has become much more cognisant of the cultural construction of socio-economic relations (Schoenberger, 1996). Treatments of gentrification, regional class ensembles, or human-nature relations in the Marxist tradition now embody a connectedness between cultural and political economic critiques. As Mitchell's (1996) reconstruction of the California landscape makes clear, a concern with political economy is basic to the new cultural geography.

If the challenges to Marxist geography in the 1990s are in part the inevitable result of Marxism's success in academic geography amidst a wider gathering conservatism, they also embody genuine shortcomings to which Marxist research must respond. Ironically, while the defeat of official Communist Parties in the Soviet Union and eastern Europe has given capitalist classes throughout the world a brief cause for jubilation, it also frees Marxist ideas from connection with a particularly oppressive social system which, however much the reality diverged from Marx's own vision of democratic workers' control, nonetheless governed in the name of socialism. Indeed, globalization represents the fruition of capitalist social relations at a global scale, making the world more not less akin to the reality that Marx critiqued (Smith, 1997). In that respect the agenda is open for a re-thought, integrative Marxism, committed still to political action as well as ideas. Perhaps the most salient feature of Marxism in geography at the beginning of the twenty-first century, however, is that its origins in activism have largely waned. If history is any measure, a forceful response to the global crisis at the beginning of the new millennium may depend on a revived connection to activism.

Bibliography

Agnew, J., D.N. Livingstone & A. Rogers: *Human Geography: An Essential Anthology*. Blackwell, 1996.

Andrews, Edgar H.: *Environmental Theory of Geography*, Presbyterian and Reformed, New York, 1980.

Austin, Steven A.: *Historical Development of Geography In Asia,* Institute for Creation Research, New York, 1984.

Bird, J.,: *The Changing Worlds of Geography*. Clarendon Press, 1993.

Blij, Harm Jan, De: *Geography: Realms, Regions, and Concepts*, Hoboken, NJ: John Wiley, 2008.

Chauhan, R N : *Basic Principles of Economic Geography*, ABD Pub, Delhi, 2007.

Cloke, P., Philo, C. and Sadler, D. : *Approaching Human Geography*. Guilford Press. 1991.

Cloke, Paul J.: *Envisioning Human Geographies*, London: Arnold, 2004.

Flowerdew, Robin : *Methods in Human Geography: A Guide for Students doing a Research Project,* Harlow: Prentice Hall, 2005.

Gosal, G.S. : *Fourth Survey of Research in Geography*, Manak, Delhi, 1999.

Habermas, Jürgen: *Communication and the Evolution of Society*, Thomas McCarthy, Beacon Press, Boston, 1979.

Harvey, D.: *Explanation in Geography*. Edward Arnold, 1969.

Harvey, David D.: *Justice, Nature and the Geography of Difference*, Blackwell Pub, London, 1996.

Hay P.: *Main Currents in Western Environmental Thought,* Bloomington: Indiana University Press, 2002.

Hubbard P, Kitchin R, Bartley, B & Fuller D.: *Thinking Geographically: Space, Theory and Contemporary Geography*. London: Continuum, 2002.

Inkpen, Robert: *Science, Philosophy and Physical Geography*. Routledge, London, 2004.

Johnston RJ.: *Geography and Geographers*. London: Arnold, 1997.

Johnston, R.J.: *Geographies of Global Change: Remapping the World*. Blackwell Publishers, London, 2002.

Kayastha, S.L. : *Geography of Population*, Rawat, Delhi, 1998.

Kidwai, Zeenat : *Environmental Approach in Geography Teaching*, Sarup, Delhi, 2004.

Kumar, Sunil : *Environmental Change in Geography*, ACB Pub, Delhi, 2004.

Mels T. *Reanimating Places: A Geography of Rhythms*, Burlington, VT: Ashgate, 2004.

Negi, Vishal : *A Modern Book on Economic Geography: Politics and Practices*, Cyber Tech Pub, Delhi, 2011.

Peet, Richard: *Modern Geographical Thought*, Oxford: Wiley-Blackwell, 1998.

Richard, B.: *Critical Ralism in Geography,* Institute for Creation Research, New York, 1991.

Sharieff, Afzal : *Encyclopaedia of World Geography*, Sarup, Delhi, 2007

Sharma, Pradeep : *Economic Political Geography*, Discovery, Delhi, 2007.

Smithson, Peter: *Fundamentals of the Physical Environment*. Routledge, London, 2002.

Soja, Edward: *Postmodern Geographies: The Reassertion of Space in Critical Social Theory,* Verso, London, 1989.

Thrift, Nigel J.: *Paradigms of Geographical Thought*, London: Routledge, 2000.

Venugopal, S : *Geography, Culture and the Environment*, Arise Pub, Delhi, 2007.

Index

M

N

O

P

R

S

❑❑❑